FOUNDATIONS OF THE AMERICAN ECONOMY

THE AMERICAN COLONIES FROM INCEPTION TO INDEPENDENCE

VOLUME III

T0326164

FOUNDATIONS OF THE AMERICAN ECONOMY

THE AMERICAN COLONIES FROM INCEPTION TO INDEPENDENCE

Edited by
Marianne Johnson
Steven G. Medema
Warren J. Samuels

VOLUME III

Colonial Money, Credit and Debt

LONDON AND NEW YORK

First published 2003 by Pickering & Chatto (Publishers) Limited

Published 2016 by Routledge
2 Park Square, Milton Park, Abingdon, Oxon OX14 4RN
711 Third Avenue, New York, NY 10017, USA

Routledge is an imprint of the Taylor & Francis Group, an informa business

BRITISH LIBRARY CATALOGUING IN PUBLICATION DATA

Foundations of the American Economy: the American Colonies from Inception to Independence

    1. Economics – United States – Sources 2. United States – Economic conditions –
Sources 3. United States – Economic policy – Sources
I. Samuels, Warren J. (Warren Joseph), 1933- II. Johnson, Marianne III. Medema,
Steven G. IV. From theocracy to secular, materialist commercial society V. Individualism and the structure of power VI. Colonial money, credit and debt VII. Mercantilism and colonialism, part I VIII. Mercantilism and colonialism, part II
330.9'73

LIBRARY OF CONGRESS CATALOGING-IN-PUBLICATION DATA

Foundations of the American Economy. 1. The American Colonies from Inception to Independence / edited by Marianne Johnson, Warren J. Samuels, and Steven G. Medema
    p.cm
    Includes index.
    Contents: v.1. From theocracy to secular, materialist commercial society – v.2. Individualism and the structure of power – v.3. Colonial money, credit and debt – v.4.
Mercantilism and colonialism, pt. 1 – v.5. Mercantilism and colonialism, pt.2.
    1. Economics – United States – History. 2. United States – Economic conditions – To
1865. I. Johnson, Marianne. II. Samuels, Warren J., 1933- III. Medema, Steven G.

HB119 .E17 2001
330'.0973'09032-dc21

             2001036917

ISBN-13: 978-1-85196-727-8 (set)

New material typeset by
P&C

CONTENTS

SEVERALS RELATING TO THE FUND
PRINTED FOR DIVERS REASONS,
AS MAY APPEAR

John Woodbridge, *Severals relating to the Fund Printed for divers Reasons, as may appear* (Boston, 1682), pp. 1–8.

This piece is the only surviving essay by Reverend John Woodbridge (1614–95). Biographical information regarding Woodbridge is scarce, but one available source is Andrew McFarland Davis's *Colonial Currency Reprints: 1682–1751*[1]. Davis credited Hammond Trumbull – trustee and librarian of the Watkinson Library in Hartford, Connecticut, in the nineteenth century – with recognising the importance of Woodbridge's *Severals relating to the Fund*. It is believed that Trumbull obtained the only surviving copy from Thomas Prince's collection of rare manuscripts, and committed it to the Watkinson Library. According to Davis, Woodbridge was born in Wiltshire, England, and after immigrating to America he became well-connected, mixing with the leading families of Boston. His relatives by marriage included three governors – one being John Winthrop, whose work is included in Volume I – who gave Woodbridge access to the political and economic decision-making powers in the colony.

Although the only existing copy of Woodbridge's *Severals relating to the Fund* is incomplete, and badly damaged in the opening pages, it is an important piece that is included here as an introduction to the discussion of money in the colonies. Woodbridge's writing was clearly influenced by William Potter, who was best known for *The Key of Wealth* (1650), which advocated the establishment of a bank of credit, where bills would be issued that were secured by land or other assets. Woodbridge met Potter in London in 1649 and they undoubtedly discussed issues of money and credit. Woodbridge suggested the creation of a bank of credit based on land, to alleviate the shortage of specie, or coined money, in the colonies. Paper money would increase the volume of trade, farming, and the settlement of lands, as well as encourage easier means of borrowing. Woodbridge argued that specie was valuable because it had inherent worth; hence, a bank based on something of such worth could approximate specie money. Woodbridge settled on the obvious choice of the time, which was land. Credit could then be issued for exchange based on the land, and transactions would be listed as 'book entries'. Woodbridge's idea was adopted in Massachusetts for a short time, but little is known about how the bank actually operated or what led to its discontinua-

---

[1] Andrew McFarland Davis (ed.), *Colonial Currency Reprints: 1682–1751*, 4 vols (Boston: Publications of the Prince Society, 22–5, 1910–11; reprinted by Augustus M. Kelley, 1964).

tion. It is only known that this bank credit, or paper money, circulated before that of the Bank of England.

Severals relating to the

FUND

Printed for divers Reasons, as may appear.

THAt the *way of man is not in himself: it is not in man that walketh, to direct his steps,* Is a Truth that all (who are not strangers to themselves) muft acknowledge; & in fpecial the Author of this *Subject:* If it be confidered,

1 That he had as little skill in, as inclination to, or need of concerning himfelf in *merchantile Affairs:* Nor came he into *New-England* with a thought to meddle therewith: as is well known to many. 2 That he fhould concern himfelf to promote *Trade* for others, and that in this Land, a place not defigned by the firft *Planters,* for *Commerce;* being better acquain -ted with *cæleftial Dealings,* than the *polities* of *mundane affairs*

3 That he fhould amongft fuch a People effay to promote a Defigne not known in the day thereof (if yet) to l in any part of the world(although fince in agitation and then furely ftrange here, where the name of benefit thereby, was hardly heard of. 4 That h

notwithſtanding the reproaches caſt upon him, & untruths raiſed & reported of this Thing, ſtil appear to juſtifie & promote
the ſame, and encourage thoſe who are ſatisfied thereof, and
join with him in this his undertaking. The riſe of which was
as followeth.

About the latter end of the year 1649. an intimate Friend
of the Author's in *London*, *Mr. William Potter*, who was likewiſe no Trader, Imparted to him a Deſigne for the accomo-
dation of Commerce, in the nature of a *Bank* of *money*; but
to be founded upon *perſonal Credit*, by a conſiderable number
of able Men Ingaging, as the *Found* thereof, to paſs forth
Credit; as a medium to enlarge the *Meaſure* of *money*, that was
known to be too little for the Dealings of that Land: Or by
depoſiting of Goods, in the nature of a *Lumber* of Merchandiſe,
to paſs out Credit thereon, untill ſold. As for a *Fund* to have
Land (the onely ſecure Depoſit) the dubious & intricat Titles
thereof, put a ſtop to any diſcourſe thereabout. And as for a
Bank of money, there was in that no certain Security; wofull
experience proving them ſubject to a rupture.

The Author ſo reſented the Notion of his Friend, (the
thing being rational, & tending much to the benefit of all men
where ſet on foot) that it became oft times when they met, the
common ſubject of their diſcourſe, in a rotation of Propoſals,
Objections, and Solutions: Leaving no ſtone unturn'd, that
might fit the deſigne to comport with that Place. *Mr. Potter*
likewiſe had about that time printed a Book *in folio*, relating
to his deſigne; one whereof he beſtowed on the Author, who
(upon the report that was given him of the Labyrinth *New-
England* was in, for want of a *Conveniency to mete their Trade
with*) gave it with good acceptance, to a Kinſman of his that
was a Merchant of this Place; the proſperity whereof he was
er to, when not likely ever to ſee It. Whether by
Book, or other accident, any motion thereabout
s unknown. But before any thing was brought to
ſeems there was; an accompt of which ſhall in
it's·

its place be given) the Author was called to *Ireland*; where he had more endeavoured the promotion of this thing, than bare -ly to hint it; had not his transient Employ prevented.

In anno 1664. His lot being here cast, he soon saw that with his eye, that did affect his heart *i. e.* The *Straits* many were in; the *Time* they consumed; and the *Disadvantag's* they were under, by higling to suit ends: And thereupon imparted to a publick-spirited Merchant, with what ease, & safety their *Measure* might be inlarged: Who likewise being sensible of the need thereof, desired to have in Writing somewhat about the same. Which being done, It was, it seems, imparted to di -vers, with approbation; and Return made, That somewhat might be done about it in due season: which the author rested satisfied with; in that there lay not now at his dore, a Thing concealed, that might tend to the welfare of the Country.

About three years after this (that foregoing being wholly buried) the author accidentally started this **Expedient**, among divers Country Gentlemen, Yeomen & others; persons not likely to lend an ear to a thing of this nature. Yet so it happe- ned, that to some one, or more of them, the Notion was of e- stimation: and spread abroad, to the occasioning of several De -bates among those who were Considerable, both in *Parts & Purse*: And stopped not, untill the honoured Council heard thereof. But before they took notice of it, One of the Magi- strates Imparted the **Designe** to an experienced Merchant, well Read in the nature of *Banks*, To have his judgement con -cerning this. Who Returned, that this *Bank* was so Stated, as left not room for a rational Objection to be made aga.nst it In that those Founded on *Money*, had only their defect, of a possibility to *break*; which this, Fixed on *Land*, was not capa- ble of. Soon after this, the Author had notice given, that the Council would send speedily for him, about this Concern: & was advised to write somewhat about it, for them. Where- upon, he set upon drawing a second Draught; in the dress of a *Proposal*. The which, before quite writ out, a Messenger was

sent

sent to call him to them. To whom he presented his (then crude) conceptions, as follows. To which some clauses, and explanations are added: but is the same for substance, with that on *File* in the Records of the General Court.

A *Proposal for erecting a FUND of Land, by Authority, or private Persons, in the nature of a* Money Bank; *or* Merchandize-Lumber, *to pass Credit upon, by* Book-Entries; *or* Bils of Exchange, *for great Payments: and* Change-bills *for runing Cash. Wherein is demonstrated, First, the necessity of having a Bank, to inlarge the* Measure *of Dealings in this Land, by shewing the benefit of* Money, *if enough to mete Trade with; & the disadvantages, when it is otherwise.*

Money is that *One thing,* which, as the *medium* of Trade, (for so *Solomon's* Assertion must necessarily, be understood) *answereth All things.* For where it is in plenty, no *Buyer* will be bound to one Person, or Market; nor purchase Credit at the Grantor's price; nor be necessitated to become Servant to the Lender, if he have Money to answer his occasions; nor will run the hazard of Trusting. Hereby also, the frequent complaints that are made, for want of present pay, are silenced & persons freed from a multitude of carking cares. It likewise, multiplies Trading; increaseth Manufacture, and Provisions; for domestic use, and foreign Returns; abateth Interest; inciteth to the purchasing of Land, and heighteneth its value; forwards the Improvement both of real, and personal Estates; promoteth the Settleing of new Plantations, and maritim Affairs; incourageth heartless Idlers, to Work; redeemeth Time Labour, and Expence, greatly consumed in higling up and down, to suit Pay to content, abrogateth the mystery of Trucking, by sinking *Barter,* and reducing all bought, and sold, to the English Standard; hindreth wrangling and vexatious Suits upon Debts contracted for want thereof, to the Scandal of a religious people, as well as the impoverishing of them,

them, and the confuming the time of their Magiftrates, that might be better fpent about ftudying the neceffary advantages of Trade, and forwarding of Manufacture, to the inriching of them. To which end moft civilized Nations fet fome apart to manage, and is the Loadftone that draweth commodities to the Market, that great conveniency of a people.

On the contrary, where *Coin* is fcarce, * all things are *dear*, & little anfwereth to content, or free from trouble, and lofs. Debts are con-tracted, dilatory, and fhuffeling pay-ments made; dexterous Traders retire or (which is worfe) deal in Money, the *medium* of Trade; young beginners are checked; good men laid open to tempta-tions, and opportunities given to bad ones, that exact from thofe who muft crave Credit, or cannot make fuitable pay. Trade is ftinted at home, and forestalled abroad; Stocks lye dead; Intrigue accompts, and perplexing Suits made. Mer-chants, and Shop-keepers, underfell one another; and piti-fully help themfelves, by beating down Craftsmen: who a-gain, through necefity, underwork others of their occupati-on; or flight over their work; adulterate Manufacture, and haften poverty on all. Nor can ever Trade be ballanced, or the advantage of *Fairs* be enjoyed, where Money is wanting. Which *the Cobler of Agawam*, before he Canonized *Pumpion*, was not fo *Simple* but underftood full well.

* This Claufe, with fome o-ther Objeĉions & Queries, ve-ry lately made, fhall receiv a full Reply in the next Sheet: if pof-fible.

Secondly, That Credit paff'd in Fund, by Book, & Bills, (as a-fore) will fully fupply the defeĉ of Money. Wherein is related, of how little value Coin, as the Meafure of Trade, need be, in it felf, what Inconveniences fubjeĉ to. The worth a Fund-Bill, or Pay-ment therein, is of: & not of that Hazard.   of

~ Although *Cafh* be fo ufefull; yet it is but a ready convenien-cy. Which hath, through miftake, its efteem; not from the ufe, (which it ought) but Intrinfic value: which is not effen-tialto a thing, meerly good for Exchange; and ferving barely

to

to procure what One wants, that another abounds with: and a-gain, to fetch for the laft, what he ftandeth in need of, where to be fpared. And this (except here were *Mines*, to tranfport bullion, for foreign Trade) *Bank-bills*, or payments therein, will effect, to all Intents, as well as plenty of Corn; which, *as money*, doth neither Feed, nor Cloath. Moreover, Treafure, not onely allures an Enemy, and is covetoufly hoarded up; & so, like dung in a heap, unprofitable: but is alfo fubject to *wear* and tearing, fires, robberies, miftakes, & the like contingencies; which, payments in this *Bank*, or bills iffued thence, are free from: having a *Fund*, or Depofit in *Land*; real, dureable, & of fecure value. And for the *Change-bills*, they may be fo con-t ived, as to be paffed with facility; and without counterfei-ting. However, fo as to prevent, or find out, any Cheat: if the Rules of them be obferved.

The other two *Sections* of the *Propofal*, muft be pafs'd to the 2d. *Sheet*, pag.. It being needful to make a *Digreffion*, to give an account of the publifhing this undertaking fooner, than intended.   In the year 74. divers well-wifhers to the *Fund*, did think it fit, to have a Narrative of it Printed. In or-der whereunto, fomething was done, in the Method before; *i. e.* the *occafion* of the Subject; and then, the *proceedings* there-on, to that time: but particular bufinefs did interpofe.   In the year 78. the author was importuned to the fame thing: which had been done, but that after-thoughts brought him to confi-der, that fo much having been agitated in Publique, about it; and the probation it had by the Referrees, and honoured Council, as to the *Theory* thereof; the *Prefs* would hardly print it into the *practic part*: and that the onely way was to fet it on foot. For, as *Good Wine needs no bufh*; fo it was prefumed, that if this were but in ufe, the *Flavour* thereof would invite enoû to, and continue them at it. Which to accomplifh, (having by accident, fom refpit time this year 1681. and accomodated with *Spirit*, *Purfe*, & *Hand*; the ingredients that muft center, as in one, for any confiderable undertaking) He did in *Sep-tember*,

tember, begin to paſs forth *Bills*, to make an Experiment of that which had paſſed the Scrutiny of above 30. years, with approbation; and had rational Grounds to conclude, that it would work it ſelf up into Credit, with diſcreet men: becauſe *Int'reſt will not Lie.* In 6. moneths, a conſiderable number eſpouſed the Deſigne; beſides thoſe that were concerned, in the years, *Seventy one, & Seventy two.* Whereupon; it became as a *Galley floating upon the ſtream of opinion, into which He, & He would thruſt an oar* And ſome that favoured not the De-ſigne, did talk to the diſcountenance of it: and wanting weigh-ty obiections, *let fly broad-ſides of Pot-gun- pellets, chained with Fallacies & buffoonry*, to impede this undertaking. Upon this, ſeveral, now engaged, think it not fit to be longer ſilent: but urge the haſtening an account of the Deſigne; that the Rea-lity, Safety, and Benefit thereof, may appear to all prudent, and unprejudic'd men. And this ſhall be endeavoured, as time will permit; though not in the mode firſt intended: Which was, to place all the Rules relating to the *Fund*, at the end of the *Narrative*; and then the Debates that are car-ried on, concerning Commerce. Which will now fall in mixt and this *Sheet* be cloſed with ſome Rules, moſt needful to be firſt known, for the directing thoſe in Company, in their mo-tion. The manner of erecting the *Fund*, which was *March*, 30. 71. and the carrying it on in private, for many moneths; and the reaſon of putting a ſtop to it, when *bills* were juſt to be iſſued forth, together with the *Preamble* of the Rules, *&c.* They may come in, in due place.

Payments on Change-bills.

That the Acceptor, who gives Credit to any Change-bill, Firſt, be aſſured that the Producer thereof, be the Perſon named in ſaid bill, or ſent by his Order. Secondly; That he Enter on ſaid bill, 1 the Time. 2. his own Name. 3. the Value he payes. Which, if it be the firſt Charge, then alſo to write the Sum, in words, above the columne: If not, then to caſt up the Total: which is to be done at e-very additional Article. & the bill to be delivered back again. Thirdly, If he pay the complement of any bill, then, to take it in.

Entries

Entries in the Creditors Leger.

First, the *Acceptor must erect an Accompt in his Leger, thus,*
The Fund at Boston in N. E. *Debitor.*   *Contrà, Creditor.*
Secondly, Enter, 1. *the Time, as in the former Rule.* 2. *thus,*
To Change-bill of *J. E. adding thereto, the number of the bill,*
& the Sum delivered. And if it be in full of the bill, Then to write
underneath the Entry, N. B. This bill taken in. *Thirdly, when*
he hath an Account in the Office, he is to write thus, N. My Accompt in the *Fund-Leger, fol.* ——

Entries in the *Fund-books.*

When the Acceptor hath given Credit to the value of five pounds,
or more: He may pass the Fund Debit into the Office, & have Cre
-dit in his Account there, as an Acceptor: giving in an Account,
as Entr'd in his Leger, with the Change-bills taken up by him, &
underwritten thus, Place to my Credit in *Fund, fol.* —— the
Sum of —— being for the foregoing Payments.
     To H. S.   *Per J. N. with the Date.*

Pass-bill Forms.

If one Fundor passeth Credit to another, it ought to be by a Pass-
bill, thus, Place of my Credit in *Fund, fol.* -,—— to Account of
D. J. the Sum of —— *Directed, & Signed, as above expreß'd.*
If the Drawer desire a Change-bill, for Pocket-Expence, Then
thus, Charge my accompt, *fol.* —— Debtor, five pounds, for
a Change bill, now received, Number, ——
Fund credit, not to be strained; nor passed, but among *Fundors.*

That no Accepter give, nor Depositor take more Fund-credits,
than they see their way how to Receive, or Pay the same again, a-
mong those in Company *with them: nor Deal in said Credit with*
any, but those Ented in the Fund-Rowl; *which all concerned. may*
take a copie of. N. *This Rule to be of force but until persons see*
it to be their Int'reß, to accept Fund-pay: *and the Credit thereof*
paß, without hazard of any prejudicing the same, through willful-
neß, or ignorance.
     To return, at length, to the *proposal,* left off *pag.* 6. .. 15.
                                   Thirdly,

A MODEL FOR ERECTING A BANK OF CREDIT: WITH A DISCOURSE IN EXPLANATION THEREOF

John Blackwell, *A Model for Erecting a Bank of Credit: with a Discourse in Explanation thereof. Adapted to the Use of any Trading Countrey, where there is a Scarcity of Moneys: More Especially for his Majesties Plantations in America* (London, 1688), pp. 1–38.

Little is known about the life of Captain John Blackwell except that he had a penchant for financial speculation. According to Andrew McFarland Davis,[1] Blackwell proposed *A Model for Erecting a Bank of Credit* to the governing council in Boston. In a similar vein as John Woodbridge's *Severals relating to the Fund*, Blackwell's proposal was to establish a bank of issue, securing the value of the bills with property or merchandise. Blackwell argues here that money is a measure of value and has no intrinsic worth; hence, paper money, as long as it was respected, would alleviate the shortage of specie. However, for reasons unknown and despite the support of the leading members of the Boston community, Blackwell's bank was never formed.

Blackwell's plan for paper currency, or credit, engendered significant discussion for over forty years. The two slightly later writings following this piece, *Objections* and *A Letter*, provide further examples of this discussion.

[1] Davis (ed.), *Colonial Currency Reprints* (1964).

A
MODEL

For Erecting a

Bank of Credit:

WITH A

DISCOURSE

In Explanation thereof.

Adapted to the Ufe of any Trading
Countrey, where there is a Scarcity
of MONEYS:

More Efpecially for his Majefties Plantations
in *AMERICA.*

Quò Communius eo Melius.

LONDON,
Printed by *J. A.* for *Thomas Cockeril* at the *Three
Leggs* in the *Poultrey,* over againft the
Stocks-Market, 1688.

A MODEL for Erecting a Bank of Credit Lumbard and Exchange of Moneys, Founded on Lands, Goods, and Merchandizes: To be undertaken and managed by Persons of good Reputation, Prudence and Estates, in a voluntary *Partnership*, as other Merchantly Affairs: Adapted for the Use of any Countrey, or Trading part, where there is a Scarcity of Moneys; and, in want thereof, they are constrained to truck, or Barter by Commodities, &c. wherein is Discoursed,

1. *Some things by way of Premise, touching Banks in General.*
2. *The Definition of such a Bank.*
3. *The Constitution.*
4. *The necessary Rules to be observed.*
5. *The particular Advantages thereof, to those that shall voluntarily deal with such a Partnership.*
6. *Some of the most material and pertinent Queries and Objections thereto, Resolved and answered.*
7. *The Conclusion by way of Animadversion, upon the whole: Briefly.*

Of the First, viz. *Some things premised for Introduction, touching Banks in general.*

Money, whether Gold or Silver, is but a measure of the value of other things; yet hath, for a long Succession of Ages especially in the Civilized and trading part of the

the World) obtained to be the ufual, and beft known means of Interchange.

' This meafure and way of Interchange, was originally occafioned by the experimented inconveniences of common Barter; in which way, unlefs both the Parties dealing, have like occafion, reciprocally, of each others commodities, the lefs neceffitous over-reaches the greater, by impofing the price of both, to his own advantage, and the others detriment, which is not Equal, nor can there be Equality, where there is no common ftandard between them.

' But, whether the Mines fail, or Men have not been fo fore-feeing and induftrious to bring in, to moft Countrys, a fufficiency of Money or Bullion, wherewith to manage their increafing trades; or, that Traders, for want of other Returns, have been neceffitated, for Ballance of the Surcharge of goods imported, to remit the Coyns of fome Countreys into others; Or, for other caufes (not neceffary on this occafion to be further inquired into) 'tis now fo hard to come by, in fome places, for carrying on of trade, to anfwer the vaftnefs of Mens attempts, and aims of increafe in Merchandize, as that its found, in in many Countreys, infufficient in this Age of the World: And that hath put divers Perfons and Countreys, upon contrivances how to fupply that Deficiency, by other Mediums; fome of which have happily pitch'd upon that of Banks, Lumbards, and Exchange of Moneys by Bills, which have thriven with them.

The

The two former of thefe, *viz.* Banks and Lumbards, have been fet on foot in divers trading Countreys, by their refpective Publique undertakings, and have fucceeded to their abundant inriching. Perhaps others have thought, that would have occafioned the overflowing of Moneys amongft them : Efpecially if they raifed the values of Gold and Silver above the common Standard ; but as they have been miftaken, or their Surfeit of trade hath obfcured the vifibility of it ; and protracted more rational Confiderations of redreffing, till it hath proved almoft Fatal, to the impoverifhing of their Countreys ; So, the other have really experimented, that their Banks have been, as well with other Countreys, as amongft themfelves, of greater value than the fpecies of Gold and Silver : And yet, fuch places drain away the faid fpecies from the other, who under thofe miftaken apprehenfious have Courted it, as the only reall good thing for a Countrey.

The Third, *viz.* That of Exchange of Moneys, hath been for the moft part managed by the refpective Merchants of all places ; who in their particular dealings and Correfpondences (fore-laying advantages to themfelves thereby) have unaccountably controll'd it, and vary it often, in each Annual Revolution.

'Tis not to be doubted, but that all three of thefe may be accommodated and improved, to the publick Advantage of any Countrey : Efpecially, if managed in Partnerfhip by private hands, being Perfons of known Integrity, Prudence and

Eftates :

Eftates: fubjecting the annual Profits accruing thereby to the anfwering the Injury, damage, or lofs, by their undertaking.

The beft Foundation for fuch an Attempt, is, that of Real and Perfonal Eftates, inftead of the *fpecies* of Gold and Silver. For, as a Bank of Moneys is liable to many cafualties and hazards; fo, the hoarding up of Moneys in Banks, neceffitates the taking out the more Bills; which is one Malady this Propofed Bank will cure.

We fhall therefore, at prefent, begin with, and principally difcourfe of the two firft of thefe: *viz.* The Bank of Credit, as it may be rendred fufceptible of the Second, *viz.* The Lumbard, conjunct: accounting both the one and the other to be founded as aforefaid, *viz.* On Lands or Real Eftates mortgaged, and ftaple durable Goods, and Merchandizes depofited: fuch as any Countreys Products and Manufactures will by Art and Induftry produce and furnifh.

Here might be alfo difcours'd, A Lumbard for the Poor, by fome called, *Mons Pietatis:* But that's fitter to be the Handmaid of the other; for, 'twill be too poor to encourage an undertaking by it felf, or for a beginning: Neither will there be any fuch neceffity thereof, when this Bank is fettled; forafmuch as this will imploy moft of thofe, who are ufually maintained in Idlenefs, if they will betake themfelves to Induftry, at fuch moderate wages as would enable them to live comfortably, without expofing their Imployers to like Poverty with themfelves.

And

And befides, this Bank of Credit and Lumbard, when underftood, and received in any Countrey with general Approbation, will in due time render that, as alfo the Third, *viz.* that of the Exchange of Moneys by Bills, the more intelligible, and as ufefull.

Of the fecond Particular, viz. The definition of fuch a Bank.

A Confiderable number of perfons, fome of each Rank, Trade, Calling and Condition, efpecially in the principal Place or places of Trading in any Countrey, Agree voluntarily to Receive, as ready Moneys, of and from each other, and any Perfons in their ordinary dealings, Bankbills of Credit, figned by feveral Perfons of good Repute, joyned together in a Partnerfhip, given forth on Lands of good title mortgaged, and ftaple unperifhing Goods and Merchandizes, depofited in fitting places to be appointed by the Partnerfhip for that purpofe; to the value of about one half, or two thirds of fuch refpective Mortgages and Depofits: Which faid Bills, through their experimented ufefulnefs, become diffufed by mutual confent; and paffing from one hand to another, in a kind of Circulation, and under reputation of fo certain a Fund, have at leaft equal Advantages with the Current Money or Coyn of any Countrey, attending them, to all who become fatisfied to deal with them.

Q. But it may be faid by fome, This is a very

very brief account, and requires further Explanation. We are yet Strangers to the Nature, and requisite Constitution of a Bank of Credit, and what lies on us to do, in order to our being made partakers of any benefits or advantages thereby, to such as shall voluntarily comply therewith; nor do we see clearly our security in so doing, nor upon what terms. Pray inform us of these things, so far as we may be safely guided into the way, and unto the end of it. Also, in case this Bank should terminate, how we shall be dealt withal, in the closing up of Accompts, so as may be without damage, either to the Bank, or to our selves. We doubt not but you have as well considered the end as the beginning. Though, if it prove useful, we can see no cause why a thing of so great advantages as are suggested, should procure any persons ill Will, or weariness of it. And we are also satisfied, that an affair of this nature, wherein the Persons and Estates of so many shall be involved (as it seems probable will be where it once gets footing) cannot suddainly be knock'd off, but with inconvenience.

Answ. The clearing these Doubts you'l find in the particulars following. Therefore now,

Of the third Particular, viz. *The Constitution of this Bank,*

IT is proposed that there be One and twenty Persons (or less) in the Partnership of this Bank : Whereof seven to be called Principal Managers ;

ſagers ; who, or any three or more of them may
have the power of managing and governing the
whole affair, according to the Conſtitution & Rules
thereof ; and fourteen Deputies, to be imployed
by them as Accomptants, Surveyors, Appraiſers,
Store keepers, &c. All of them to be Perſons of
good and general Reputation for Integrity, Prudence and Eſtates : But, foraſmuch as, at the firſt
entrance upon ſuch an affair, it may not be needful to ingage ſo many ; That any three, five or ſeven of them (more or leſs) may be conceived ſufficient to begin the ſame ; and manage it until, by
the coming on of buiſineſs, it ſhall be judged neceſſary and incouraging, to ſettle the full, or ſome
greater number of them. Theſe may all be in-
gaged by Articles of Agreement, and Covenants
in Partnerſhip, to attend thereon, and be reſponſible
for their doings, according to ſuch Conſtitution
and Rules in that behalf.

Theſe are to receive all Propoſals from any
Perſons touching their having ſuch Credit thereout
as they ſhall deſire upon their ſaid Eſtates of Lands
or Goods reſpectively ; and to contract and agree
with them therein, at ſuch values, and for ſuch
time as they ſhall judge the ſecurity propoſed of
either kind will admit, and to draw up, and perfect ſuch Bank-Bills, Bills of Sale, Mortgages
Grants and Defezances thereof, as Lands or Goods
reſpectively ſhall require ; and perfect the Coun-
terparts thereof, to the Mortgagers and Depoſi-

They are alſo to cauſe the ſaid Mortgages and
                                                    Depo-

Depofits to be laid up and ftored, refpectively, in as fafe and convenient Rooms, and Warehoufes, &c. as fhall be without exception, to prevent damage of Weather, Robbery, Fire, Water or Vermin of any kind, whereby they may be impaired, or dampnified, and all this under the truft and cuftody of fuch numbers of the faid Partners, as no opportunity can be taken to impair or leffen the fecurity, unlefs they fhould all agree therein; which cannot reafonably be imagined, being fuch as are propofed. But for the better fecurity thereof, there may be continual watching on all fuch places; and it will be the Intereft of all perfons, any way concerned in the affairs and profits of fuch a Bank, to be careful to prevent, and to give Advertifement of any attempt made to the impairing and prejudicing thereof, for that their livelihood and dependences will much confift, in their preferving it in the greateft Repute; which upon the leaft violation, by thofe who are engaged in the management and truft thereof, will be utterly loft, and the Bank fall to the Ground.

These Partners aforefaid, muft alfo enter into and oblige themfelves by Covenants to, and with other Perfons to be called Affeffors of the Bank, and Confervators of the Conflitution, Rules, and Inftructions to be obferved in the management thereof, for their diligence and faithfulnefs, in the difcharge and Execution of their refpective trufts, according to the faid Conftitution: and irviolably to obferve the fame, and all the Rules thereof.

The

The said Affessors have also the Oversight and Controll of the whole Affair : To see the same be so managed : and to that end are daily to inspect the management thereof; and that the said Rules be duly observed on both parts, *viz.* as well on the part of the persons dealing with them, as of the managers themselves, in every branch of the Bank, that all be done with Justice, and Impartiality between them ; to settle differences, in case any happen ; and in the absence of the Managers, may supply that defect, by their personal transacting the same things, or allowing others as their Deputies. Also,

Each of the said Partners must deposit Moneys and other Estate in the Bank as a Stock or Fund, of their own ; which be a further Security and Obligation upon them, for their upright dealings : For thereby every of themselves become personally Interested, and concerned to be careful in every thing, that they keep the Rules; and all Persons concerned in the yearly profits thereof are liable, according to the Constitution, to answer the damages, as far as their respective shares thereof extend.

Of the fourth Particular, viz. *The necessary Rules to be observed in this Bank.*

1. I*Nprimis*, That the Partners in the management of the affairs of the said Bank do live in some convenient place, of the chief trading Town of each Countrey, from day to day, and at

at such hours as the bufinefs and occafions thereof
fhall require; to receive Propofals from any perfons, touching their having fuch Credit as they
fhall defire; and for drawing up and perfecting
fuch Bank-bills, Mortgages, Bills of Sale and Defezances thereof, as Lands or Goods refpectively fhall require; Alfo for giving information and
fatisfaction concerning the fecurity, benefits and
advantages accruing thereby, to fuch as fhall defire to deal with them therein; and to take Subfcriptions for that purpofe.

2. *Item*, That whatfoever Perfon fhall propofe
to Mortgage or Depofit any ftaple Goods or Merchandizes, Lands, Tenements or Hereditaments of
a clear and good title, to the faid Partnerfhip,
may have fuch and fo many Bills delivered to him
as fhall amount to about the value or fum of one
half, or two thirds of the faid Eftates; or more
or lefs according as his occafions fhall require;
and the nature of the Depofitors fecurity will admit. Paying for the ufe of the faid Bills, after
the rate of four pounds *per Cent. per annum*, in like
Bills, at the end of every fix Months, for fo long
time as he and they fhall agree for the fame.

3. *Item*, That if at the Expiration of the term
agreed for, the Mortgager or Depofitor fhall defire the continuance thereof, for fuch further time
as the Partnerfhip fhall judge the nature thereof
will admit, the fame fhall be allowed upon the
fame terms; and if any perfon fhall defire to
redeem them fooner than the time agreed on, he
fhall have liberty fo to do, paying only for fuch
time

time as they continue depofited or unredeemed. And fhall be allowed to pay in any Even fumms (not being under ten Pounds) in part thereof, if he fhall think fit fo to do, to leffen his Debt and charges.

4. *Item*, That the Redemption the reof be by Bank bills'of Credit, or fuch other Depofits as the Partnerfhip fhall approve of. But if by Moneys in fpecie, that there be an Addition of Forty Shillings more in every hundred Pounds paid in Money, than in the faid Bills. For they defire not the ingroffing of Coyn, or ftreightning mens occafions thereby.

5. *Item*, That if it fhall happen that any payments fhall be made in ready Money, fuch Perfons as having any of the faid Bills in their hands, which they would have Exchanged, to anfwer their occafions for Money, and fhall feafonably defire the fame, fhall be accommodated therewith, upon the delivery up of Bills to fuch value.

6. *Item*, That there be One or more Perfons allowed by the Partnerfhip in the Nature of Merchant-brokers, to correfpond between the Perfons who have, and who want Moneys, and Bills refpectively, to affift their refpective occafions.

7. *Item*, That if any Perfon fhall not redeem his pledge, or pay his Intereft at the refpective times agreed on (being of Goods or Perfonal Eftate, the continuance whereof may be hazardous) the Partnerfhip, giving notice thereof, may Sell the fame at the beft Rates they can get, either in ready Moneys, or Bank bills, rendring the Overplus to the Depofitor.   8. *Item*,

8. *Item*, That if any Person be Rob'd of, or lose any Bill or Bills, by accidents of Fire, Water or otherwise. He may have them renewed, if he forthwith apply to the Partnership, and make a voluntary Oath thereof, before a Magistrate, expressing the Number, Value and Date of each Bill or Bills; and securing the Partnership against all after-demands for the same Bills: It appearing by the Bank-books, that such Bill or Bills were issued thereout, and have not been returned.

9. *Item*, That all Bank Bills of Credit be Signed by two or more of the said Partners, (whereof one to be a principal manager) who are thereby held, to oblige themselves, and all and every their Partners of the said Bank, to accept the same for so much Currant Moneys as shall be in them respectively mentioned, in Payment, for Redemption or purchase of any Estate in the said Bank, according to the Rules thereof: and that all such Bills be duly entred, in Books to be kept for that purpose, and the Indented Counter-part thereof filed, before the same be issued.

10. *Item*, That all Goods deposited, be laid up and stored in such safe and Convenient Rooms, Warehouses, or Cellars, Yards or Docks respectively; for preventing damage of Weather, Robbery, Imbezlement, Fire, Water, or Vermin of any kind, whereby they may be impaired, and be under such custody and continual care, as will probably render them more safe than in any Persons particular Custody, or Ware-house.

11. *Item*, That the Charge of Warehouse-room be

be reasonable, with respect to the bulkiness or value of the Deposit; and be agreed upon between the Parties to, and inserted in, each Contract. In which respect it will be easier to many than to hire Warehouses of their own.

12. *Item,* That all persons having any Deposits in Bank-warehouses, &c. may have liberty, at seasonable hours, and in the presence of known persons, to be intrusted for that purpose, to view their Goods, that they be not imbezled, or dampnified, and to provide against the same: Also to shew them to their Chapmen; and shall be assisted therein by the Rommagers or Porters imployed by the Partnership

13. *Item,* That in case the Creditors of this Bank shall agree to desire, and accordingly Declare in Writing, That there be a Determination put thereto: Or if on any other account whatsoever, the Determination thereof shall be judged necessary, by the Proposers and Managers of this Bank, and so declar'd in Writing (which cannot be without allowance and ascertaining of a reasonable Time betwixt the said Creditors and Partnership or closing up the same, and the Accompts thereof, so as may be without damage to any or either of them,) That, as no person is or shall be compelled to accept Bank-bills of Credit, unless he shall voluntarily agree so to do, and for no longer time, nor otherwise than he shall so consent: so, no man paying his *præmium* and charges aforesaid, for the Credit he hath, shall be compelled to Redeem his Pledge, being of Personal Estate, sooner than the time contracted for, and the na-

cure of the Deposit shall require: And to the End the Mortgager of Lands, of unquestionable good title may not be distressed, to his undoing, in case he should, by reason of such Declaration, be suddainly call'd upon to Redeem the same, (which may be impossible for him to do in some years, through the scarcity of Moneys) That all & every Mortgager of Lands in such case, shall or may have and take six years time, from and after such Declaration aforesaid, to be allowed unto him, his Heirs and Assigns, for Redemption of his Lands; He or they paying after the rate of six pounds *per cent. per Annum*, in ready Moneys, at the end of every six Months, for the continuance of the Credit he had thereupon, from such time as the said Declaration shall be perfected, until he shall redeem the same: and that the Partners of this Bank shall or may have and take one full years time more, from the Expiration of the said six years, to be allowed unto them, for selling the said Lands, or such of them as shall not, within the said six years be redeemed; whereby they may be inabled to receive, In, and Exchange all Bank bills then granted forth, into the now current Coyn or Moneys of this Country, or other moneys being not of more intrinsique value than what now passes: Or otherwise satisfie for the same by such proportions of the said remaining Lands or other Effects, as shall be judged to be of equal value : Or by assigning or transferring to such Creditors the then Remaining Lands or other effects, at the same Rates or Values for which they were respectively Mortgaged or deposited·   And in the mean time Paying to all the Creditors who shall then have any

Bills

Bills in their Hands, after the fame rate of Intereft, for fo long time, after publifhing the faid Declaration, as the faid Bills fhall remain in the faid Creditors hands, unoccupied; with Deduction and allowance only of the *Præmium* contracted for, as aforefaid; and that fuch Bank-bills, as before fuch Declaration made, have been given forth, upon the real or perfonal Securities aforementioned which remain in the Poffeffion of the faid Bank, may and fhall be efteemed, and pafs as Currant Moneys, of the value of the prefent Coyn, in all Receipts and Payments whatfoever, during the faid Term.

14. *Item*, That the foregoing Rules be attended and obferved by all and fingular Perfons concerned therein, and who fhall propofe to deal with, and accept the Bills of Credit iffued by the Managers of the faid Bank of Credit, Lumbard and Exchange of Moneys propofed to be erected in any place, and managed by Perfons in Partnerfhip, as other Merchantly affairs.

Of the fifth Particular, viz. *The Particular Advantages of fuch Perfons as fhall voluntarily deal with the faid Partners, in thefe affairs; which will appear in feveral Inftances.*

Firft Inftance.

A Country Chapman hath Lands, fuppofe worth to be fold for 400 *l.* and being willing to inlarge his Trade and Dealings, or make improvement on his Lands, as far as his Eftate will inable him; Or, having bought Goods, which he is indebted, and

can-

cannot otherwife pay for, he mortgages his Land to the Partnerfhip for 200 *l.* more or lefs; and thereupon receives feveral Bank-bills of Credit, for 200 *l. &c.* of feveral values from twenty fhillings, and fo upwards, to anfwer his occafions.

With thefe he buyes fuch Goods as he pleafes, or payes his Debts for what he formerly bought of the Wholefale Shop-keeper, or Warehoufe-keeper, in **fuch Town or Towns of Trade as fhall fall into this way of Dealing**; and, having Bank-bills to deliver for them, which are of better value by 40 *s.* in the 100 *l.* than Moneys, with this Society, as is herein evinced; he buyes much Cheaper than he could upon his own Credit, or with Moneys in fpecie.

The Shop-keeper goes to the Merchant, who thus agrees, and buyes of him other Goods, with the fame or other like Bills; wherein he reaps the fame advantage as he gave his Chapman.

The Merchant buyes Corn, Beef, Pork, Fifh, Hops, Lumber, Pitch, Tarr, Rozin, Skins, Furs or any other of the Countreys Products or Manufactures, of the Husbandman, Grazier, Artificer, or maker thereof.

The Husbandman, *&c.* If a Farmer of Lands, payes his Rent, and purchafes more young Cattel of his Neighbour, for Breed or Fatting, Or,

If an Owner of Land, and hath not fufficient ftock to improve it, he alfo Mortgages his Land, and has Credit to furnifh himfelf. Or,

If he hath fufficient Stock, and perhaps more than his prefent Farm can maintain, he hath his Eye upon a neighbouring Farm, or piece of Land

that

that would be fold; he Mortgages his own Land in the Bank, and hath Credit to buy the other.

If then he want Stock, he may also Mortgage the Farm or piece of Land last purchased; and have Credit to inable him fully to improve and stock both : Whereby he doubles his yearly advantages, and if he can then content himself to live as frugally, and be as industrious as before, he may soon compass to pay off his Debt, and redeem his Land. Or, he may continue the Credit he had, and take out more upon the Additional improvement; and thus increase his purchases and Estate, as long as such an help is afforded.

Second Instance.

The like may be done for carrying on the opening and working in any Mines, Minerals or Quarreys of Stone, Lead, Tin, Iron, Copper, &c. thus, viz. The Mine and Lands wherein the same is, may be Mortgaged as aforesaid, to supply the Owner thereof with Bills of Credit, for paying his Workmen, in any summ of Twenty Shillings, or above.

As fast as any of these Metals, &c. are wrought fit for Sale, if a Chapman be wanting, the Metal may be brought into the Bank, and the Owner Receive Bank-bills to the value of about two thirds thereof, as aforesaid, to enable him to proceed on his Works : And the Metal lying in Bank is there readier for a Market than elsewhere, in his own Private House or Ware-house, at very reasonable rates for lying there, and may with allowance of the owner, be sold in his absence, by the Merchant-Broker before mentioned, at such current Rates

as

as he fhall fet, and he become Creditor for fo much, to be difcompted or paid him, whenfoever he fhall call for it.

Third Inftance.

A Weaver of Cloth, Serge, or Linnen, &c. is imployed in any Work-houfe erected or to be erected, to carry on thofe refpective Manufactures : Alfo other Manufacturers, and Artificers, in Rope-making, Cables, Rigging, Sails, Anchors, or any other materials for the Fifhing trade, Merchants, or building of Ships, &c.

The Owner of fuch Work-houfe, or materials refpectly, confents to Mortgage the fame, for one or two hundred pounds, more or lefs, in Bank-bills, as the work fhall require, and the value of the houfe or materials will admit.

With thefe Bills, the Work-mafter or Overfeer, buyes Wooll, Worfted, Yarn, Hemp, Flax, Dying-ftuffs, Iron, Timber, Lumber, &c. of the Merchant, Ware houfe-keeper, Countreyman, or other Seller ; and finifhes 40, 60, or 100, peices, &c. more or lefs of any the faid Commodities ; which when wrought up for a Market ; if he want a Chapman, he brings into the Bank Ware-houfes, as aforefaid ; or fuch Yards, Docks, or other places as they fhall appoint or agree : Takes up new Credit upon them, and leaves them there to be fold, at his own rates, as aforefaid. On

A confiderable parcel of Wooll, Cotten, Yarn, Flax, Hemp, Oyl, Dying-ftuffs, or other Goods for his ufe, are offer'd to Sale ; he may pay one third thereof by his wrought up Goods unfold, and bringing thefe Commodities into the Bank,

may

may receive Bills of Credit for paying the other two thirds ; which he may take out, in parcels, as he brings in any new wrought up Goods, or hath occasion to use them for working up more ; and the Bank-ware-houses will be to him as *Blackwell-Hall*, &c. in *London* to the Clothiers, to affift his fale of them, without his trouble : For thither will all Merchants have incouragement to come, to feek fupplies for Tranfportation, and find Goods always ready.

Other Inftances might be multiplied, but by thefe it appears,

1. That the Manufacturer, &c. lofes no time in looking out a Chapman.

2. Is always furnifh'd with Credit to buy his Materials at the beft hand.

3. The Merchant never trufts, nor Ware-houfe keeper ; Or, if he do, the plenty of Bills expedits his Chapmans Sale, and confequently his payments. Whereby,

4. He has incouragement and ftock prefently to look out for more of the fame, or other ufeful Merchandizes.

5. Sends forth the faid Metals, Clothes, Stuffs, Linnen, &c. amongft other Merchandizes of the Product of his Countrey, or imported.

6. Makes return of Bullion, Moneys, or other ufeful Goods, which are prefently bought off with Bank bills. Or,

7. He may ftore them up in Bank Ware-houfes, and receive prefent Credit, wherewith to fend out again. And,

8. Thereby is inabled (at leaft) to double, or
treble

treble his yearly dealings, and receive proportionable advantages. This,

1. Increases and quickens Merchandizing and trade.

2. Promotes Shipping and Navigation. Which;

3. Increases the Publique Duties, and consequently the Revenues.

4. Imploys the Poor in the mynings and manufactures forementioned.

5. They get Moneys by these Imployments.

6. That inables them to buy up all necessaries for Cloathing, Victuals, paying of Debts, &c.

7. This helps the Consumption of, as well their own Commodities, as other imported goods and Merchandizes: for no Man, that hath wherewith to buy, will go naked or be hungry, &c.

8. This helps to civilize the Ruder sort of People; and incourages others to follow their Example in Industry and Civility.

9. Thus all sorts of Persons become inabled to live handsomly, and out of Debt; and that prevents multiplicity of Law Suits, and troubles to the Government: but none of these advantages may be expected, out of the small Pittance of Cash, that now is, ever was, or likely will be in any Countrey, unless assisted in Trade, and inriched by the help this Bank proposes. And so we pass to the Consideration.

Of the sixth Particular, viz. The answering some few of the most material Pertinent Queries, and Objections touching this Bank, viz.

Q. 1. Can I have Moneys for Bank-bills, when have occasion ?   *Answ.*

Anfw. 1. 'Tis not propounded to be a Bank of Moneys (which is liable to inexpreſſible and unforeſeen hazards) but, of Credit to be given forth by Bills ; not on Moneys advanced, as in other Banks, but (on Lands or Goods, as aforeſaid,) to ſupply ſuch as cannot get Moneys (by reaſon of its ſcarcity) with whatſoever may be had for Moneys. Yet,

Anfw. 2. As oft as any Perſons redeem their Lands, or Goods, they muſt do it in Bank-bills, or with Moneys. If in ready Moneys, the Partnerſhip may exchange Bills therewith, to ſuch as deſire it ; as is afore provided by the Rules.

Anfw. 3. However, this Bank is no occaſion of ſtreightning men that would have Moneys ; but leaves them free ; and in this caſe, the Merchant-brokers of the Bank will be helpful, between thoſe who have and who want Moneys, and Bills reſpectively ; as is likewiſe aforementioned in the ſaid Rules. But,

Anfw. 4. If it be made appear to you, that others who have Moneys, will be willing to change your Bank-bills into thoſe ſpecies of Gold and Silver, and thank you for offering them the occaſion (though the Bank Partnerſhip do it not) you'l have no cauſe to decline the other advantages Propoſed : Eſpecially if you may both be gainers by the Exchange. Now, if I ow'd you 500. *l.* to be paid in Silver, which I could not do, but ſhould propoſe to pay you in Gold, at the intrinſique coyn'd value, which if you part with again will yield you five pound profit, or more : Would you then refuſe Gold ?

Obj.

Obj. But how will you apply this, to make it Credible?

Sol. Thus, Whoever hath any payment to make in Bank, which (in probability if such Bank take effect in any Countrey) will be every Man that deals in above twenty Shillings at a time) will find, that we muſt pay forty Shillings more, in every hundred pounds of ready Money, than in Bank-bills of Credit; (as *per* the forementioned Rules of the Bank) which is about five pence be-nefit to the Exchanger, in every 20. *s.* No doubt then of having Moneys (by a little inquiry of the Merchant-Broker) at the value contained in the Bills, of all ſuch as muſt redeem their Mortgages, and Depoſits. But,

Bills, wherever Banks have been erected (though Money Banks) have always been of better value than Moneys in ſpecie. Whereof three Reaſons may be given.

(1.) For the eaſe of Compting and Carriage; and preventing damage to the Receiver, by Coun-terfeit, Clip'd, Light or baſe Coyn : (Which is obvious to all.)

(2.) For ſafety in Travelling, laying up, *&c.* As viſible as the other.

(3.) For the advantage that is to be made by the Exchange, on the account of ſuch Conveniences. Whereof take two Examples, *viz.*

(1.) The Bank-bills of *Holland* are ordinarily better than Moneys, by at leaſt three pounds *per Cent.* And,

(2.) Thoſe in *Venice,* by twenty pounds *per Cent.* and Laws made there to keep them from riſing

fing higher; for they were once at 28. *l. per Cent.* and not without fome difficulty Reduced to twen-ty; fo that each Bill of 100. *l.* is now Current at 120. *l.*

Obj. But how is that poffible or Credible?

Sol. There is this account rendred of it (which has confirmation by many other Inftances that might be given, concerning the Current Prices of many Commodities, which have not fo much of in-trinfique value in them,) *viz.* The State of *Venice* propounded the Erecting a Bank to confift of two Millions of Duckets: Accordingly Moneys were brought in, Bills given out for the fame value; and a ftop put to the receiving, or giving out any more of either.

The ufefulnefs of thefe Bills was fuddainly found to be fuch in the practice and imployment of them, upon the three forementioned Accounts, that every Man, at one time or other, found his affairs required them; So, that at firft, fuch Bills would not be parted with for Money, under ten Shillings *per* hundred pounds; And no fooner was that become the Current rate, but they were fuc-ceffively raifed, by ten Shillings at a time, till they came to be, in every one's Eftimation, 28. *l. per Cent.* better than moneys in fpecie; and fo paft accordingly. Whereupon,

The State of *Venice* enacted feveral Laws againft their paffing fo high: which failing to accomplifh what was required, at length they conceived it neceffary, in order to the bringing down the price, to propofe the giving forth Bills for three hundred thoufand Duckets more: By which means they
brought

brought it back to twenty pounds *per Cent.* (which pleafed the People) and there fixt it, as to it's rifing higher afterwards, by a fevere Law; fince when, it ftands fo to this day: And this is no more than what is familiar in the price of other things, *viz.* Diamonds, Rubies, Pearles, Horfes, Pictures, *&c.* which have their Eftimation from the various Pleafures and Fancies of men, *&c.*

And, if it be demanded, what induced that State to allow it fo high?

The Anfwer is eafie, *viz.* The State of *Venice* had made ufe of the Moneys depofited, in their publick occafions (where obferve the hazard of a Money Bank) and, having Promifed, for fatisfaction of Creditors, to raife the like fumm, if they fhould have occafion for it, reap this advantage, of their Peoples high opinion of Bills, that, they are thereby affured, that, never, will any Creditor come to ask them 100*l.* for a Bill of 100 *l.* when he may have 120 *l.* from any other hand. A notable way to pay a vaft debt. But, by means hereof, the Creditor has no other Fund or Security but the States Word: For, there is not one Ducket for them in Bank.

Q. 2. My Lands or Goods are already Mortgaged for Moneys, at a higher Rate of Intereft; and the Mortgagee will not take Bills. Can fuch a Bank help me?

Anf. There may be Perfons, of whom you may be informed at the Bank, who will advife and affift you therein: If there be Moneys in the Countrey to be had.

Q. 3. I have neither Lands nor Goods, but a
Trade,

Trade, by which I could live comfortably if I had a small Stock; and I could afford to give a greater Intereſt, and have Friends that would help me ſo pon my own bond: But they have not Moneys. Which way ſhall I be help'd?

Anſ. If your Friends have Lands or Goods, they may have theſe Bank-bills of Credit, at four Pouhds per Cent. *per Annum*, to lend you at ſuch Rates as you can agree: Whereby they alſo may be gainers, and have incouragement to help you.

Much more might be ſaid upon this Subject, but theſe ſeem to be ſufficient, for incouraging an attempt: And, the experiments of the things ſuggeſted will give ſuch clear Demonſtrations of the Uſefulneſs, advantage, neceſſity and ſecurity of ſuch Banks, in moſt places, beyond all others that have been hitherto put in Practice, as thoſe who are not ſo prompt to receive things into their urderſtandings by the Notions of them, or are prejudiced by miſtaken apprehenſions about them, and, thence raiſe many impertinent Objections (not worth ſcribling) may be preſumed will follow others Examples, in wel-doing, when thoſe are obſerved to thrive who go before therein.

We ſhall therefore, for the Concluſion, which is the laſt Particular mentioned, to be Diſcourſed, ſumm up all, in this General Aſſertion, viz.

THat there will ariſe many more Conveniences and advantages, by this Bank, to ſuch Countreys where they ſhall be erected, than have been enumerated, in the ſeveral foregoing inſtances; or, well, can be.   1. **By**

1. By this, the Trade and Wealth of any Countrey is establish'd upon it's own Foundation; and upon a *Medium* or Ballance arifing within it felf *viz*. The Lands and Products of fuch Countrey and not upon the Importation of Gold or Silver or the Scarcity or Plenty of them, or, of any thing elfe imported from Forreign Nations, which may be withheld, prohibited, or enhanfed, at the Pleafure of others.

2. The Native Commodities of fuch Countrey will thus become improved to a fufficiency (at leaft) for their own Ufe ; and thereby afford a comfortable fubfiftence to many ingenious and induftrious Perfons, in fuch Countreys; who know not how to fubfift : Efpecially fuch as are Banifh'd, or inforced to forfake their Native Countreys, by reafon of the heat of Perfecution, upon the account of Religion.

3. It will not be in the Power of any, by Extortion and Oppreffion, to make a Prey of the Neceffitous.

4. The Fifhery of fuch Countreys, as lye convenient for it, may be improved : and the Navigation and Shipping increafed, for Ufe or Sale.

5. The Publick Revenues thereof, in confequence of thefe, will be augmented.

6. The Rents of Lands, yea, the purchafe value thereof, will rife ; For, the Plenty of Money, or a valuable Credit equivalent thereunto, and the Lowering of Intereft, muft neceffarily have that effect

7. It will fupply the defect or fcarcity of Moneys in fpecie until by the fetling of Manufactures, *&c.* (which this Bank propofes) the Products of fuch Countrey for Exportation fhall come to Ballance or exceed the value of it's Importations ; which

which afterwards will neceſſitate the bringing in of Moneys, as faſt as the want thereof hath carryed it away. For, the true Ground of the Plenty or Scarcity of Moneys in any Contrey, is not the high or low value of the Money (as ſome erroneouſly conceive) but, that the value of goods imported from other parts hath been greater than that of the Export. The ballance whereof muſt neceſſarily be anſwer'd with Moneys, and for the ſame Reaſon, Revers'd, the Export of goods when brought to exceed the value of the Import, muſt, as neceſſarily bring it back again to ſuch proportion as the Export can be raiſed. And whatſoever other means may be ſuggeſted for furniſhing of Moneys, muſt be fruitleſs, for, there will abide no more than ſuch proportion ; let what value will be put on Moneys above the currant price thereof in other Countreys with whom they ſhall Trade ; which may be further evidenced, if this hint thereof be not ſufficiently intelligible. To which may be added, That the leſs need there is of Moneys in ſpecie, by reaſon of ſuch Currant Credit, the more will be the increaſe of Money it ſelf; as is manifeſt in *Holland, Venice,* and all places where Bank-Credit ſupplies the Defect of thoſe ſpecies ; at leaſt, the Money that remains in ſuch Countreys, will be at greater liberty for ſuch petty occaſions as cannot be ſo well accommodated by Bills.

In order therefore, and as Prævious to the entring upon ſuch an affair, 'tis requiſite that other Queries be propounded and reſolved, *viz.*

Q. 4. How ſhall it come to be known whether a ſufficient number of Perſons, of all Ranks, Trades

and

and Callings, will deal with this Bank ? The Reafons of which Inquiry are thefe, *viz.*

(1.) It will be of ufe to the undertakers of fuch Bank to know it, for their incouragement in their entrance upon this affair.   And,

(2.) To fuch others as would take the Bills, if they were fatisfied they could buy fuch Goods, *&c.* as they want, with Bills, at as eafie rates, as if they had ready Moneys to give.

Anfw. 1. It will be requifite, that a fhort Declaration be tendred to be fubfcribed by fome Perfons of all Ranks, Trades and Callings; fignifying that they will accept the faid Bank-Bills of Credit, in their ordinary future dealings of buying and felling, or other traffiquing affairs, whereupon they are to receive Moneys, for fo much ready Moneys as fhall be in fuch Bills mentioned, upon the terms and according to the Rules of the Bank : Saving to every Man his fpecialties, and particular Contracts.

Anf. 2. That fuch as fhall fo declare themfelves, by Subfcription (or otherwife) may be put into Alphabetical Lifts ; and, fuch as take forth Bills may be informed of the Names of the faid refpective Perfons, their Trades or Callings, and Places of Habitation.   But,

Q. 5. It may be further inquired, *viz.* What if fome forts of perfons requifite for a univerfal Circulation of Bills, will not, in all cafes, ingage to accept Bank-bills : but fome will wholly Refufe them, and cry up moneys, inhans'd to a higher Rate than they pafs at in other Countreys, *&c.* Others will be for either, or both, as they find it for their advantage, *&c.*

Anf.

Anf. It's not neceffary that all fhould, in all cafes, oblige themfelves ro Bills, as long as there is moneys to be had: But if there be not a fufficiency of that for carrying on of Trade, &c. as, this Bank hinders not the Currency of moneys, but that may be imployed as far as it will go, (which, for the moft part, during the fcarcity of it, will be in fmall dealings,) fo, the Bills will be found ufefull to fupply the defect. The needful proportion whereof will foon be underftood; and each Perfon will caft his bufinefs, and make his Contracts accordingly : And confequently, this need not hinder, or difcourage the attempt; if there be a competent number of each, or moft forts, that cannot, otherwife, deal as they would.

Q. 6. And, if any fhall inquire, What number of Merchants and other Tradefmen may be fufficient (at firft erecting fuch a Bank) to affift a Circulation of Bills in Trade, in cafe fome fhould, not only withdraw from, but, obftruct, and mifreprefent the Affair, or perfons managing it, as not having the publick approbation, or Sanction of the Authority of a Countrey, which they may fuggeft to be neceffary ? It's anfwered,

Anf. 1. A few Merchants in any Countrey who are General Traders (by the help this Bank propofes, in the foregoing Inftances,) may be fufficient to give encouragement for the Entrance upon this Affair; and fo many Shop-keepers, Artificers, &c as muft and will deal with them. For,

Anf. 2. It may reafonably be prefumed, that, many, in the practice of the thing, will apprehend

hend the neceffity, ufefulnefs, and fecurity thereof, who cannot eafily take it up in the Notion,
or by difcourfe; and that fuch will come in by
Degrees: for, if, (being Merchants) they ftand
out, fuch of their Chapmen as fhall find it their
intereft to fell for Bills, muft buy again of others
who will take them in payment; and finding themfelves well ufed by fuch, will hardly return where
they have been refufed: and, if of other Profeffi-
ons, they muft either fell little, or do it on Truft,
or wait for payment till moneys grow more plen-
tifull; whileft others carry away the whole trading amongft them.

Anf. 3. This part of the Merchants Calling, is,
in every refpect, as Free and lawfull for any to
undertake, and needs no more of publick encouragement or Countenance, than that part of buying and felling (at home or abroad) with or for
ready money, time, or barter, which they better
underftand and practife. And the managers hereof
may as well expect a benefit by it as the others:
Forafmuch as it will no lefs take up their time to
attend; and will be an improving the trade of any
Countrey, no lefs than the other: And laftly, has
' its hazards attending it; for the profits accruing
thereby, are, in the firft place affigned, by the Conftitution and Rules thereof, for making good all
loffes and damages that may happen, in the management of this Affair.

De te Narratur, N. A.

FINIS.

A Supplement *or* Appendix *to the Treatise Entituled,*

A MODEL for Erecting a Bank of Credit, &c; Or, An account of some of the many Prejudices that will Inevitably ensue, as well to His *Majesty* as to his Subjects by enhansing the value of Spanish *Coyns* &c. above his *Majesties*. Together with the most probable means for Preventing thereof, without damage to any. *viz.*

Prejudice. 1*st.*   To the KING ; and that in a double respect.

First, In point of Honour and Royal Dignity. *viz.*

1. *That the Stamp or Coyn of any Prince should be preferr'd to his Majesties, Especially by his own Subjects, it being so sacred a Badge of Royalty and Dominion.*
2. *That any part of his Dominions should, by so doing be proclaim'd to be reduced to such indigence, in Scandal of Government.*

Secondly, In point of Profit. *viz.*

I: THat any European Princes should so far divide or Share with his Majesty in the Royalty and Profit of Coynage; and be thereby invited, not only to put off their Moneys to so great enriching themselves, and impoverishing his Majesties Subjects: But to raise the value of their moneys upon all other Princes: To the confusion of trade, by altering the agreed or used measure or standard amongst them.

2. That by such a course (Especially at such a time as this, wherein his Majestie is setling and Establishing his Revenue) the whole should be Regulated by a Temporary advance (for a present turn) which, when Reduced to his Majesties Standard (as no doubt it will soon be judged fit to have it so) will be Detrimentall to his Majestie in all future times.

Prejudice. 2d. *To his Majesties Subjects.* viz.

1. To such as have contracted for money, current at the time of the Contract, and by this means shall come to be paid in other moneys really less in value; which carrys great injustice in it; whether such contracts be for goods or Merchandizes, ancient Rights and Rents on Leases, Annuities or Perpetuities. &c.

2. To such as live upon Pensions, Salaries, Wages; Civill, Military or Ecclesiasticall, Establish'd by Law or otherwise. Also to Handicrafts

dicrafts men, Artificers, Labourers Servants, &c,
who will (in time) become pinch'd thereby,
viz. Upon Raising the Prices of Victualls,
Cloathing, and other Commodities (an usuall
confequence of raising moneys) which will
be a great Oppreffion. &c.

3. To the whole Community and body of
his Majefties Subjects inhabiting fuch Country
(except the firft importers of fuch Coyns) For,
they muft all Expect to pay for what imported
Goods they need, proportionably to fuch advance of Coyns : as is apparent in the advance
of *Twenty-Five Pound Per-cent* on all goods
imported into *New-England*.

Object. 1. *But will they not all have opportunities of paying away the money they receive, at
the fame Rates they receive it ?*

Aufw. Though they do, That will help little : For, they cannot buy the fame Comodi-
ties with it, as they might have bought with the
moneys for which they Contract d : and confequently will be Damnified fo much more
thereby, as the Prices fhall be raifed.

Object. 2. *Princes and States may give what
values they pleafe to moneys by enhanfing or Lowering of them : And (fay fome) by this means,
we fhall not only have moneys brought in, but keep
what moneys we have from being Transported, which
occafions our prefent Scarcity and decay of trade.*

Anfw. The Queftion is not about the Power,
but profit of Princes, in giving new rifed
values to other Princes moneys. And the Objectors

ļ:ctors Affertion is a great Error. For he con-
fiders not,

1   What it is that is the Real caufe of the Scarcity of moneys, *viz.*   The Actual Transporting
the Ballance or Over plus of the value of goods
imported, above the proportion of the value of
the native products exported ; which (Exceeding) muft of neceffity be anfwered by moneys in specie; and confequently, what ever
rate moneys be current at (though it fhould
be double the ufuall value) it will be exported ; and the higher the rates be, the more
muft be Transported for the ballance. Nor,
does he confider,

2   That money will retain the fame proportion in value to other things, as, the Gene-
rall confent of other Nations and Countrys with
whom the dealings are, does give it. By
which it comes to pafs, That if the price of
moneys be raifed by any Prince or ftate to
any proportion whatfoever, above the common
and intrinfique value, the Price of all forreign
goods impoited into fuch Country,   will be
proportionably raifed upon the People by the
Importer. For Example, Imagine any Country fhould have it's Coyn raifed from *Five
Shillings per ounce,* Sterling Silver (which is
Three pence each penny weight) to *Six Shillings
Eight pence per-ounce,* or *Four pence* each penny
weight, which is one fourth part (*as in New-
England*) the Importer muft and will fell his
goods there, at above one fourth part more
in

in price than he was wont to do ; or he shall lose by his Commodity. And therefore the first thing he will consider in his Sale will be, the intrinsique value of the payment, whether it be in money or goods ; and hee'l be sure so to deal as to lose nothing by either ; but the Country shall pay the more, which he'l take away with him, in the money so raised in Denomination.

Obj. 3. *But you'l say, perhaps, as imported Goods will be raised in value, so will Exported : and that will counterpoise the Damage.*

Answ. 1. Suppose that, yet it will not keep the overplus of the ballance in such Countrey; which is the evil predicated. But,

2. It will be difficult for any Country, (and especially for *New-England*) to raise its wonted known price of its NativeCommodities, for a considerable time ; perhaps for some years : which the present circumstances of *New-England* cannot bear : for, while the grass grows, (as the proverb is) the Steer will starve. And 'tis more probable, that as the Country grows more populous and improved, its products will multiply ; and consequently abate in price: But suppose the price to rise proportionably with the mony ; 'twill then bear hard on most of the parties before enumerated, whose settled wages, Rents, &c. will remain what they were.

Quest. These are Labrinths it's confest. But it's evident (may New-England-men say) *that we cannot hold out long under such pinching circumstan-*

ces

ties as we are reduced unto, for want of Moneys. We must therefore run the hazzards ; unless some expedient be suddainly applyed: The Shop-keepers must break ; and they'l break their Merchants ; and they their Principals, &c. Is there any Remedy ?

Sol. The most probable, is humbly offered in the particulars following, *viz.*

1 **By some Act or Proclamation, That in all payments on future contracts, all sorts of forreign Sterling Silver shall pass by weight, at the value of his Majesties Englifh Coyn.**

2 By sumptuary and Trading-Laws for Ballancing the importations of such Commodities as are most useful, with the Exportations of the manufactures and products of the Country that may be best spared, after the utmost improvement made of them: which may be easily contrived to become practicable.

3 Now, That there is so little of the Coyn of this Country remaining in Trade, it may be the easier reduced to pass at it's equal intrinsique value compared with his Majesties *English* Coyn ; by passing the several pieces here Coyned at the several values respectively adjoyned as followeth, *viz.*

The

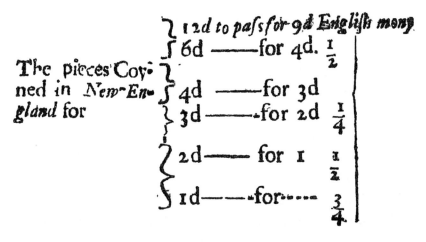

The pieces Coyned in *New-England* for
- 12d to pass for 9d *English mony*
- 6d ——— for 4d. $\frac{1}{2}$
- 4d ——— for 3d
- 3d ——— for 2d $\frac{1}{4}$
- 2d ——— for 1 $\frac{1}{2}$
- 1d ——— for —— $\frac{3}{4}$

But thefe things, and the manner of doing them effectually, are confiderations fit to be fubmitted to his Majefty and Councill, who beft know how they will comport with his Royal Intereft and Leagues with other Princes, &c.

2. Will not this be unjuft? efpecially to fuch as have ftore of thefe moneys lying by them?

Sol Not at all : for, they now pafs really for no more than according to thofe rates propofed, *viz.* Twelve pence for Nine pence, &c. The difference lying not in the intrinfique value or current ufe, but in the Denomination only, *viz.* That nine pence is ftampt and. called twelve pence : They will ftill buy as much therefore, for their fhilling when called nine pence, as they were wont to buy when called twelve pence ; but,

Obj 4. This will caufe all the prefent moneys of this Country to be tranfported ; and what fhall we do then?

Anfw That's anfwered and provided for.

4 By

4. By the Bank of Credit ; *Lumbard* and Exchange of moneys propounded, which will both supply a neceffary proportion of Credit as good as mony for carrying on of Trade, till the ballance of Trade be fettled: and then caufe moneys to be brought in as faft as ever it went out. For, as hitherto the Import of Goods, having been of greater value than the Export, hath drawn away the moneys of this Countrv, for the neceffary ballancing of Accompts ; & will fo do whatever the value of the Coyn be fet at (as is before fhewed) fo, for the fame reafon (Revers'd) the Export of *Goods* thence, when it fhall come to be of greater value than the Import (which fuch Bank will affift, in the way and manner, and by the means fuggefted) muft as neceffarily bring it back again to fuch proportion as the Exports can be raifed ; to the enriching and Flourifhing of his Majefties *Subject:* in this his Territory of *New-England.*

He that cannot fee this is darkened by unaccountable prejudice, &c.

F I N I S.

OBJECTIONS TO THE BANK OF CREDIT LATELY PROJECTED AT BOSTON

[Paul Dudley], *Objections to the Bank of Credit Lately Projected at Boston. Being a Letter upon that Occasion, to John Burril, Esq; Speaker to the House of Representatives for the Province of the Massachusetts-Bay, in New-England* (Boston, 1714), pp. 3–32.

Following the revival in 1714 of a plan to create a bank of credit along the lines suggested by John Blackwell in his *Model for Erecting a Bank of Credit*, anonymous objectors published *Objections to the Bank of Credit Lately Projected at Boston*. We now know that the author of this piece was Paul Dudley (1675–1751), the attorney general of Massachusetts and son of the governor Joseph Dudley. Paul Dudley later became the chief justice of Massachusetts despite the hostility of Increase and Cotton Mather's faction, who maintained their political enmity against Joseph Dudley through his son.

    Objections contains two main complaints. The first questions whether the government ought to own or regulate the bank, rather than leaving the responsibility to private owners who may have ulterior motives. Further, it is argued that such an enterprise ought to obtain permission or a charter from the crown, given that the general assembly and council in Boston were dependent governments. The second complaint centres on the definition of money; the author of *Objections* argues that only silver and gold truly constitute money because of their intrinsic worth and universal value. While bank notes could serve as a medium of exchange, their value could only be guaranteed by the crown, rather than private owners of the bank. In defence of his position, the author ends his letter by delineating a number of practical concerns about the management of such notes, including interest payments and insurance against mismanagement.

Objections

TO THE

𝕭ank of 𝕮redit

Lately Projected at

BOSTON.

Being a LETTER upon that Occasion, to *JOHN BURRIL*, Efq; Speaker to the Houfe of REPRESENTATIVES for the Province of the *Maffachufetts-Bay*, in

New-England.

Better is a little with Righteoufnefs, than great Revenues without Right.

BOSTON:
Printed by *T. Fleet*, in *Pudding-Lane*, near *King-Street*. 1714.

A
LETTER, &c.

SIR, .

I Believe it can't be unknown to you, That fome time the laft Summer, I prefented a *Memorial* to His Excellency the *Governour* and *Council*, referring to the *Bank of Credit*, Projected by a Number of Gentlemen, Merchants, and others among us; and you muft needs have feen in the Publick *News-Paper*, an Order of *Council* that was paffed upon that Occafion; whereby the Projectors were directed to *Proceed no further in that Affair, until the next Seffion of the General Affembly,* That fo the whole Government might be of Advice in a Matter of that Weight and Confequence. Notwithftanding all which, (I am loth to fay in Contempt of it) the Perfons Concerned, are openly carrying on their *Bank* with utmoft Vigour and Expedition; as Suppofing, and indeed Affirming, That the Government have nothing to do with them in that Affair: So that 'tis very much to be queftioned, whether the Projectors will

will make any Application to the *General Assembly* or not; looking upon themselves very Well and Sufficient without it. But does it follow, S I R, That the Government must fit still, and neither *Say* nor *Do* any thing, when they fee and hear of a Projection that is just ripe for Execution, which so very much Imports the Prerogative of the *Crown*, the Constitution and Laws of this Province, the Estates and Liberties of the People, and that not only for the present, but succeeding Generations? No, it can't be!

I doubt not, but that before I have finished this Letter, to prove beyond all Question, and that by very good Reason, That as it Principally, and in the first Place behoves the *Government*, and *General Assembly* of the Province, so it really Concerns every Man that has any Interest in this Country, with great Application to Enquire into, and feriously Confider the Nature and Confequences of this *Bank* of *Partnership*, and that before it take Effect, and there be no Remedy: For, do but fuppofe, S I R, This *Pandora's Box* once opened, and Two Hundred Thousand Pounds of thefe *Bank-Bills* Iffued and Circulating upon *Loan*, or otherwife, and the Government at home should afterwards, in their Great Wifdom Difapprove and Suppress 'em, or it should otherwife Mifcarry and come to nothing, by any unforeseen Accident; into what irreparable Mischiefs, Confusion and Misery would every body be Involved, that had to do with 'em? and the Blame and Reproach of it finally (with too much Reason) be thrown and Center on the *General Assembly*: For it will be Natural for every one then to say, *Ay! Why did not the Government Interpose and Prevent this?* And it was this very Consideration that principally Determined me at this time, freely to Communicate my Thoughts upon this Matter: And I could not, I am sure, think of a more suitable Person to Offer 'em to, than One, who has deservedly so good a Character and great an Influence in his Country.

But before I proceed any further, I must pray you not to mistake my Design; for my Intention is not so much to sit in Judgment upon this *Bank Projection*, as to Awaken the Government, (Pardon the Expression) and to Convince the Projectors, that not one Step in an Affair of this Consequence, ought to be taken without the Knowledge and Leave of His Majesty's Government of this Province, and that for these two Reasons: Principally,

First. Because we are a Dependent Government, and must in all things Conform our selves to the Laws of *Great Britain*, and the Instructions of the *Crown*; and therefore must

muſt expeƈt to give an Account of all our Matters. And then,

Secondly. Becauſe the People of this Country have their next and immediate Dependánce on the *General Aſſembly,* who are therefore to ſee to it, (as they will anſwer the Truſt repoſed in them) that the *Common-Wealth* receive no Damage by their Means. But to proceed in what I have further to ſay, I ſhall take this Method. Firſt I ſhall give you a ſhort Abſtraƈt of the Projeƈtion it ſelf, and then ſome of my Sentiments or Refleƈtions upon it.

The Projeƈtion in ſhort, as I underſtand it is thus: *A, B, C, D, &c,* to the Number we'll ſay of one Hundred, by a certain Policy of their own Framing, Aggregate or Join themſelves together into a *Company* or *Partnerſhip,* in Order to make a *Bank of Credit,* as they call it, by Subſcriptions, amounting to Two Hundred Thouſand Pounds; which Sum they propoſe to make into *Bills,* of *Pounds,* and *Shillings,* and to let 'em out at Four Pounds *per Cent.* Intereſt; the Subſcribers themſelves being obliged to take out one quarter Part of their reſpeƈtive Subſcriptions, and give good Security accordingly; the other three Quartérs to be let out upon good Land Security, to ſuch as will borrow 'em; the Profits ariſing from time to time, upon the Loan of
the

the *Bills*, to be to the Community or *Partner-ship*, excepting some Proportions thereof, which they propose for the Use of the Government, the Town of *Boston*, and some other Publick Uses, after the Expiration of such a Time, and on certain Conditions therein Expressed. And for the better Management of their Affairs, they have their *Treasurer*, *Directors*, and other Officers, &c. But for your further Information of the Projection, I will now Insert the Form of one of their *Bills*, *Viz.*

s.

(20)

*T*HIS *Indented Bill of Twenty Shillings, Obliges us, and all and every of us, and all and every of our Partners of the* Bank of Credit *in* Boston *in* New-England, *to Accept the same in all Payments, according to Covenant made by us, on Publick Record; and that it shall be accordingly received by the Treasurer for the Redemption of any Pawn or Mortgage in the said* Bank. Boston, &c.

Now in the first Place, *SIR*, How Plainly and Greatly must the Prerogative of the Crown, and the Honour of Government, be affected

affected by, and concerned in this Projection?
Dare any Man of Law, or will any Man
that loves or underftands any thing of Government, Say, or Imagine, That fuch a *Bank*
as this, may Safely, or can indeed Poffibly be
fet up, and carried on without a *Charter* from
the *Crown*? Shall a Number of Perfons, of their
own Head, Form themfelves into a Company, by a Conftitution of their own making,
and Erect themfelves into a *Body Politick*, and
Corporate to all Intents and Purpofes in the
Law, fo as to Sue and be Sued, to. Purchafe
and Grant Lands to take in Succeffion, with
the Power of Making and Lending at one
Stroke, the Modeft Sum of *Two Hundred Thoufand Pounds*, and afterwards as much more as
they fhall fee meet? Certainly, Men that
Talk at this Rate, muft be abfolute Strangers
to the Conftitution and Laws of *Great Britain*,
the Honour of Government, the very Notion
and Nature of Corporations: For any one
that has but lookt into the Hiftory of *England*
and *London*, will find that the feveral Companies, Fraternities, and Corporations there,
have been all of them Created, either by
Charter from the *Crown*, or by Act of *Parliament*, and fome of 'em by both; and neither
have, nor pretend to any other Powers, Franchifes or Liberties, than fuch as are Given
and Limited to 'em in and by their feveral
Char-

Charters. And indeed it is altogether as Abfurd in the Law, for a *Body Politick* to Create it felf, as in Philofophy for the *Body Natural.*

The *Law-Books* of *England,* do all *Una Voce* Proclaim it as an undoubted Truth, That all *Powers Politick,* all *Franchifes, Liberties, Charters Corporations,* and the like, are Derived from the King, as their Original Fountain. And I believe this is the firft time that ever any thing to the Contrary entred into the Reafon of any Man out of *Eutopia.* I am fure the Great and Famous *Bank of England* was firft Founded, and is ftill Supported on the ftrength of an Act of *Parliament,* and a *Charter* of the late King *William* and Queen *Mary* of Glorious Memory; as may be feen at Large by the faid Act of *Parliament* made in the Fifth and Sixth Years of that Reign: Whereby Their Majefties were Impower'd to Incorporate a Number of Gentlemen, Merchants, &c. by the Name of the *Governour and Company of the Bank of England;* who were to Govern themfelves by certain Rules and Limitations, made partly by the faid Act of *Parliament,* and to be made by Their Majefties in the *Charter,* and which was finally Subject to the Condition of a Redemption by *Parliament.*

But

But our Gentlemen, it feems, have found out a nearer way to a *Bank* and *Corporation*, than the Tedious. and Troublefome one of a *Charter* from Home, or Acts of *Affembly* here; and not only prefume to Incorporate themfelves, and make their own Rules and Orders, but alfo very Dutifully foreclofe and fhut out the Government from any Power of Redemption, or indeed any other Concern with 'em.

Poffibly thefe Gentlemen may fay, They don't pretend to Incorporate or make themfelves a *Body Politick*, *&c.* but to Obviate that Objection, I fhall give you the Notion, and Nature of a Corporation, as I find it in my Lord *Cook's* Inftitutes, and then leave you to Judge how Inconfiftent this Objection is with their Policy or Projection.

My Lord *Cook* fays, ' A Corporation is a ' Body to take in Succeffion, Framed as to ' that Capacity by the Policy of Man, and ' called a Corporation, becaufe the Perfons ' are made into a Body, and fo are of Capa- ' city to Take or Grant, *&c.* with Powers to ' Sue or be Sued, *&c.* Now 'tis eafy to obferve, how fully the Projectors, in their Scheme, have come up to this Defcription of a Corporation.

As

As to their *Bank-Bills*, I readily grant they are not Money; for indeed nothing can be Money properly, and in the Law of *England*, but *Silver* or *Gold* (both which are of an Intrinsick and Universal Value) that has the Imprefs of the Prince, and made Current at a Rate, or Value fet by Act of *Parliament*, or Proclamation of the *Crown*. However, thefe *Bills* will have as much the Face and Signatures of Money, as even the *Bills* of the *Bank of England*, or the *Bills of Credit* of this Province: For they are to be *Printed*, to be *Stamped* with an *Efcutcheon*, to be *Mark'd* with *Pounds* and *Shillings*: They are to be Let out at Intereft, and finally, the Projectors themfelves tell us, They are to ferve as a *Medium* of Exchange, which was the Firft Rife, and ftill continues the End and Ufe of Money. But that which I Infift on under this Head as before, is, That no Perfon, or Number of Perfons whatfoever,, can Affume, or may Dare to take this Power to themfelves, but muft Derive it from the *Crown*.

But befides what I have faid of the Prerogative, the Nature of *Corporations* in General, with *Political Powers, Liberties, &c.* and in Particular of the *Bank of England*, I muft needs obferve to you, an Act of *Parliament* made in the Sixth Year of the Reign of our late

late Sovereign Lady Queen *Anne* of Bleſſed Memory, wherein it is Enacted, *That during the Continuance of the* Bank of England, *it ſhall not be Lawful for any Body Politick or Corporate, other than the ſaid Company of the* Bank, *or for other Partners exceeding Six in* England, *to Borrow, or Owe any Sum on Bill or Note Payable en Demand, or at any time leſs than Six Months from Borrowing thereof.*

Now I ſhan't trouble you or my ſelf, to Argue how far this Projection would be a Breach upon the Conſtitution of the *Bank of England*; yet I think it is very fair and eaſy to obſerve, that ſo great a Number of Perſons, as our Projectors conſiſt of, may by no Means, without a ſufficient Power firſt had, preſume to Make or Iſſue theſe their Joynt *Bills* or *Notes.* For certainly, if the ſame Fact committed in *England,* by a Number exceeding Six, would be a breach of Law, much more may we ſuppoſe it forbidden and made Unlawful for an Hundred to do it here.

We frequently meet in our *Law-Books,* with Informations in the Nature of *Quo Warrantos* againſt Corporations, and Bodies Politick, for Uſurping Powers, Franchiſes and Liberties not belonging to them; or for abuſing and acting contrary to thoſe that do. And the De-

Defence generally made in thofe Cafes, has been Founded on their feveral *Charters*. But now fuppofe fuch an Information were Ordered to be brought againft thefe Projectors, what Defence in the Law could poffibly be made by them, or for them?

I now proceed to the next General Head which I propofed, and that is, How far the Government, and the very Conftitution of this Province may be affected by, and therefore ought thoroly to Inform themfelves about this Projection: And I think nothing can be plainer, than that the *General Affembly* of the Province, are under a neceffity of Enquiring into the Legality, the Juftice, the Safety, and Publick Advantage of this *Bank,* and if judged otherwife; by fome proper Act, or Publick Order to Declare againft, and forbid it, until His Majefties Pleafure may be known upon it. And as no wife Man, or good Subject can queftion the Power or Juftice of the Government in fo doing, fo 'tis much to be feared on the other Hand, in Cafe they fhould be wholly Silent, they might be called in Queftion at Home, for any ill Confequences of their Neglect therein: For I can't agree by any means with thofe Gentlemen that Argue, Becaufe the *Bank* is Private, and the Government as fuch not In

tereft

Interested in it, that the whole Blame and Damage will fall on the Projectors. Can it be Imagined, that when this Affair has been so Publick, the Government Notified of it so Effectually, and the Projection it self of so high and extraordinary a Nature, That upon the whole, no Account will be demanded by His Majesty of the Government, what Methods they took upon this Occasion, to secure the Honour of the Crown, and the Safety of the Subject. But be that as it will, I think it very Unreasonable, and absolutely Inconsistent with the Honour, the Power, and Wisdom of this Government, to suffer any Projection whatsoever, tho' otherwise never so well Framed, to be set up and carried on, and they have no Advice about it, no Authority over it, nor so much as a Power to Redeem it, in case they see good. This will be in effect, to suffer a Number of their own People to set up an absolute Independent Government, which like a Fire in the Bowels, will Burn up and Consume the whole Body. If such things as these may be Tolerated, 'twill be a vain thing any longer to talk of Government, a Power of making Laws, Regulating Trade, &c. For they that can make at one Dash, the Sum beforementioned, and as much more when they please, will quickly Govern the Trading part, and by degrees

get

get the Land, of the Country Mortgaged to them, and so at length bear down the Government it self, *and nothing be restrained from them*. For which Reason I hope, and doubt not, but that the *General Assembly* of the Province, will upon this great Occasion, exert their proper Powers, as they have once and again heretofore, when they have been under any apprehensions of Danger, either to the Government, or the Publick Good. Two notable Instances whereof you'll find in the *Memorial*, one with respect to the making of Money, and the other of a Partnership or Company, both which are Published among the Printed Acts.

As to the Act of Parliament of the Sixth of the late Queen beforementioned, the Act of Parliament of late also made referring to Money in the Plantations, the several Laws of our own Province, with respect to Money, and the Interest of it; as also those that concern the *Bills of Credit* Established on the Province; all of which will more or less be Affected, Invalidated, and broke in upon by this Projection. I have taken so much Notice of them in the *Memorial*, that I shall forbear saying any thing more on that Head here, save only to Remark, That as the *General Court* or *Assembly* of the Province, so

cer-

certainly no particular Number of Perfons in a Company or Partnerfhip, can Pretend, or muft Prefume to Inftitute or Eftablifh any thing Repugnant to the Laws of *England*. And fo I pafs on, in the laft Place to Confider the Frame and Nature of this *Laudable Projection*, as fome are pleafed to call it; and my Objections to it are fuch as thefe.

Firft. Its abfolute Independency on the Government, either as to its Regulation, or the power of Redemption; which, as I obferved before, is a thing Intolerable, and without Precedent, and never fo much as entred into the Minds of the Projectors of the Great *Bank of England* to Ask, much lefs of the Government to Grant.

Secondly. I cannot fee the Reafonablenefs and Juftice of it, betwixt the Subfcribers and Borrowers: For, as I have Remarked already, the Subfcribers are obliged to take out but a Quarter part of their Subfcriptions, the other three Quarters is to be Let out at four *per Cent*. Intereft, upon good Security. Now, according to the common courfe of Intereft, in lefs than Twenty Years, and if the Company fhall pleafe, by iffuing out a greater Quantity of *Bills*, in a third part of that Time, the Subfcribers will have cleared their

own

ówn Mortgages, draw out their own Stakes, and fo have the Intereft of the whole to fhare among themfelves, and the *Bubbled Borrowers* pay Intereft for their own Eftates. Pray where's the Juftice of this? Why fhould not the Borrowers when it comes to that, have fome of the Profits of the *Bank*, when their Eftates are the only remaining Fund? I confefs, it may feem a very eafy and fhort Way of getting an Eftate; but fure no Projection can expect to Succeed, that is not Founded in Commutative Juftice and Common Honefty.

I fhould be glad to know of thefe Gentlemen, that pretend to be fo Publick Spirited in this Bufinefs, whether they could be Contented, and have the fame Opinion of this *Bank*, if their Names were taken out of the Policy, and an equal Number of others put in, and I fuppofe, without any Reflection, as Good may be found, and fo inftead of being Lenders, they would become Borrowers of thefe *Bank-Bills*? I am afraid not! For the Bufinefs is, and very good Bufinefs it would be, in one Day to be Mafters of 150000 *l.* and without any Rifque at all, or any other Charge or Trouble, except the Printing and Signing a few pieces of Paper, to accept of Six Thoufand Pounds *per Annum* Intereft: By which

which Method, in effect, the Projectors would immediately have the Profits of other Mens Estates; and finally, as the Matter may be managed, the Estates themselves, without a valuable Consideration; their *Bank-Bills* being but pieces of Paper that have no other Value, but what the Borrowers give them. And yet we are made to believe, that the Borrowers are well dealt with, if tho' they pay Interest, yet they may at last have their own Estates or Pawns back again, upon bringing in the Bills. If this be not the *Philosopher's Stone*, there is no such thing in the World.

Thirdly. It must, I think, unavoidably prove a great Snare and Mischief to People that want Money to pay their Debts or otherwise, for whose Ease and Advantage nevertheless the *Bank* is Projected: As for Example; A Man owes me one Hundred Pounds upon Bond, in the *Bills of Credit* of the Province, and very readily pays me Six *per Cent.* Interest; to Discharge which, he repairs to the *Bank*, and Borrows 100 *l.* in their *Bills*, and comes to take up his Bond: Can any Man in Prudence or Justice think, that I shall take one Hundred Pounds in *Bank-Bills*, that will fetch but Four *per Cent.* for one Hundred Pounds in *Province-Bills*, that People so willingly give Six *per Cent.* for? No sure. I must at least have

have as many of the *Bank-Bills*, as will fetch Six *per Cent*. And if the *Bankers* should out of their great Generosity, and in Compassion as they pretend to such as want Money, Let their Interest at three, or two *per Cent*. Interest, the Case would be so much the worse.

Fourthly. What Security will the last Possessor of these *Bills* have to depend upon, in case this *Bank* should be broke up, either by the Government, or its self? As for Example: A Man has one Thousand Pounds of 'em by him; what shall he do with 'em, when the Credit of 'em is come to nothing? For, by the Tenour of the *Bills*, as you see, they are only obliged to accept of 'em for the Redemption of Pawns or Mortgages; and this Possessor has neither to take up. Possibly you'll say the *Bankers* will Assign him over a Mortgage: To that I answer, That th Foundation being gone, every thing else will fall with it. I doubt our Courts would never Adjudge those Mortgages to be good in the Law, being for no Valuable Consideration, so that the Lands so Mortgaged, would Revert to the Original Owners, like the Year of *Jubilee* among the *Jews*. And then as to the Possessors Suing of the Company to make good their *Bills*, first there will be no such thing in case they be Dissolved by Order of Govern-

Government; fecondly, If in the other Cafe, it fhould fink of it felf, they may prove Infolvent, and fo the Poffeffor be finely *Lurched*. For which Reafon, all Wife Men will be afraid to meddle with them, or be fure to get rid of them as faft as they can.

Fiftbly. The Name and Stile of this Projection, is a *Bank of Credit*: Now I take it for a certain Rule, That no *Money-Bank*, as we may call it, can or will poffibly have any *Credit* that is not Equal, either Really, or in Reputation, to the True or common Current Money of the Country, or Place where fuch *Bank* is Erected: And You may depend upon it, *SIR*, That if the *Bills* of the *Bank of England* it felf were not looked upon as good as *Specie*, and in effect a *Money-Bank*, the Credit of 'em would quickly come to nothing. For which Purpofe there are always kept in the Office of the faid *Bank* in *London*, vaft Sums of *Silver* and *Gold*, to Exchange for their *Bills* to any one that demands it. Befides which, the *Exchequer*, as you may fee frequently by the *London-Gazett*, is always ready for that End to Affift 'em with whatever Sums they may have Occafion for. But now our Projectors don't fo much as pretend to have the leaft Doight of *Silver* or *Gold*, or even a Stock of *Bills of Credit* of this Province

to

to Anfwer, in Cafe of Neceffity, or to fupport the Credit of their *Bills* withal. And I
am fure they have no reafon to expect the
Affiftance of the Government upon any
Emergency, fince as yet, they have not fo
much as Confulted them in the whole
Affair.

Sixthly. I cannot but think, the Making
and Iffuing fo great a Quantity of thefe
Bank-Bills, will be attended with a great deal
of Mifchief and Confufion as to Money in
General: Now Money is of the greateft
Importance, and laft Confequence to a *Common-Wealth*; for as 'tis the Sinews of *War,* fo
'tis the Strength of *Peace*: For which Reafon,
we can't have too much of that which
really is Money, but we may very eafily have
too much of that which is not fo.

The pooreft Country-Man in the Province,
is not convinced to this Day, but that *Silver,*
tho' never fo Rough and Unpolifhed, is preferable to the fineft *Paper-Money* that ever
was feen. We have had too much Confufion
already in the Province, by the Difference
that has been made between *Silver-Money* and
our Publick *Bills of Credit,* (when yet they
were fupported by the Government) and are
hardly got over it to this Day. But into what

a Gulph of Mifery by *Stock-jobbing* Difference of Money, and innumerable other Mifchiefs fhall we be plunged think you, when fuch a Flood of Private *Paper-Money* comes to be poured out among us? 'Tis now more than Twelve Years fince the Government firft began to Make and Iffue the *Bills of Credit* ; and tho' the Occafions and Neceffities of the Province have been very Preffing and Urgent, yet in all that time, they have made but about Two Hundred and Forty Thoufand Pounds: But as if that were a fmall Thing, our Gentlemen propofe at once to Make and Iffue out 200000 *l.* And by the fame Reafon that a *Bank* is fet up in *Bofton*, feveral others may go on in the feveral parts of the Province ; and what can the Confequence of this be, but to Confound the People, and make Money Vile and Contemptible ; and as much as in them lies, to Alter and Deftroy the very Nature of Money ? So that inftead of Anfwering all things, as it has always done, and ought to do, it will now Anfwer nothing, and be worfe than every thing elfe ; For that which really makes the Value of Money, among other things, is its Rarity : So that upon the whole, the Remedy propofed by thefe Projectors, will be much worfe than the Difeafe. As to the Bufinefs of Trade, for the Eafe, Benefit, and Advantage whereof

this

this Wonderful *Bank* is Projected, it would be well Confidered, Firft, Whether we have not generally run upon too much Trade for our Profit, already? For if I am not miftaken, tho' I am no Merchant, the greatnefs of the Credit given in Trade, has in a great Meafure, brought this want of Money upon us.

I confefs, as to the Encouraging the Produce of our own Country, and our own Manufactures, the Exporting of our own Commodities we cannot well exceed; but if we Import from Abroad, more than we can Pay for, by what we Produce our felves, or Purchafe from others with our own Commodities, we fhall unavoidably grow Poor, and a Million of *Paper-Money* won't help the matter at all : So that the lefs we Import from Abroad, the lefs Money or Medium of Exchange, the Trading part will want. And here indeed has been our great Improvidence and Unhappinefs in this Country, (of late Years efpecially) that the greateft part of our Confumption in *Bofton*, and other Sea-port Towns, almoft to Food and Raiment, has been of Foreign Commodities, when the fame things might be raifed among our felves, were the Produce of our own Country Encouraged, at leaft, fo much as to make a Ballance of Trade in our Favour. Befides all which, I cannot but think it the Duty and Interest of our Merchants and Traders, who have been the great Occasion of the Loss of our *Silver*, to Project some way of Recovering it again, and manage the Trade, so as that a good Proportion of *Silver* and *Gold* might once more find the way into *New-England*, and there remain for the Honour and Service of the Government and Country, who have Suffered and been Exposed too much already for want of it; and had not the absolute Necessity of the Government and People Required it, it had been better (in the Opinion of many Wise Men) for the Province, they had never made any *Bills*, or *Paper-Money* at all.

I might also mention the great Extravagance that People, and especially the Ordinary sort, are fallen into, far beyond their Circumstances, in their Purchases, Buildings, Families, Expences, Apparel, and generally in their whole way of Living: And above all, the excessive Consumption of *Rhum* and *Wine*, as one of the greatest Sources and Causes of the present Distress: Hereupon it must be granted by every one of common Sense and Observation, That if the Importation of Foreign Commodities were less, and especially those two

two Branches beforementioned, *viz*. *Rhum* and *Wine* Reduced to what only might be Necessary. Were but a tolerable Proportion of *Silver* brought in to us, which might be effected with Ease and Profit, were Frugality and good Husbandry Universally in Fashion among us, there would not be such a Clamour for want of a *Medium* of Exchange. I confess, as things are at present Managed and Circumstanced among us, both *Silver* and *Paper-Money* is become very scarce; tho' really more in *Boston*, and among the Trading part, than in Proportion, in the other parts of the Province. And the last Session of the *General Assembly*, when I had the Honour to be one of an Extraordinary *Committee* raised for that Purpose; I gave it as my Opinion, *That considering the Demand of the Government as to the Taxes, and the great Occasions of the People as to their Trade, it might be convenient to Make and Issue out a further Quanty of the Publick* Bills of Credit, *&c. in such a Method as was then agreed on*: And of the same Opinion were all of that *Committee*, save Two, as I Remember, and they consisted of Thirteen : And accordingly a Report was made by the *Chair-Man*, in the Name of the rest. But how that Matter dropt when it came into the *Lower House*, I shall not take upon me here to say, tho' it may easily be guessed at. However, I persuade my self, felf, that when the *General Affembly* comes to Review that *Report*, the Scheme then Agreed, will be found the beft, if not the only Expedient to Relieve the prefent Diftrefs; and the Gentlemen that Oppofe it, will I'm Confident, have no Thanks from thofe they Reprefent.

SIR, I do not pretend in all, or any thing that I have faid, to be againft a *Bank of Credit* in General, were ·it well Founded, well Limited, and Regulated by the Government, and Equal to our own *Current-Money*, as fuch a *Bank* ought to be: But I am utterly againft this prefent Projection, for the Reafons I have given, and many others that might be Mentioned: And fince, as I faid before, and I really am of that Opinion, That there is a Neceffity of Supplying the People with a further convenient Quantity of *Bills of Credit*, for the better Payment of their *Taxes*, and the eafe of Trade. I am abfolutely for its being done by the Publick, and for fuch Reafons as thefe.

Firft. We have had Twelve Years Experience already of the *Publick Bills*, with great Honour, Safety, and Succefs; Whereas the Private Projection, is a Path that has never yet been Trod, and what the Confequences may be, we don't know.

Second

Secondly. The *Bills of Credit* upon the Province, are Equal even to Seventeen Penny half-penny Weight, as to the Publick Tax, and by a late Act of the *General Assembly*, they are made a good Tender in the Law, as to all Debts Contracted in the Common Course of Trade, and by that means upon the Matter, made of an Intrinsick Value, and so the Credit of 'em Firm and Necessary.

Thirdly. The Profits in Case the Government Issue the *Bills*, will always Redound to the Publick, and so every one will have a Benefit thereby. And again, we may reasonably suppose, that the Government would be more Sparing and Cautious, and not so Lavish in Launching out their *Bills*, as a Private *Bank* would be, not being under the like Temptation: By which means the Credit of the *Bills* would be the better preserved. Besides which, the Province has once and again made good Counterfeits, and further provided against 'em, as you may see by a Private Act made in the Third Year of the late Reign, and a Publick Act made the very last Session of the *Assembly*: Whereas there is no Provision at all against Counterfeits in this Private Projection. And to mention no more upon this Head, the Fund of the Publick *Bills of Credit*, being the Province in General, according to the ordinary Course of Things, can never be doubted, or in Danger.
I

I know very well what the *Bankers* Object to all this, *viz.*

Firſt. That as by the Conſtitution, it is in the Power of the *Governour* and *Councſl* to draw out the Publick Money, ſo it would be much more in His Power to lay His Hand on the Money ſo made and Let out, it being not raiſed for His Majeſties Uſe, and Appropriated, and thereby Endanger the Liberties of the People. To this I Anſwer, Firſt, That according to the Scheme agreed on, and Reported by the *Committee,* The Principal and Profits of that Money were ſo Settled and Secured, that nothing leſs than the *General Aſſembly* could Diſpoſe of either. Secondly. As the Projećtors have Ordered their *Bank,* 2000 *l.* of their Yearly Profits they deſign to preſent to the Government: Now what they mean by that, is uncertain. Firſt, If they mean a Governour that they ſhall pleaſe to like, I'm ſure it would be a very effećtual way to Enſlave this Country, by an underſtanding between ſuch Governour and the *Bank.* Secondly. If they intend the *General Aſſembly,* then I ſay as in the *Memorial,* That this Government neither can nor ought to be Maintained in any other Method, than by the *Charter,* and Inſtructions from the *Crown.*

Secondly. That the Government have no Power to do any ſuch thing, as to Make and

Lend

Lend out any *Publick Bills*; but with what Defign they make, and how well they Enforce this Objection, I leave the World to Judge, and with their Favour, I fhould think the *General Affembly* as Capable of knowing and underftanding their own Powers, as the Projectors for 'em. I am fure it was the Opinion of the *Committee* beforementioned, That the *General Affembly* of the Province, were fufficiently Impowered by the *Charter*, whenever the neceffary Support of the Government required it, to Make and Iffue thefe *Bills of Credit* in the Method then propofed. And their Opinion was Founded upon that Claufe in the *Charter*, referring to impofing reafonable *Affeffments*, *Taxes*, *&c. In the neceffary Defence and Support of the Government, and the Protection, and Prefervation of the Inhabitants there*, &c.

Now Firft, There's nothing in the *Charter* Repugnant to the Governments Iffuing a further Sum of *Bills*. Secondly, It has been done, once and again, upon great Occafions, and the Government not blamed for it, that I know of. Thirdly, If the neceffary Support of the Government of this Province, and the Prefervation of the People, (for thofe are the Words of the *Charter*) require the Making and Iffuing a further Quantity, then 'tis directly within, and well Warranted by the *Charter*. Now I think we are all agreed in this, That neither

the

the Government nor People (as to their Trade and Bufinefs) can well be Supported and carry on their neceffary Affairs much longer, without a further Supply of Money, or *Bills of Credit*. Befides which, the Projectors would do well to tell us, how it comes to pafs, that they fhould have fo great a Power of Supplying the People with Money, and the *General Affembly* have none at all. But certainly, if the *Bankers* are fo wife and Cautious as to the Powers of the Government, for fear they fhould be exceeded, and the Conftitution thereby Endangered; it much more behoves the *General Affembly* of the Province, to Exercife this Caution, with refpect to this Projection, and effectually fecure the Honour and Safety of the Government, the Eftates and Liberties of the People, which is the very thing I Contend for, And that which Comforts me in what I have faid and done upon this Occafion, whatever the Event prove, is, That I have had no Private View, or Seperate Intereft, much lefs any Prejudice to the Gentlemen concerned; among whom I have many particular Friends; but have Sincerely aim'd at the Publick Good. *SIR*, It was the Excellent Character of the Heads of the Tribe of *Iffachar*, in *David's* Time, and Recorded for their Honour, and our Imitation, 'That they were Men of Underftanding in the Times.

Times, to know what *Israel* ought to do, I earnestly Desire, and Believe, That the Heads of our Tribes like them, upon this great Occasion, may and will Discern both Time and Judgment; know and seek the true Interest of their Country: And I shall be glad, if I may in any wise contribute to so good an End, by what I have here Offered. You'll please to Excuse the Trouble of this long Letter, and Communicate it as you think Proper.

I am, *S I R*,
Your very Humble
and Affectionate Servant.

Boston, October 22.
1714.

P. Dudley.

POSTSCRIPT.

SINCE the Date and Delivery of this Letter, I understand the *Bankers* have new Modelled their Projection, and Reformed it, as they reckon, in two Articles: But how long this new Scheme will hold, is uncertain. First, Instead of Four,
they

they now propose to have Five *per Cent*. Interest; but they would do well to tell us by what Law, or with what Justice they can pretend to ask or receive one *per Cent*. or indeed any Interest at all, for their own *Bills*, which (as before is observed) are nothing in themselves, have not the Foundation, the Advantage and Value of the Publick *Bills of Credit* on the Province, nor ever can without the Government, and must be wholly obliged to the Borrowers for their present worth or Currency. And I believe this is the first time that ever Interest was asked for any sort of Money or Bills that had not the Stamp or Authority of a Government.

Secondly. They have Reformed the Fund also, in obliging the Subscribers to give in Real Security, to the Value of 200000 *l*. the full Sum of the Bills proposed to be made, and so not to be obliged to the Borrowers for any part of the Fund. I confess, there seems to be some Justice in this, and serves to prove, that there was Reason and Weight in my first Objection to the Nature and Frame of the *Bank*; And when they have Answered the rest, and made a thorow Reform of their Projection, so as it may be Consistent with the Honour and Safety of the Government, the Liberties and Properties of the People, and agreeable to the Rules of Reason, Justice and Equity, I believe every one will Encourage and give in to it.

F I N I S.

A LETTER FROM ONE IN BOSTON, TO HIS FRIEND IN THE COUNTRY

A Letter from one in Boston, to his Friend in the Country. In Answer to a Letter directed to John Burril, Esqr. Speaker to the House of Representatives, for the Province of the Massachusetts-Bay in New-England (Boston, 1714), pp. 1–37.

As the debate over the bank of credit continued in Boston, one defence of the bank came in the form of this anonymous *Letter from one in Boston, to his Friend in the Country*, which was addressed to John Burrill (1694–1754), then speaker of the House of Representatives in Massachusetts Bay Colony. This piece addresses the root problem for the colonies: that there was a pervasive shortage of currency. This was problematic because currency as a medium of exchange, according to the anonymous author, 'gives life to Business, Employs the Poor, Feeds the Hungry, and Cloathes the Naked'. The shortage of currency was not only limiting trade, but was also preventing the payment of debts and taxes and thus holding up the legal system – for which the debtors could not be blamed, as they could not pay without specie. A bank of credit, by providing an additional medium of exchange, could stimulate Boston's economy to everyone's advantage.

A
LETTER,

From One in

BOSTON,

To his Friend in the

Country.

In Anſwer to a Letter directed to

John Burril, Eſqr.

Speaker to the Houſe of Reprefentatives, for the Province of the *Maſſachuſetts-Bay* in *New-England*.

Printed in the Year 1714.

SIR,

UPON your fo earneftly repeating your Defire to me, to give you my Thoughts, or the Thoughts of the Gentlemen of this Town, relating to the Bank of Credit Projected; and to a Letter directed to the Speaker of the Houfe of Reprefentatives againft it, and the Objections made againft it with no common Applaufe, cryed up by the Court Intereft as Unanfwerable ; tho' I readily acknowledge my felf as unfit a Perfon, as you could have Writ to about it, being not concerned with the Gentlemen in the Projection, and but little converfant with them, and in that I pretend to little or no acquaintance in State Affairs, or in Trade ; yet when I fat my felf down to Read that Letter, it appeared to me fo trifling, and below the Character of the Gentleman that Subfcribed it ; that it confirmed me in my thoughts, that the Caufe was not fo good, as fome Others he has pleaded, and invited me in a few Remarks to comply with your Requeft.

I frankly acknowledge, that I have been Sometime of the Opinion, that a Bank of Cre-

dit,

'dit, well Founded and well Regulated, would be of the greateſt Advantage imaginable to this Country; and therefore it was a real pleaſure to me, when I firſt underſtood that a Number of Valuable Gentlemen were Concerting proper meaſures to accompliſh ſo deſirable an end. But I muſt confeſs my ſelf to have been at a Loſs when they had given the finiſhing ſtroke to their firſt Scheme, wherein I apprehend they had left the foundation too fluctuating and changeable for a Land Bank, and that, tho' the Poſſeſſor of the Bills Emitted, had good Security, yet it ſeemed to me that they had not ſecured it well againſt one another, but had left it too precarious and dependent on the Caprice of every Accident, and the Probity and Juſtice of they knew not who, which might come after them, yet I am very ready to excuſe them that they did not arrive to the beſt method in their firſt Eſſay; but ſince this great Miſtake is Corrected in their laſt Model, *viz.* by every ones Mortgaging a Real Eſtate in proportion to the Intereſt he is to have in the Bank, and ſo to abide during its Continuance; hereby there is ſuitable proviſion made not only for the Credit of their Bills and Notes, but a ſufficient Obligation upon them to do Juſtice to each other, & to every man that ſhall be concerned with them, in caſe the Bank or Partnerſhip ſhall come to an end; which the Author of the

Letter

Letter himſelf allows to be good; which in my Opinion before was not: All that I have to do is to blow off the Cloud of Duſt and Smoke, which the Author of the Letter has covered the Bank with; that when it comes to ſtand in its native light, we may be the better able to paſs a Judgment upon it; and that I may have the advantage of ſtanding on my own ground, (and be freed from the incumbrance of making good any of his) it will not be improper to tell you, how far I can agree with the Author of that Letter, *viz. That the People as to their Trade and Buſineſs, cannot well carry on their neceſſary Affairs much longer, without a further Supply of Money, or Bills of Credit*, page 30. *But there is a neceſſity of ſupplying the People with a further convenient quantity of Bills of Credit*, page 26. The Queſtion then is, Whether the Publick ſhall Emit theſe Bills of Credit; or whether it had not better be done by a Company of men in the nature of a Private Bank of Credit. I agree with the Author alſo in this, *That I am not a-againſt a Bank of Credit in general, were it well founded, well regulated*, page 26. I leave out the words (by the Government,) becauſe the Conſideration, whether by the Government, or otherwiſe comes under the foregoing Quæry; ſo that the Queſtion here is, *Whether or no this Projection for a Bank of.*

Credit

Credit be well Found•d, well Limited, and Regu-
lated? And here I cannot avoid doing the
Gentlemen that Juſtice to ſay what ſome of
their Number have informed me, namely that
when they firſt waited on his Excellency with
their firſt Scheme, they were deſired to leave
the Limitation to the General Court, that it
was a proper Compliment to pay them, to deſire them to ſet the Sum, which was one reaſon why there was no Limitation ; but this
by the way.

We agree thirdly, *That the Projection of a*
Bank of Credit, very much imports the Prerogative
of the Crown, the Conſtitution and Laws of the
Province, the Eſtates and Liberties of the People ;
and that not only for the preſent, but Succeeding
Generations, page 4. For I take it, that the
word import when ſo uſed, generally means
to be of advantage ; however to deal fairly,
it ſhall be the queſtion, *Whether it imports to*
their advantage or diſadvantage, and which does
moſt of all import them, the Publick or the Pri-
vate Bank? I agree with him alſo, *That it be-*
hooves the Government and General Aſſembly of
the Province, and really concerns every man, that
has any Intereſt in the Country, with great appli-
cation to enquire into, and ſeriouſly conſider the
Nature and Conſequences of this Bank or Part-
nerſhip, page 4. And ſo Sir, I am ſufficiently
warranted to make my Enquiry, and endeavour to ſet things in a true light ; but to find
theſe

these things wherein we agree so confusedly jumbled together as they are in Mr. *Attorneys* Letter, that they might appear a sort of dark Arguments against a Bank of Credit, is such a fine Amusement to the Ignorant and Injudicious Reader, and such an odd way of reasoning, that we could have expected it from none, but he that had lost his own eyes, or thought every body else was blind. And to be plain, when I heard of such a Letter published in Mr. *Attorneys* Name, I expected to find the strongest Arguments, and the fairest Pleadings that could be, against the Private Bank of Credit, from a Gentleman of so bright Parts, and so Learned in the Law, as is his general Character : Yet I must assure you, that I had not read over the first page, before I had altered my mind, and received this settled Idea of the whole Piece ; that I should find nothing in it but Evasions, Doublings and Misrepresentations, and some few amusements ; for I was astonished to see so fair (not to say false) a light given to the Order of the Governour and Council, which being Publick, every one has the opportunity to see and judge of the fallacy. He tells us, page 3. *That the Projectors were directed to proceed no further in the Affair, till the next Sessions of the General Assembly ; notwithstanding all which (I am loth to say in contempt of it) the persons concerned are openly carrying on their Bank with utmost Vigour and*
Expedi-

Expedition. How could he Sir, so openly give us this wrong Account of the matter? My News-Letter Printed by Authority, *August* 23. tells me, that upon Reading, *&c.* Ordered, *That the Projectors or Undertakers of any such Bank, do not proceed to Print the Scheme, or put the same on Publick Record, Make or Emit any of their Notes or Bills, until they have laid their Proposals before the General Assembly of this Her Majesties Province, who are always ready to Encourage and Countenance any Proposals,* &c. *I. A.* Secr. Which Order, as it was far from forbidding their proceeding any further in that Affair; as to the digesting their thoughts upon it, and filling up their Number, *&c.* but rather suppos'd they ought to wade through all the difficulties, and bring their Scheme to its perfection, that it might be fit to lay before the General Assembly; so was it, as I have been well informed, in every Article complied with, in Duty to the Government; and even to this day have neither Printed their Scheme, Put it on Publick Record, Made, nor Emitted any of their Notes or Bills; so that really Sir, what has been done by the Projectors, won't bear so much, as a, *notwithstanding,* much less, *a, leth to say in contempt.* Indeed, I have heard it whispered, that they have thought the Order very hard, in that they were denied the benefit of the Press, and the benefit of Publick Records,
                                                    which

which I fhall leave: And now Sir, after fo plain, and publickly known, a falfe Comment, upon the Order of the Governour and Council, and the Actions of the Projectors in the very Entrance of the Letter; what can be lookt for, but Arguments of the fame Kidney thro' the whole: And I Confefs, when I had Read the Letter out, I fhould verily have thought it had been Calculated to Lull the Government into a profound Sleep, if I had not remembred that he faid page 5. *his defign was to Awaken it;* fo eafily do we miftake things till we are informed better. But not to give you or my felf any further trouble about the defign of it, believing it is not laid fo deep, but your penetration without being put to the Wreck will fathom it. I Return to the firft Enquiry, fince 'tis agreed there is a neceffity of a certain number of Bills of Credit, or Notes to be Emitted, as a Medium in Trade, *viz. Who fhall Emit thefe Bills ?* Had the Government of the Country beft take it on themfelves? or would it not be fafer to permit particular Perfons in Partnerfhip to Iffue out, and give a Currency to their own Notes, founded on their Lands, under the name of a Bank of Credit ? This is the main Enquiry which now falls under every Bodies Examination, and becomes the debate of the Town this Winter Seafon ; and that I may give you my thoughts upon it freely, I fay

with

With all due Deference to Government, by all means let the Governments Notes, Emitted to pay the Publick Dues, and called in by Taxes granted as a Fund for them, have all poſſible Honour and Credit amongſt us ; and if in their great wiſdom they ſhould ſee meet to make it a Publick Charge, to Emit a certain number of their Notes in Erecting a Bridge over *Charles*-River, and make it a Toll Bridge, with ſuitable Allowances to the Colledge at preſent ; and ſuppoſe that *Forty Thouſand Pounds* were Iſſued out to make it a ſubſtantial and firm Bridge ; and that a Toll upon every thing paſſing and carried over, ſhould be a Fund to Call them in gradually ; and after that it had cleared it ſelf, it ſhould be taken off from Paſſengers, and left only for Carts, Horſes, &c. And the Colledge have the Income for ever, or any ſuch Publick Charge, as Fortifying the principal Town by Sea, Erecting Stone Fortifications or Garriſons on the Frontiers, or Erecting Light Houſes, for the Security of Trade ; and the Re-ſettling the *Eaſtern* Parts of the Country in a Defenſible manner, in giving a Bounty for the encouraging the Sowing, water-rotting, and well curing of Hemp ; the encouraging them that ſhould make the beſt pieces of Hollands-Duck : Which two Articles alone, it is thought might ſo effect the ballance of our Trade, as to bring us in *Silver* Money ; eſpecially if a Reward of *Three Pounds*

per Head were given for all **Male White Ser-**
vants, that fhall be Imported into this Province, and Bound out from the **Age** of **Ten** to
Eighteen Years ; the Reward to continue the
Term of Twenty Years ; and this would furnifh us with Sailors, with Labourers in Huf-
bandry & Fifhery, & Soldiers for our **Defence,**
whofe Polls in a few years would pay it in :
And whereas now they are Sold for a Term
of years, for *Fifteen* and *Twenty Pounds* a Head ;
fuch a certain Reward would induce men to
bring in fuch Numbers, that they would be
Sold for *Five Pounds,* as they are in *Penfilvania,*
and other Places, where fuch certain Encou-
ragements have been given. The Debts Contracted by thefe Emiffions would be the real
Credit of the Country, both Serviceable and
Honourable, the Strength, Support, & Exter-
ternal Glory of a Country ; and whereas the
Trade wants a Medium to Circulate it, there
would be no neceffity of Laying heavy Taxes,
& the Funds might be carried forwards as the
Government would fee caufe ; for I believe by
this time moft men of thought may fee, that
fince Paper Notes are our only Medium, that
Day we are out of Debt, we are out of Credit, and muft unavoidably fink, unlefs there
fhould be found out fome other way to fave
us from Ruin. So the Queftion comes the
fairer in view, *Whether is the better of the Two,*
a Publick or a Private Bank ?

I ſhall therefore in the next Place, give you thoſe Reaſons that are of weight with me againſt a Publick Bank, and Reſcue the Private from the Authors Objections : For theſe Reaſons may not the Publick Bank be Objected againſt ? May there not be a danger if the Publick ſhould go on to Emit Bills on Intereſt, that it will be too great an Invaſion of the Prerogative of the Crown : For I am apt to think every body will grant, that the Stamping of Money is a Royalty inveſted in the Crown ; and I am prone to imagine, that Bills Emitted by Publick Authority to Lend at Intereſt, will carry with them many ſignatures of Money ; eſpecially ſince the Act of this Province makes them a Legal Tender, ſo far as no man may be Impriſon'd for Debt that Tenders them ; eſpecially if we Conſider the difference in the Emiſſion of theſe Bank Bills, that they are not paid out of the Treaſury, as the Notes Obligatory of the Government to thoſe they were Indebted unto, with the Publick Faith, plighted to Call them in by Taxes ; and ſo tho' they are of the ſame Tenour, yet the manner of the Emiſſion, with that Law cited, gives them the character of real Money ; for I cannot perſwade my ſelf to ſay with Mr. *Attorney*, that nothing can be Money properly, but Silver and Gold, becauſe that both Copper & Braſs have had the Royal Stamp, and Copper paſſes in ſmall Payments, as other Money in

Great

Great Britain at this day; and I have also heard, that Leather was once the current Coin of *Rome*: And I am very much inclined to think, if the Crown of *England* saw cause, they could make Paper Bills, so stamped, as properly Money, as any Money whatsoever. Now is there not ground to fear, when the Sovereign has been pleased to indulge us with the Priviledges of Emitting Publick Notes for the defraying the necessary Charge in the Defence and Support of the Government, and to Confine us to those Occasions in the Taxes and Assessments allowed to be made on the Inhabitants; would it not be looked on as an Incroachment in very deed on the Royal Prerogative for us to exceed, and what the Consequence of that will be, you are a much better Judge than I am; (and I have been informed that the Gentlemen concerned, have had Letters from their Friends at Home, advising that by no means the Government would be Concerned in such a Fund) but if it should not in all the signatures of Money be a direct Invasion of the Prerogative, on the account of its being really Money, yet would it not be a going beyond our Last? and a doing what we had no power or warrant for; for I look upon it a weak & foolish plea, some peoples mouths are filled with, *viz.* That we ought not to debate about the Power of the Government, that it tends to weaken us, and that there are

enough

enough that do that, and the like. I think
the way to have our Powers rendred ftrong &
durable, would be to Confider what they are,
and ufe them, and not go to the brink, or one
hairs breadth beyond them : And truly I fear
there is fome defign in raifing all this fmother,
to blindfold us, and lead us whence we cannot
fo eafily return. I take it that our Charter
fets us the bounds of our Power, and tells us
how far we may go, and all withbut that is
forbidden ground; now it is a plain thing,
that the Governments Emitting Bills of Publick Credit on Intereft, is not to be found, neither granted or warranted by the Charter, the
boundaries thereof are *Affefsments and Taxes, in
the neceffary defence and fupport of the Government, and the protection and prefervation of the Inhabitants there.*---Mr. *Attorney* has given it us,
page 29. He was fo well apprized of this Objection, that he lays out his ftrength to remove
it; tho' I think he has not been able to make
it ftir one inch. He tells us, *there is nothing
in the Charter repugnant to the Governments Iffuing a further fupply of Bills,* page 29. It is
very true upon the Foot or Fund of Affefsments, as they have been hitherto Emitted,
for Paying the Debts, and Defraying the neceffary Charges of the Province; but once
for all, the Charter may well be allow'd to
be repugnant to all that is not fairly Contained in it. He fays fecondly, *That it has*
been

*been done once and again, on great Occasions,
and the Government not blamed for it.* The
Government has Emitted their Bills to pay
their Debts, but never to Lend at Intereſt,
before his Letter was written, which is the
matter in Controverſy. The Bills the Merchants Lent to the Treaſury, and the Treaſury in Return, Lent the Merchants by Order of Government on that great Emergency, were for the paying Her Majeſties Soldiers, and would not have been Emitted,
but in ſuch an Extraordinary Caſe, and upon that bottom, ſo that it can never be
made the preſident to Lett out Bills at Intereſt : and then he would perſwade us (not
himſelf) that the words the neceſſary Support of the Government, protection and pre-
ſervation of the People, will allow it, and
ſo forſooth with an (if) it is *&cra,* then
it comes within the Charter ; and I am
verily perſwaded (if) he were of Councel
againſt us, he would with all imaginable
Juſtice declare, as every reaſonable man elſe
(eſpecially a Gentleman of the Law) would,
that the evident meaning of theſe words are,
the Charges of the Government and the
War, even all ſuch Charge as the Inhabitants ſhall be Aſſeſſed and Taxed for, and
that they have not the leaſt aſpect upon a
Fund for Trade, or the ſupplying the People with a Medium of Exchange, & there-
fore

fore his thrufting the word, Government, and into a parenthefis, *as to their Trade and Bufinefs*, into the Sentence at *page* 30. is as arrant a piece of Sophiftry as can be, akin to his fore-mentioned Arguments, and what I told you at firft you muft look for; I readily grant the General Court here muft be Judges of their own Power; and there is no Doubt but that it is poffible alfo they may have been, by this Letter under the Attorney Generals Hand, induced to believe that they have more than really they have. I am informed, that in *May* Seffions, the Sufferers by the late dreadfulFire applied to them forRelief toLend them Money on their Lands, they did not apprehend it in their prudent Power fo to do; & fome of as good Councel as any in this Province, have declared it as their Opinion, that the Country had, not the Power to form themfelves into a Publick Bank, and Emit Money at Intereft, and how the Wifdom of the General Affembly came to be of that fide, I cannot fay whether it is hard or eafy to guefs.

I cannot help reciting the words of the Charter here : *We do*, &c. *Giue, Grant*, &c. *To Make, Ordain, and Eftablifh all manner of Wholefome and Reafonable Orders, Laws, Statutes, and Ordinances, Directions and Inftructions, either with Penalties or without, fo as the fame be not repugnant or contrary to the Laws of*
this

this our Realm of England, as they shall judge to be for the Good and Welfare of our said Province or Territory----And for the Welfare, Support, and Defence of the Government thereof. And a little after this General Clause, comes the Power of Imposing Taxes. *To Impose and Levy proportionable and reasonable Assessments, Rates and Taxes upon the Estates, and Persons, of all, and every the Proprietors, or Inhabitants of our said Province or Territory, to be Issued and Disposed of by Warrant, under the Hand of the Governour of our said Province, for the time being, with the Advice and Consent of the Council, for our Service in the necessary Defence and Support of our Government, of our said Province or Territory.*

Upon which, and the Publicks Emitting Bills of Publick Credit upon Interest, we may make a few Remarks, for the Investigating of Truth, so much embarrassed by the Letter.

1. In the first place then, I would Remark, That by the Charter we have a Power to impose reasonable Taxes, to be disposed of by Warrant under the Hand of the Governour, with Consent of the Council, for Defence and Support of the Government, &c. This being our Power and Limitation, no Act of ours can alter the Power of Disposing: for the following words according to such Acts, can be understood I presume, no otherwise than for the Uses Raised, yet no ways alters the foregoing Clause of the Governours and Councils Power of Judging & Disposing of it. That the Clause for Imposing and Levying
Taxes

Taxes coming after the General Power of Making Laws in the Charter; can be I think understood in no other sense than a Limitation of the foregoing Power, and the path of our Duty, in that of Taxing the People.

3. That the Credit of every Freeholder is as much his Property as his Lands. Suppose a man gives his Obligatory Bill or Note to pay an *Hundred Pounds* on Demand, or to take again in Payments, tho' he does it to serve a Friend in Distress, yet so passing his Bill in his own Name, becomes the principal Debtor, and the Possessor can look for no other, though the Person takes private Security for himself.

If the General Court Emit Bills Obligatory upon the Province, whether they are not bound in Justice and Honour to make them good as much as private men; and whether it is not creating a Debt upon the Province for such Sums as shall be so Emitted, which they must make good to the Possessor, which is a burden, and may be called a Tax with a Witness. Now it may well be Quæried, How far a Representative Body or Free State has a power over, & a right in the Credit, and the Properties of the Principals they represent? Whether a free People submit their Estates any further to their Deputies, than to pay the Proportion of the Charge that arises for their mutual support and Defence? Whether it would not be entring in such a State on the Properties of every particular Person, who is Lord of his Penny, and only

only has a right of Difpofing of his own. It is true, that the Reprefentative Body are faid to be the Keepers of the Peoples Purfe ; but that can be underftood by any Freeman I believe in no other fence, than for what is, or fhould be a common Charge ; and to ftate the proportion, if it is queftionable, in a free State : May it not be much more fo in a depending Government, whofe Powers are Limited by Patents, and are accountable for Ufurped Powers ; but fome fay the Province runs no rifque, for they are to have the Profits, which are four & an half *per Cent.* for all Emitted, which will pay all the Charge of the Government, and the People be fet free in their Taxes, and that they may gain a Stock in the Treafury---- A Golden Bait. As for the Rifque the Province runs in the Principal and Intereft, it is not yet determined ; it is judged by fome, and thofe not the moft unthinking, that it is great ; in that the Security taken by the Truftees if it comes to be fued out, would be claimed for the Crown ; for in our Charter we have not ; as Sir *Ferdinando Gorges* had in his, the grant of that priviledge of the Forfeitures and Reverfions of Lands ; befides the Collufion that may be introduced, by fuffering Lands to be forfeited and redeemed at half price ; that as to the Profits and Income which is for His Majefties Service in the Support of the Government, it being a Revenue to the Crown ;

Crown ; how natural does it ly instead of a Salary for a Governour to ask at Home, in a Line or two of Instructions for himself and all his Officers, as *Lieutenant Governour, Secretary, Judges, Attorney General, Captain of the Castle, Surveyor General,* &c. which is not I hope the end intended, or the most grateful : Other difficulties referring to the Borrower, not proper to be mentioned may arise ; the Crown will not want Occasions of Disposing of their Revenues, which may seem on due reflection to over-ballance the gains proposed : May it not be thought an hazard, if they should go on to Emit greater Sums on such a foundation, that the Crown may be invited to take away the Charter, and that for the sake of the Money Emitted as forfeited ? And may not the Confusion be better thought on than expressed on such en event ? May not the old Maxim be of use to us here ? that in doubtful Cases the negative is the safer. I am in duty bound, to suppose what has been done, was thought necessary by the Government in their distress ; unto whom I am sensible we owe all possible deference and respect ; and I assure you, none is more ready to pay it than I am ; yet in such a weighty case, truth stands the clearer in view, on a free, modest and rational enquiry : And since the Interest arising from those Bills they say will be for the support of the Government, if they will take the Attorney General's ral's Opinion ; he has given it, page 28. *That this Government neither can, nor ought to be maintained in any other Method, than by the Charter, and Instructions from the Crown,* and I presume this method is neither. And to Conclude this Argument, we have heard Sir, of Informations in the nature of *Quo Warranto's* ; and this very Country has felt the weight of one, and upon the very score of Invading the Prerogative, in the Article of Money, and doing what was said we had no warrant from Charter to do ; and certainly no Lover of this Country can wish them to take such methods as may be tho't to put it in any hazard of a second *Quo warranto* ; no, none but such as have not scope enough already to get Money, *&c.* extending Law Suits, to the enriching none but themselves. I assure you Sir, I am the plainer on these Heads, in that I value the Liberties of my Country so dearly, as never to esteem such its best Friends, that are willing to part with them ; and yet does not the disputableness of this Power, if we should go on in such a method, shew that at least we run the risque of a second ; which if it should take place, would not the Country (and with just cause) cry out, Ah ! why did the Government hearken to Mr. *Attorney's* Letter ? Ah ! Mr. *Attorney,* why did you so amuse and slily argue them into it ? And by the way, the very notion of a second *Quo warranto,* confirms what I ground much of this

Argu-

Argument upon, *viz.* that what is not within the Grant of the Charter, is forbidden to us, and to be avoided. If after all that has been said to the Power and Safety of the Publick going on to Emit Bills Obligatory on the Country, which is making the Country Principal Debtor, and to Let 'em out on Land Security, where is the Limitation of the Power? the Gentleman would do well to explain it; if the paying the Publick Charge and its Defence be not the boundaries and limitation, why may they not Emit *Five Hundred Thousand Pounds* as a Fund of Trade, & appoint Factors for the Government, that they may have the Profit? the difference seems only to be in the prudence, not in the power; how safe then is it Living in a Community where the Estates may be charged to answer more than the value upon such Projects, does not such a Power render mens properties in their Estates very precarious? especially since it is hinted, that the Representatives may be kept by the Charter as long as a Prince lives; we may open a door wide enough for the getting Estates; it is but dividing a number of Bills amongst themselves, and call it for the support of the Government, according to that argument, and it is done. We have always looked upon it, That an empty Treasury is very much our Security; This Government thought it so when they appointed a Committee to burn the Pub-

lick

lick Bills that were returned into the Treafury
during the recefs of the General Court ; and
prevents many fine Schemes of Arbitrary Power ; a full Treafury by a ftated Revenue has
the contrary confequences, and may foon in-
volve the poor people into unknown mifchiefs.
No fays the Letter, page 28. *The principal Profits of that Money, according to the Scheme agreed
on, reported by the Committee, were fo fettled and
fecured, that nothing lefs than the General Affembly could difpofe of either.* This is his main Argument againft the Objection to the Supply,
&c. The Governour and Council has the
draught of all Moneys that are Raifed by the
Government according to the Charter, as I
obferved before ; and fhould the Publick Emit
a large Sum as is neceffary for a Publick Bank,
the Income thereof would be inviting, and I
doubt not of the ways being prefently found to
it, for a Law contrary to the Charter being
void of it felf, would be no boundary ; and
fuppofing it were not fo, is not the Governour
an effential part of the Conftitution, and is
not his Council neceffary ? Has he it not then
in his power to come to terms for his own allowances ? Will there be any room left for
Contefts about fettling Salaries ? Will it not
be done to hand ? I befeech you Sir, to Confider when this *Pandora*'s Box fhall be once o-
pened, what unforefeen accidents, what irreparable mifchiefs, confufion and mifery would
this

this whole People be in? This is true, I we may take what the Author of the Letter fays, they intend to give the Government *Two Thousand Pounds* a year. I cannot tell whether they were to fence out to make such an offer; *if they mean a Governour by Government, it would be an effectual method to Enflave this Country* fays the Letter. Indeed I never knew that Governour and Government, were one and the fame word; yet it is Obfervable, that the Author of the Letter makes them fo. If the General Affembly fays the Author of the Letter, *then they neither can, nor ought,* &c. Yet I believe all Government have Liberty to accept of Donations; but be it fo that they cannot, then neither can the Government be fupported by the Profits of the Publick Bank, for this is not in the Charter; and if the Authors Arguments were good, that the Publick could not make ufe of it; the Governour as he affures us, will be fole Heir of it: and then what will the gain of the Country be? Whilft I retort this Argument, I had almoft forgot the Claufe in *Hudibras*, that, *no man turns the Cafe upon his own Concerns.* What would become of the Fund, if the Crown fhould forbid it? Will not the Confufion be great on the Borrowers? *Juftinian* was of Opinion, that nothing could be a Law that was not juft. The Gentlemen who fhould

pro-

promote fuch an one, furely would have no
thanks from them they reprefent, when they
come to feel the ill effects of it; but I hope no
fuch thing will take place. Thus Sir, I have
given you fome of the thoughts of the Town,
and the Reafons in particular, that fway with
me againft a Publick Bank. The Reafons why
I prefer a Private Bank, are fuch as thefe.

1. That there will be no Invafion of the Prerogative; for every body as well as Mr. *Attorney* will readily accknowledge that, *they are
not Money,* page 11. And they may have the
face and fignature of Money, as much as the
Bank Bills of *England,* that is none at all; for
they carry nothing of Authority with them,
but are only Notes on the Bank, paffing from
one to another, for fo much value as is expref-
fed in them; which value being depofited in
the Bank, either in Lands or other imperifhable
Eftate as the Original Fund, and the Obligation
of the feveral Partners, to take 'em in all Payments, except Specialties, under a great penalty, gives Credit to the feveral Bills or Notes
iffued from the Bank.

2. Nor will a Private Bank open a door of
Arbitrary Power to invade the Liberties of the
People, by a Governours handling at his own
pleafure fuch Sums as he has occafion to make
ufe of, to promote his own ends.

3. Nor is there any infringment of the Liberty of the People, there is no Tax requifite to
make

make good the fall of the Bank, no Publick
Warrantee to fecure it, but only the Eftates of
fuch Gentlemen as are willing of their own
accord to Mortgage 'm; that by the Security
given, and their mutual agreement, their Notes
fhould have a Currency, that they might ferve
the Country, and themfelves in promoting the
Trade of it; fo that if the Bank be fuppref-
fed, it would hazard only their particular E-
ftates.

4. It may be Carried on as other Merchant-
like Affairs, by Factors or Truftees, without
offence to the Crown, or Government; This
being the head of Argument that bears the
Countenance of reafoning in Mr. *Attorneys* Letter, which I fhall Remark : I take it for
granted, that it is the Natural Right of *Englifh*
to Trade, and to carry it on in fuch Methods,
as they fhall conceive to be moft advantageous to
them; and that in order thereto, they have a
right to take one anothers Word, Note or Bond,
as the Cafe may require, with due regard had
to Juftice, and the power of the Legiflature, to
enlarge and limit this Trade, as fhall be tho't
moft fuitable to the Honour of the Crown, &
the Publick Weal : It is in the liberty of any
in Trade, to enter into a Covenant, to take one
anothers Notes, and that they might be better
known, they may agree upon fome perfons to
form thofe Notes under their hands for them;
& on their making over fuch Security as there
is

is required, for their mutual safety, for such Sums as they shall emit or take, and may agree to pay such an Interest as may support the Charge, and Lend of their Credit to others for their benefit, since there is no Statute Law broken, & nothing contrary to the Common Law; so that the difference between us is not, Whether the Government cannot crush such a Partnership, for no body denies that? but whether such an Affair may be carried on in a Company, without being Incorporated, without being a breach on the Prerogative of the Crown? Thus the Private Bankers in *Lumbard-Street* Emit their Notes, and that on Interest too without being tho't so; Our Fathers about Twenty eight years ago, entred into a Partnership to Circulate their Notes founded on Land Security, stamped on Paper, as our Province Bills, which gave no offence to the Government then, and that at a time, when the Prerogative of the Crown was extended further than ever has been since; What Mr. *Attorney* says of the Bank of *England,* that they obtained an Act of Parliament for their Support is true, yet proves nothing to his purpose; for altho' a Company can manage their Affairs better, and in a shorter method, for their mutual Security by a Patent or Charter of Incorporation, and with the greater Security by an Act of Parliament as the Bank of *England,* by the loan of *One Million Two Hundred Thousand Pounds* to the Nation

on obtained, yet it proves nothing that such Companies were any breach on the Prerogative; the Act of the Sixth of Queen *Anne*, quoted by the Author of the Letter, viz. *That during the Continuance of the Bank of* England, *it shall not be lawful for any Body Politick or Corporation, or other than the said Company of the Bank, or for other Partners exceeding six in* England, *to borrow or owe any Sum, or Bills, or Note Payable on demand, or at any time less than six months from the borrowing thereof*; is so far from proving against the Partnership, that strong Arguments may be drawn from it, of its Lawfulness: As,

1. It appears plain, that the Limitation of the Act is to *England*, and that during the Continuance of the Bank; and so is of no force in the Plantations or *Ireland*.

2. That it is lawful now for the number of six.

3. It implies that they might do it, before this Act was made in favour of the Bank of *England*, and consequently lawful for us, where that Act never was in force, which is what we Contend for.

4. It implies that the Law of *England* does not look on every number of Partners to be a Corporation purely for their being Partners; and Mr. *Attorney* quoting my Lord *Cook*'s description of a Corporation, and his applying it to the Gentlemen concerned in the Projection, is nothing but an amusement, and deserves no Answer, in that none of the Essentials to such a Body was pretended to by them: for a Pattent from the Crown, which gives the Form and Being to a Corporation, was but hoped for.

But what I would Remark with the greateſt Complacency, is the applying this Law to us in *New-England* ; for he tells us, page 12. *If the ſame faċt committed in* England, *by a Number not exceeding ſix would be a breach of Law, much more may we ſuppoſe it forbidden, and made unlawful for an hundred to do it here.* A nice way of Arguing, that concludes ſtrongly, and deſerves thanks for the new Invention : Becauſe Gunning upon *Boſton* Neck is forbidden by a Law, therefore in every Town of the Country, I am apt to think that any man that is able to carry a Gun, may ſee the folly of ſuch an Argument : Truly it gives me a merry turn of thought to entertain the Idea, how Mr. *Attorney* would crow to hear his Antagoniſt at the Bar plead a deſperate Cauſe with ſuch a mighty dint of argument as this ; 'tis well he did not proceed, to give himſelf any further trouble to argue with the ſame velocity and ſtrength, how far the Projeċtion would be a breach on the Conſtitution of the Bank of *England* ; for we are not able to ſtand before the whiz------But did the Author of the Letter, who quoted the Law, in very deed believe it poſſible that it ſhould have any influence ſo far over the Water ? I wonder then how it conſiſted with his Conſciencious regard to it, to adviſe the Publick to Ereċt a Publick Bank of Credit ! for I would put it to his Conſcience, whether this Law is not as point blank

levelled

levelled at the Corporation, (which the Government is) in cafe they fhould have the
thoughts of doing any fuch thing as private
Partners, and whether it is not as poffible for
the Government to Set up & Eftablifh things
contrary to the Laws of *England* as for private Perfons ? and whether the offence would
not be as great ; and becaufe I do not know
but that the Supream Authority may fee caufe
to crufh any Bank fet up here, I will add, that
there is no reafonable man, nor man of Law,
nor man acquainted with the nature ofGovern-
ment dare fay, that it will be of equal pernicious confequence, for private Perfons to fet
up, as for the Publick ; for no act of private
Perfons can forfeit our Charter, it muft be a
Publick Act to do that ; all the mifchief of
the Private's being condemned, would be that
the Bank would fall, and that the Bankers
muft make good their Notes ; but if the Publick Bank fhould be fet up and Condemned,
by that means we fhould be endangered in our
Charter : And I am afraid there are fome
men in the world that would gladly lay hold
of the firft opportunity to deprive us of it.---
The Tendency of a Publick Bank, as have
been propofed, is to Unite the Power of the
Country and the Cafh together, which all wife
people have endeavoured to keep afunder, in
order to preferve their Liberties ; it tends
to bring all the People into a dependency upon

on the Court Intereſt; and conſequently to
render them Abject and Servile, which I
think no Lover of his Country ſhould promote: As it is propoſed at preſent, it tends
no way to help the Landed Intereſt in the
ſtocking and improving their Lands, but only ſerves to remove the evil day a little,
very little further off, and then runs them
into greater diſtreſs. On the contrary, the
Projection for a Private Fund of Credit,
which ſince I began this Letter, I hear is
coming out in Print, that all may judge of
it, and no doubt will be acceptable to the
Country; is ſo well founded and ſecured,
that were they permitted to proceed and
Emit their Notes, would furniſh us with a
Medium of Exchange; the Landed man
might either be Concerned in the Foundation, or might borrow Credit without any
fear of a ſudden or ſurprizing demand, to
the prejudice of his Affairs, might Stock
his Farm, and be able to leſſen his Principal, as his Product would enable him; it
would be a certain reſort for men to borrow Credit on any Emergency; it gives the
Induſtrious an opportunity of improving their
Lands to greater advantage, which would
increaſe the Export of the Country; it
could hurt none but the envious, who will
do no good themſelves, and yet are grieved
at what their Neighbour does. The Publick

lick Charities are not inconfiderable, that are
Eftablifhed in it ; in a word, without it, we
cannot fo comfortably enjoy the Outward
Bleffings that Heaven has indulged us with.
With it we may enjoy all the Conveniencies
of a Plentiful Cafh, without running the risk
of being a Prey to an invading Foe ; and in
that as well as in every other refpect would
anfwer our Occafions as the Mines of *Peru* or
Potofi : But I think I hear you in the Country
fay, they will not pay our Rates, and therefore will not anfwer our ends. In anfwer to
which I would fay, that the Bills of Credit of
the other Provinces do not pay our Rates, yet
have a general Currency amongft you ; that
the Gentlemen concern'd to promote the Projection fay, that whilft there is any of the Province Bills ftirring, they would change them
gratis, when they fhould grow fcarce that the
People could not obtain them ; there is no
doubt, but that the Government would Order
the Treafurer to take what would anfwer their
Occafions, that would pay the Souldiers and
the other Officers of the Government, and the
other Charges ; then they would not have the
occafion to be at the Charge nor Rifque of
making Bills of Credit if they faw good ; it
would revive the Trade of the Province, and
enable them to pay their Debts ; for as things
are now, they cannot make Money but with
a fmall part of their produce, they are forced

to

to Truck them away, fo that fome are not a-ble, and others take the opportunity to defraud the Country Trader, and he of Confequence is not able to pay the Merchant in *Boſton*, to the great Damage of the whole Country, as well as a Difcredit to our Trade ; for the badnefs of the Pay for want of a Medium, obliges the Merchant to make a great Advance on the Sale of his Goods, that they are as dear now as in the heighth of War ; the Country in Courfe ask dear for their Produce, which occafions a great Lofs in Returns, and the Dearnefs of both affects the Tradefman, and makes him ask dear for his Labour, without which he is not able to Live ; fo that as the ſtate of our Commerce is now, every thing tends to drive away the Trade from us to our Neighbours : The Fifhery will fail, becaufe they have no Money, for it, and all Induſtry is very much crampt ; in that when men have Laboured, they are obliged to go to a Shop for Goods for their Pay, which often invites, if not neceffitates 'em to fpend more than they want of *Engliſh* Goods, to the hurt of their Families ; and by that means brings us more in Debt to *England* ; all which would be remedied by the Eſtablifhing the Land Bank : And whereas the Gentlemen are applying Home for a Charter from the King to Incorporate them, that they may be the better enabled to fecure the Foundation and the Credit of the Bills : I wifh them
good

good fucce{s, and doubt not the whole
Country, (when they have a clear view of
their be{t Intere{t) will fay, *Amen*.-----And
whereas fome of you in the Country obje&,
that if fuch a Company goes forward, they
will have all the Lands in the Country : In
anfwer to which Obje&ion, it would be
worth while to Confider the Scheme how
it is guarded, and it will eafily be apprehended that the Charge is groundlefs ; for
the Lands will be taken in at little more
than half the value, and whilft the Borrower pays his Intere{t Money, the Bank will
never trouble him ; if he negle&s that, he
will {tand a year longer before he can be
Sued for it ; and no man will let his Land
go at half the value ; his Neighbour will
fooner buy it of him than let it go at fo low
a rate ; but if the Bank recovers it, they
mu{t Sell it, for they have not asked leave
to purchafe Lands ; then there is three years
right of Redemption left to the Owner : if
the Land fells for more, the Bank returns
the Overplus, which I think fufficiently
takes off the weight of that Obje&ion : Befides, as it is propofed by the Publick, there
will be but few Borrowers, but what are in
d;{trefs to put it off the further, becaufe
they are fure of being {traitened at the expiration of the five years to pay it in ; yet
in this Proje&ion, every Partner is obliged
to

to take out a quarter part of what he Subscribes, to bring out a Medium of Exchange: But I shall tire your patience in enlarging on the pleasant Subject, in which we have a prospect of relief under the present and growing distress: I shall make a few more transient Remarks and Close. The Letter says, page 15. *That the several Laws of this Province respecting the Money, or the Interest, are broke in upon by the Projection:* It is so far from being so, that it directly has a contrary view; the Act of the Fifth of *William* and *Mary* about the Interest of Money is broke in upon, because we fix the Interest at less than six *per Cent.* when the preamble of the Act says, for as much as the abatement of Interest has always been found beneficial to the Advancement of Trade, and the Improvement of Lands by good Husbandry; which is the very thing we have consulted. I have with care examined all the Laws of this Province, relating to Money or Bills of Credit, and the several Acts of Parliament quoted in the Letter too many to be recited, and cannot for my life imagine that any Lawyer besides Mr. *Attorney* could find that they were invalidated, or in the least broke in upon by this Projection; and now that any person acting as he apprehended in his Office as Attorney General, should insinuate to the Government, and publish to the World in Print, that they have

been

been all broke in upon is very ftrange and un-accountable : His Infinuation, page 18. *That the Bills being but pieces of Paper, have no other value than what the Borrower gives 'em,* is a ve-ry ungrounded (I am loth to fay falfe) Af-fertion, in that they are Notes Iffued out un-der the Hands of them that are abundantly fufficient to make them good, and who were obliged not only to that, but under a *Fifty Pound* Penalty to take them in all Payments, and the Borrower being at his liberty, muft be bubbled indeed to take them out, if they would not anfwer his Occafions, in *page* 19. he afferts, that the Projectors are only obliged to accept of them for the redemption of Pawns and Mortgages ; and fuppofes that the Pof-feffor has neither, referring to the Tenour of the Bill : See his own recital of theBill,*page* 7. Obliges,*&c.* to accept the fame in all payments, according to Covenant made by us ; (or rather fee the true Form or Tenour of the Bill in the Scheme Printed) both which fo manifeftly contradict his Affertion, and at firft fight tend-ed to miflead the Honourable Houfe of Re-prefentatives in Matters of Fact, that it is un-accountable, he fhould offer it. As for his grofs Charge of Contempt of Government, I fuppofe the Gentlemen will vindicate them-felves ; I have heard fay, they are fufficiently able, as well as obliged : his breviate of the Scheme, and his Tenour of the Bill being a

grofs

grofs mifreprefentation, and his reflections
made thereon, confequently ill grounded, I do
not trouble you with a Confutation, they fall
of themfelves, *page* 13. He fays, *That the Gene-*
ral Affembly are under a neceffity of enquiring in-
to the Juftice, Legality, the Safety, and Publick
Advantage ; wherein I agree with the Author,
and I believe the Gentlemen concerned, would
have been glad if it had been duly weighed,
and fully confidered before they had been prohibited ; and whereas no man has ever proved
it to be, either unjuft, illegal or unfafe, or not
for the Publick Good ; and the contrary I
think, is fufficiently evident to any
difinterefted ; the Gentlemen that they
might proceed in their Affair without offence,
(fince he defires that it might be forbidden,
until His Majefties Pleafure is known ;)
have agreed by a Humble Petition, to lay it
before His Majefty, praying for a Charter of
Incorporation, to enable hem with the more
fecurity to Circulate their Notes founded on
their Lands : The Author, *page* 20. and 18.
feems Concerned about the Credit of the Bank
Notes, and that for two Reafons ; the lownefs
of the Intereft, & the Foundation being Land
and not Money, to anfwer the Notes : As for
the Intereft which is fet at *Five per Cent*, it is
what the Publick has feen reafon to fet theirs
at, and therefore may be fuppofed their reafon
was good ; the value of Money or Notes never

ver was founded on the Intereſt, but what they would purchaſe of Land or Merchandizes; the Intereſt is juſtly lower'd by the abundant Security required, which is conſidered in the nature of a Sum paid in hand by way of fine, as in the Leaſes of Lands to lower the Annual Rent. As for Land Foundation, the only meaſure of valuation we have left, and the beſt (in that Silver has altered four parts in five within this two hundred years, as is affirmed by good Authors) to found our Notes on, in that our Trade will be governed according to our produce either in our own growth, or what by our Induſtry we Import from others, to Export by way of Returns to *Great Britain*, which wholly takes off the common cry by way of amuſement againſt it, that we are extravagant in our Conſumptions, and Over-traded, which tho' they may be true in themſelves, are nothing promoted by this, in that the Notes cannot be ſent off. Mr. *Attorney* tells us, page 30 *that in what he has done, he had no private view, or ſeparate Intereſt, nor any prejudice to the Gentlemen concerned, among whom he has many particular Friends, but has ſincerely aimed at the Public Good.* I believe the Gentlemen concerned do not think he has treated 'em like Friends, who they ſay never came amongſt them to reaſon about the Scheme; but In his Lette has dreſt them Alamode the *Spaniſh* Inquiſition, with horrid pictures on their Deſign that
they

they might be delivered over to the Secular Power, to be punifhed. And as tor his defign and feparate Intereft, being one that improves his Stock by Letting Money at Intereft ; if he had not told us fo, we fhould have been apt to have believed the contrary, and may be worthy of a fecond view and Reflection by him, as well as the Portion of Sacred Writ, fo much abufed as to be fet in the Frontifpiece of his Letter, which I fhall take the freedom to repeat to his Confideration in the very words, *That better is a little with Righteoufnefs, than great Revenues without Right.* And now Sir, I have given you a few of the many dark thoughts of the Town, relating to the Letter, and the Publick Bank Projected ; as alfo fome of their hopes of the Succefs of the Private. If what has been written may contribute to the fetting Truth, and the Intereft of theCountry in a clearer Light in your Parts, it will be a fufficient Reward, and an entire Satisfaction,

To your Humble Servant,

New-England,
Anno 1714.

F---l. B---t.

A VINDICATION OF THE BANK OF CREDIT

A Vindication of the Bank of Credit Projected in Boston from the Aspersions of Paul Dudley, Esqr. in a Letter By him directed to John Burril Esqr. Late Speaker to the House of Representatives for the Province of the Massachusetts-Bay in New-England (Boston, 1714), pp. 1–20.

A Vindication of the Bank of Credit was written by those who proposed the bank of credit, in support of *A Letter from one in Boston to his Friend in the Country*. In particular, *A Vindication* was meant to be an attack on the author of *Objections to the Bank of Credit* (reproduced in this volume and attributed to Paul Dudley). Supporters of the bank included Samuel Lynde, Edward Lyde, John Coleman, Elisha Cooke, Jr, John Oulton, Timothy Thornton, Oliver Noyes, William Pain and Nathaniel Oliver. These men were economic and political leaders in Boston, though they were not part of the elite. Most of them held modest political offices and were either professionals or involved in some aspect of trade.

    A Vindication, like *A Letter from one in Boston*, spells out the shortage of currency in the colonies and attempts to clear up any misconceptions about how the bank of credit would operate. A primary problem for these supporters was the simultaneous proposal of a public bank of credit. A public bank had greater support, as it would be regulated by the government of the colony, therefore avoiding the risks of a bank under private management.

A
VINDICATION
OF THE
BANK
OF
Credit

Projected in *Boston* from the Aspersions

OF

Paul Dudley, *Esqr.*

IN A

LETTER

By him directed to *John Burril* Esqr. Late Speaker to the House of Representatives for the Province of the *Massachusetts-Bay* in *New-England.*

Printed in the Year 1714.

A

VINDICATION

OF THE

Bank of Credit, &c.

To *John Burril*, Efqr.

S I R.

MR. Attorney General, by his Letter of the Twenty Second of *October* laft paft to your Self, as Speaker to the Houfe of Reprefentatives for this Province, having moft unaccountably, with an uncommon Freedom, taken upon him to Infult and Arraign a Confiderable Company of Gentlemen Merchants, &c. (as he is pleafed to ftile them) Projectors of the Bank of Credit, and call them to the Bar of that Honourable Houfe, Charging them with the many High Crimes and *Mifdemeanours* following.

Firft, That they are openly carrying on their Bank with utmoft Vigour and Expedition, in Contempt of an Order of Council; and indeed affirming, that the Government

have

have nothing to do with them in that Affair:
And that they look upon themfelves very
Well and fufficient to carry it on without making any Application to the General Affembly. *Vide* Page 3, 4.

Secondly, That their Bank is *Pandora's Box*,
Page 4.

Thirdly, That their Projection is juft Ripe
for Execution, which will more or lefs affect,
invalidate and break in upon the Prerogative
of the Crown, feveral Acts of Parliament,
the Conftitution and Laws of this Province,
the Eftates and Liberties of the People; and
that not only for the prefent, but fuccceding
Generations. *Page* 4, 7, 15.

Fourthly, That their Projection is a thing
Intolerable, *Unreafonable and Unjuft*, not founded in *Commutative Juftice*, and *Common Honefty*;
and muft unavoidably prove a great Snare and
Mifchief to People that want Money to pay
their Debts, or otherwife for whofe eafe and
advantage the Bank is Projected. *Page* 16, 17,
18.

Fifthly, That the Bufinefs of the Projectors
is in one day to be Mafters of *One Hundred
and Fifty Thoufand Pounds*, without any Rifque,
or any other Charge or Trouble, than the
Writing and Signing a few pieces of Paper,
to Accept *Six Thoufand Pounds* Intereft *per
Annum*; whereby they would immediately
have the profits of other Mens Eftates, and
finally

finally the Eftates themfelves, without a valuable Confideration. *Page* 17, 18.

Sixthly, That their Projection will be in effect the fetting up an *Abfolute*, *Independent Government*, which like a Fire in the Bowels, will Burn up and Confume the whole Body. *Page* 1.

Thefe Articles being Intermixed and Cloathed with fo many Invective Sarcafms, Opprobrious Language and Undue Reflections, the Gentlemen Concerned hold themfelves Obliged in Juftice to themfelves, and the Truth, and in Honour to your felf; that you and every one elfe may be Un leceived, and that the whole Matter may be fet in its true light, do Affirm and Declare,

That two or three Gentlemen in the Town of *Bofton*, difcourfing of the Difficulties that Trade laboured under, for want of a Medium of Exchange, the Silver being fent Home for *England*, and the Bills of Credit on the feveral Provinces daily Called in by the Funds on which they were Emitted; thought it proper to confult fome other Friends, and to Meet together, and Confider of a fuitable Remedy for the prefent and growing Inconveniencies and Difficulties. At which time fome were defired to Commit their thoughts to Writing, in order to be confidered of at a Second Meeting, which was accordingly done; And after feveral Meetings, agreed on a Land Security,

as

as a Fund for Bills and Notes to be Circulated; and Minutes then drawn up, for the Regulating and Carrying on that Affair, but all with an intire dependance upon on the Government for their Favour and Countenance in promoting it, and furnishing them with all such necessary Powers as might enable them to carry it on with safety to themselves, and the Possessors of their Bills or Notes. And therefore immediately they desired some of the Gentlemen to wait upon His Excellency the Governour for his Advice, Favour, Countenance and Direction in their Projection; who accordingly the very next Morning before they had taken a fair Copy of their Minutes, waited on His Excellency; so careful were they of paying all due Respects to Government, who were well Received by him, and Encouraged to proceed. And at the same time their Scheme being first laid before his Excellency; his thoughts were desired, whether it was practicable for the Publick to come into a Fund themselves, to which he was pleased to Answer, No, by no means; The Country is greatly Indebted already, and if such a thing were proposed, any Landed Man might come into the General Court, and enter his Protest against it; Neither would it be safe for that a Governours Fingers could not be kept out of it. And there then being further discourse about the power of the Government

ment to Lend at Interest on the Publick Credit; He Replied, That what the Government could not do wisely, equitably and safely they could not do; and that the Method that they had Projected for Relief in that Affair, he well approved of; withal adding, that he would be the first Person that would take out *Three Hundred Pounds* of their Bills to promote their Credit, and encouraged them to proceed to take Subscriptions, in order to lay it before the General Assembly for their Allowance; and that he would do all that lay in his power to promote it; assuring them that he would Write Home in their favour, by setting forth the Necessity of such a Projection: And directed them to wait upon Mr. Secretary *Addington* for his Advice, which they did, who was of Opinion that the Government would not Raise Money or Bills to Let out upon Loan. They then, and at sundry other times consulted him about their Scheme, committed it to him to peruse, correct, alter, amend and frame as he should think fit, which he accordingly did. Whereas if the Projectors had been discouraged in their so early Attempts, it might have prevented any further proceedings: And the said Scheme was laid before the General Court at their Sessions in *February* last past, together with a Petition, Subscribed by most of the Undertakers

kers of that Affair, for the granting them such neceſſary Powers, as they ſhould think meet to carry on the ſame.

Sir,

The foregoing being Matter of Fact, and the exact ſteps taken by the Gentlemen concerned in the Projection of the Bank. It cannot be ſo much as imagined, that the Author of the Letter, his Poſt and near Relation to the Governour Conſidered, ſhould be ignorant thereof. However it fully proves that part of his Letter reſpecting their *Slight, Neglect and Contempt of the Authority and Government* to be a deſigned Miſrepreſentation, and therefore Abuſive of the Gentlemen concerned ; ſome of whom on ſeveral accounts are Superiour to him.

Now Sir, If you will pleaſe to Conſider his Argument, whereby he would ſeem and pretend to prove his Charge of *Contempt*, &c. you will find it as Unfair and Fallacious as his *Charge*, which is that which you muſt needs have ſeen ' in the Publick News-Paper, or an ' Order of the Governour and Council paſſed ' upon the Occaſion of the Projection of the ' Bank of Credit ; whereby the Projectors ' were directed to proceed no further in that ' Affair, until the next Seſſion of the General ' Aſſembly ; that ſo the whole Government ' might be of Advice in a Matter of that ' Weight and Conſequence. Notwithſtanding

' all which, I am loth to lay, in Contempt of
' it, the persons concerned are openly carrying
' on their Bank with utmost Vigour and Ex-
' pedition, and supposing, and in leed affirming
' that the Government have nothing to do
' with them in that Affair.

Is not this a bold and wilful Misrepresenta-
tion of the Matter ? Whenas the Order of
Council, which the Government Ordered to
be Printed in the Weekly News-Letter, is in
the Words following.

At a Council Held at the Council-Chamber in
Boston, upon Fryday the Twentieth of
August, 1714.

UPon Reading a Memorial, *Presented by the
Queens Attorney General, setting forth that
upon good Information, a certain Number of Gentlemen, and Merchants are Projecting a Bank of
Credit as they call it, designing speedily to Make
and Emit a quantity of Bills to a great Value ;
which is a Matter of Importance, and will necessarily be of General Influence.*

Ordered, *That the Projectors or Undertakers
of any such Bank do not proceed to Print the
said Scheme, or put the same on Public Record, Make or Emit any of their Notes or
Bills, until they have laid their Proposals before
the General Assembly of this Her Majesties
Province ; who are always ready to Countenance*
and

and Encourage any Proposals that may be of be-
nefit and advantage for the Publick ; or for the
promoting and encouraging of Trade amongst Her
Majesties Good Subjects of this Province ; And
that this Order be Printed in the Weekly
News-Letter. Isaac Addington, *Secr.*

Now by what Words in this Order can Mr.
Attorney support his Argument, to prove the
Projectors *Contempt and Insinuated Disobedience,*
which as it did not forbid their proceeding a-
ny further in that Affair, but rather encourage
and direct them to compleat their Subscriptions, and perfect their Scheme, so as it might
be fit to lay before the General **Assembly** ; so
was it punctually complied with, in that the
Projectors neither Printed their Scheme, or
put the same upon Publick Record, Made, or
Emitted any of their Notes or Bills ; but Re-
considered and New-Modelled their Scheme,
and took many more Subscriptions, and so far
perfected it, as to lay it before the General
Assembly, which they did at their last *October*
Sessions ; hoping for their Countenance and
Authority, for that because a certain number
of the Gentlemen concerned were appointed
to attend his Excellency with the present
Scheme, which they carried to him on the
Morning of the Day they presented another of
the same to the House of Representatives,
who then freely declared, that he would favour

vour the Defign, if the Houfe of Reprefentatives and Council would come into it, and
that the Publicks Raifing of Bills to Let out,
to him had its dark fides ; for that if any Perfon fhould borrow of the Publick Bills, and
Mortgage his Eftate for payment, and fail of
making payment, whereby the Bftate fo Mortgaged fhould become forfeit, the Eftate fo
forfeited would belong to the Crown ; and if
he were their Governour, he fhould think
himfelt obliged to lay his Hands upon it,
till the Kings Pleafure could be had; who
would have the intire difpofition thereof.

And now after fo fair a Glofs and falfe
Comment upon the Order of the Governour
and Council, and the Actions of the Projectors in Conformity thereto in the very beginning of the Letter ; what can be expected but
the like Arguments .throughout. And indeed
here you may fee *Ex Ungue Leonem.* Is not
this too much like prevaricating talk in a bad
Caufe. Wherefore it is now to be Noted,
that notwithftanding the Gentlemen concerned, had made feveral Alterations in their Projection obliging every one that Subfcribed
thereto, to give good real Security, to the full
value of their feveral Subfcriptions, to Lie as a
Fund or Security, to anfwer all the Notes or
Bills Iffued from the Bank ; and to make good
all Deficiencies, whereby the Poffeffors or
Borrowers of the Bills or Notes were in no
danger

danger of being wronged, with some other
Amendments: The want of which Security
in the first Projection, is one of the most popu-
lar Arguments Mr. *Attorney* hath made use of
to cry down the same. Now he being well
Informed of these Alterations before he Published ; Nay, before he delivered and sent his
Letter to you, whereby he certainly knew his
short Abstract of the Projection, and his Form
of the Bills, with his Addition of an Escutch-
eon, and consequently all the fine Structure he
builds thereon, to be but upon a sandy Foundation ; tho' he would have the Honourable
House of Representatives believe it.

And then he does in effect tell you, that the
Projectors of the Bank have of their own
heads formed themselves into a Company, by
a *Constitution* of their own making, and Erecting of themselves into a *Body Politick and Corporate to all Intents and Purposes in the Law* ;
and then calls in the Prerogative and the Honour of the Government to his Aid and As-
sistance. It's true, they have by a Constitution
of their own making, formed themselves into
a Company and Co-partnership, and that they
take for granted they well might do without
the least affront to the Crown, or this Government, or else had never attempted it ; for
what's more common and usual then for Merchants and others to enter into Partnership,
make their Rules, and oblige themselves to
the

the due obfervation of them. And does this make them a Body Politick, and Corporate to all intents and purpofes in the Law, or encroach upon the Prerogative, or difhonour this Government? What is it then the Projectors have done, that makes them fuch a Body Politick as Mr. *Attorney* pretends they are. Certainly no man but one in *Eutopia* could make fuch an Interpretation of their Articles as he has done. The Projectors, as he rightly obferves, do not pretend to Incorporate, or make themfelves a Body Politick; neither does his partial defcription of a Corporation, which he fays is my Lord *Cooks*, with all the *&crs.* he has put into it prove they have.

We agree with him, that all Bodies Politick are derived from the King as their Original Fountain; but it does not thence follow, that all Banks of Credit and Companies are,for that there have been fuch as never were Incorporated: And does not the Sword Blade Company in *London*, continue even unto this day, to Emit their Notes to a very great Value by Truftees, and not Incorporated as a Bank of Credit; fo that their Emitting Notes or Bills is not in *England* accounted a *thing intolerable, Unreafonable and Unjuft*, and abfolutely inconfiftent with the Honour, the Power and Wifdom of that Government,nor to fuffer a Number of their own People to fet up an *Abfolute Independent Government*, which like a Fire in
their

their Bowels, would burn up & confume their whole Body. But Mr. *Attorney* it feems is wifer, & fees further into the Matter, than the Government of *England* doth. And then again to prove the Erecting this Bank a Breach of Law, he brings in an Act of Parliament, made in the Sixth Year of the Reign of Queen *ANNE*, to wit, *that during the Continuance of the Bank of* England, *it fhall not be lawful for any Body Politick or Corporate, other than the faid Company of the Bank, or for other Partners exceeding fix in* England *to Borrow or Owe any Sum on Bill or Note, payable on demand, or at any time lefs than fix Months from the Borrowing thereof.* Now it is to be obferved, that this Law does not make any Number of Partners to be a Body Politick or Corporate, for their being in Partnerfhip; Neither doth it forbid any fix, or any other Number of Partners to Borrow or Owe any Sum on Bill or Note, payable at any time longer than fix Months from the Borrowing. Moft certainly that Law was made in favour of the Bank of *England*; So that even in *England* it felf before that Act had its force, it was lawful there for any Body Politick or Corporate, or Partners to Borrow or Owe any Sum on Bill or Note, &c. And therefore will be Lawful again at the determination of that Bank. Then why may it not lawfully be done here, fince that Act no ways affects this Province; For can Mr. *Attorney* imagine,

gine that setting up a Bank of Credit in *New-England*, would in the least measure, prejudice the Bank of *England*: However, tho' he says he will not trouble himself to Argue how far this Projection would be a Breach upon the Bank of *England*; yet tells you, *page 12. That certainly if the same Fact committed in* England, *by a Number exceeding six would be a Breach of Law; much more may we suppose it forbidden and made Unlawful for an hundred to do it here.* Certainly, this is a fine and accurate Mode of Reasoning and Pungent Argument.

Because our Law forbids us Building of Wooden Houses in *Boston*, therefore we must not Erect one in *Lynn*, or the Province of *Main*.

As to what he says of the Projection not being founded in *Commutative Justice* and *Common Honesty*, and that he can't see the Reasonableness and Justice of it, betwixt the Subscribers and Borrowers; and therefore must unavoidably prove a *great Snare and Mischief* to those that want Money, &c. To make a shew of the Proof thereof, he Argues from his own false Abstract of the Projection, so that he disputing *Ex non Concessis*; all he draws from thence, together with his *Hypothesis*, grounded thereon, must needs fall of it self, & come to nothing. And it is plain, his design was only to amuse the People, but more particularly the House of Representatives: Now since the
Projection

Projection obliges every Subscriber to Mortgage a Real Estate, of the full value of what he Subscribes for, to make a sufficient Fund for the Credit of their Notes and Bills; as likewise to Answer all Deficiencies arising by any defect or default of the Projectors in the aforesaid Scheme; Whereby the Borrowers or Possessors of the Notes or Bills are sure to have Justice done them; and all concerned with them, in case the Bank should come to an end, even then will the last Possessors of their Bills or Notes have good Security to depend on: Notwithstanding all the Objector hath said, or possibly can say: They still having their Credit and Value from the Intrinsick Value of the Bank, and not from what his Bubbled Borrowers give them, as he groundlesly asserts. He must needs suppose the House to be asleep, and so to need awakening, as *page* 5. when he asserts, *page* 19. that by the Tenour of the Bills you see, they are only obliged to Accept of them for the Redemption of *Pawns* and *Mortgages:* When in his Reciting the Tenour of the Bill, *page* 7. He owns that we oblige our selves to Accept the same in ALL PAYMENTS according to Covenant made by us on Publick Record, *&c.* Which how directly he Contradicts himself, & endeavours to Mislead the House, we leave you and the World to judge: Not would the Projectors have the Profits of other Mens Estates, ftates, much lefs the Eftates themfelves without a valuable Confideration, nor make themfelves Màfters of any Eftates but their own, which they willingly Depofit and Mortgage for a General Benefit for the Loan and Credit whereof it's as lawful for them to take Intereft, as it is for Mr. *Attorney* for his Bills of Credit on the Province. The Bank Bills having a better and more certain Security than the Publick Loan Bills, and more eafily obtained, In Cafe that late Act fhould be Repealed: And for that Reafon his Argument againft the Private Bank is of far greater ftrength and force againft the Publick Bank.

Mr. Attorney *is pleafed often to put you in mind, that this Projettion breaks in upon, and Invalidates the Conftitution of this Province, page 4. 15. The Act of Parliament of late made Referring to Money in the Plantations, defigning thereby to awaken the Government upon this great occafion, to Exert their proper Power, and not fuffer the Projettion to proceed, but by fome proper Act, and Publick Order, to declare againft, and forbid it, left thereby the Conftitution of the Government of the Province be broke in upon, and endangered: Becaufe we are a Dependent Government, and muft in all things Conform our felves to the Law of* Great Britain, *and Inftructions of the Crown, and therefore muft expect to give an Account of all our Matters.*

Now if the fuffering of this Private Bank to be
Erected,

Erected, is such an Encroachment upon the Prerogative, and a breach of the Law of *England*, as to endanger the loss of our Charter, & the Liberties and Estates of the People, which to prevent, Mr. *Attorney* tells you, was the very Confideration that principally determined him at that time so freely to Communicate his Thoughts to your self in that Matter ; with the several other fine flourishes and plaufible Infinuations, whereby he would induce you to believe that in all this Affair that he hath fincerely aimed at the Publick Good, and effectually to prevent any Attempts that might be made againft our Liberties and Priviledges, which no doubt he is intirely fond of, & always was vigilant & induftrious to maintain and defend. If he has fincerely given you his Opinion refpecting the Private Bank, and the direful effects of it, with what fort of fincerity did he when he fays he had the Honour to be of an Extraordinary Committee Raifed for that purpofe, give it as his Opinion, that considering the demand as to the Taxes, & the great occafion of the People, as to their Trade, it might be convenient to Make and Iffue out a further quantity of the Publick Bills of Credit : And now in his Letter fpend fo much time, and take fuch pains, and argue to perfuade the General Court to fet up a Bank of Credit themfelves, Emit their Bills, and take Intereft for the fame. Is it not as poffible for the Government to Erect,

Set

Set up and Eſtabliſh things contrary to the Law, as for a Number of Private Perſons; and does not the Law of *England* which he ſaith would be broke in upon, by Erecting a Private Bank, much more reſpect a Corporation than Private Perſons; and which he himſelf readily grants it doth. Is not this then one effectual way to endanger the Conſtitution of the Government, the utter Ruin & Loſs of theCharter, & the manyLiberties we hold & enjoy thereby. For if a Number of private Perſons break in upon the Law of *England*, they may be ſeverally puniſhed therefor; But if a Corporation or Government like Ours, Set up and Enact things contrary to the Law of *England*, doubtleſs the way to puniſh them would be by Loſs of their Charter and Priviledges granted thereby. So that upon the whole Matter, whether his Letter was not rather to Lull you aſleep if poſſibly he could, that then he might bring you into the Practice of ſuch things, which hereafter you, and all of us might have ſufficient Reaſon to lament and be grieved for, but when too late; than in the leaſt meaſure to awaken the Government that they might be upon their Guard againſt any Attempts to undermine them. Becauſe having lately ſeen a Book Printed in *London*, *Anno* 1708. Intituled, *The Deplorable State of* New-England, *&c.* In which is a Letter in the Words following.

Boſton,

Boston, January 12th, 1703, 4.

Dear Kinsman,

I Confess I am ashamed almost to think I should be at Home so long, and not let you know of it till now; Tho' after all, a New-England Correspondence is scarce worth your having------ I Refer you to *Mr.*------for an *Account* of every thing, *especially about the Government and the Colledge, both which are discoursed of here in Chimney Corners and Private Meetings as confidently as can be. If there should be any occasion you must be sure to stir your self and Friends, and shew your Affection and Respect to my Father, who loves you well, and bid me tell you so.----This Country will never be worth Living in for Lawyers and Gentlemen, till the Charter is taken away. My Father and I sometimes talk of the Queens establishing a Court of Chancery in this Country. I have Wrote about it to Mr.* Blathwayt: *If the Matter should succeed, you might get some place worth your Return, of which I should be very glad. If I can any ways serve you or your Friends, Pray signifie it to*

Dear Sir,

Your Affectionate Friend,

and Humble Servant,

Paul Dudley.

Surely

Surely fuch a particular Favour done this Country, loudly calls upon every good Inhabitant within the fame, to be always paying his proper thanks : And may it not very juftly raife fome doubts of his fincerity in feeking the true Intereft of this Country ; or at leaft whether he doth not vaftly differ in his Opinion from the moft and beft of Men among us, concerning what are our good and valuable Liberties and Priviledges.

Sir, We take no Pleafure in Rehearfing thefe things to you, but were neceffitated thus to do, left by the aforefaid Letter in which he afferts, *page* 21. that as yet they have not Confulted the Government in the whole Affair ; We might be thought to be in any wife endeavouring to break in upon the Conftitution of this Government, and confequently the Priviledges and Liberties we enjoy by the Charter, which we highly efteem of, and fhall never be wanting to do what in us lies for the long and well fecuring thereof.

A very confiderable part of his Letter being on the praife of Money, Silver and Gold, and his Contrivance to ftore the Country with it, Regulating the Trade of the Country, and the Extravagance of the Inhabitants far beyond their Circumftances in their Purchafes, Buildings, Expences, Apparrel, &c. being not to the prefent purpofe, we fhall not trouble you with an Anfwer thereto.

We

We doubt not but upon your Reading this our juſt Defence, you will be ſufficiently enabled to make proper Thoughts upon the whole deſign of that Gentleman, as well as our Projection; which ſeeing it hath laboured under ſo many needleſs Aſperſions, ſhall take this occaſion to Print the ſame; that every one that pleaſes may have the Peruſal and Examination thereof: whereby they will perceive his Letter to be *Pandora's Box*, and not the INNOCENT PROJECTION.

Dated at Boſton, *in* New-England, Decemb. 20 1714.

We are, Sir,

Your very Humble Servants,

Samuel Lynde,
To the Contents, except the Letter taken out of a Book.

E. *Lyde*
John Colman
Eliſha Cooke; jun.
J. Oulton
Timothy Thornton
Oliver Noyes
William Pain
Nath. Oliver.

At the Deſire, & in behalf of the Partnerſhip.

A PROJECTION FOR ERECTING
A BANK OF CREDIT

A Projection for Erecting a Bank of Credit In Boston, New-England. Founded on Land Security (Boston, 1714), pp. 5–22.

A Projection for Erecting a Bank of Credit is an anonymous tract in support of a bank of credit based on land ownership. The primary complaint is a familiar one – covered in *A Letter from one in Boston* and *A Vindication* – where there is a shortage of specie in the colonies, limiting trade as a result. This piece spells out in more detail the abstract of the plan for a bank of credit as presented in *A Vindication*, although support for a private bank of credit had decreased by then, due to the establishment in Boston of a public bank of credit in November 1714.

A PROJECTION

For Erecting a

BANK

OF

CREDIT

In *Boston, New-England.*

Founded on

LAND

Security.

Printed in the Year 1714.

A

PROJECTION

For Erecting a Bank of

Credit.

To all to whom thefe Prefents
fhall-come, We whofe Names
are hereunto Subfcrib'd, and
Seals affix'd, fend Greeting.

WHEREAS there is a fenfible
decay of Trade within His
Majefties Plantations in
New-England, for want of a
Medium of Exchange, where-
with to carry on the fame ; the Running Cafh being
Exported, and confiderable Sums of the Bills of
Credit put forth by the Government, which had their
Circulation

Circulation and supported the Trade being already drawn in, and the remaining leffening Yearly, by the payment of the Taxes, and other Publick Dues; fo that without a Medium, the Trade muft neceffarily decay, to the unfpeakable detriment of the Landed Intereft as well as the Trading Party; and there being no other Expedient in our view for the Reviving and Encouraging of Trade, and facilitating Returns for Goods and Merchandizes Imported from Great Britain, but by Eftablifhing a Fund or Bank of Credit upon Land Security, which may give the Bills Iffued there-from a General Currency amongft us.

We therefore the Subfcribers, Parties to thefe Prefents, for the more effectual Erecting and fure Eftablifhing of fuch a Fund or Bank of Credit, do Mutually Covenant, Confent and Agree as follows:

THAT the Subfcriptions fhall be taken to a Value not exceeding *Three Hundred Thoufand Pounds*, and that every Subfcriber fhall Settle and Make Over a Real Eftate, to the value of his Refpective Subfcription, to the Truftees of the Partnerfhip or Bank, to be and remain as a Fund or Security for fuch Bills as fhall be Emitted therefrom; which Emiffion fhall not exceed the Subfcription, and will make good all deficiencies that fhall arife from any Neglect, Default

Default or Mifmanagement of any of the Officers or Members of this Partnerfhip or Bank.

2. That no Perfon fhall Subfcribe above *Four Thoufand Pounds*, nor under *Two Hundred and Fifty Pounds* ; and each Subfcriber fhall take out and keep for two years at leaft, one quarter part of his Subfcription, and not exceed one half part by virtue of his firft Mortgage, paying Intereft there-for, according to the Rules of this Partnerfhip.

3. That we will from time to time, and at all times for ever hereafter give Credit to the Bills Emitted from this Fund or Bank, equal to what is given to the Bills of Credit on the Province of the *Maffacbufetts-Bay*, and to accept the faid Bills in all Payments (Specialties and Obligations for any other Specie excepted) upon Forfeiture of *Fifty Pounds* for each refufal, until the Refufer has forfeited his whole Security and Profits ; and every fuch Perfon having fo forfeited, fhall no longer be accounted a Member of this Partnerfhip, but be deemed *ipfo facto* difmift, and lofe his Intereft therein.

4. That it fhall be free for any Perfon or Perfons not being of this Partnerfhip or Bank, to borrow Bills, or have Credit out of faid Bank,

Bank, giving Security according to the Rules hereof, and on payment of the Principal and Intereſt, their Mortgage or Depoſuit, ſhall be releaſed and diſcharged.

5. That in all Matters to be Tranſacted and Voted in the General Meeting of the Subſcribers of this Partnerſhip or Bank ; every ſuch Perſon who hath Subſcribed *Two Hundred and Fifty Pounds*, ſhall have one Vote, *Five Hundred Pounds* two Votes, *Seven Hundred and Fifty Pounds* three Votes, *One Thouſand Pounds* four Votes, *Twelve Hundred and Fifty Pounds* five Votes ; and no perſon ſhall have above five Votes, how great ſoever his Subſcription to, or Intereſt in this Bank is, or ſhall be.

6. That the Intereſt to be paid on all Bills Iſſued out, whether on Perſons Mortgages or Depoſuits, ſhall not exceed *Five Pounds per Cent per Annum*.

7. That there ſhall be at no time Emitted from this Partnerſhip or Bank, any Bills of Credit, but upon good Security, to the acceptance of the Directors for the time being, at the Rates and Values following,

  On Rateable Eſtates two Thirds of the Value.

  On Wooden Houſes without Farms, not exceeding the Value of the Lands belonging to them.
            On

On Brick Houses not exceeding the Value of the Land belonging to them, and half the value of the Lands: according to their different Circumstances.

On Gold not exceeding *Five Pounds Ten Shillings per* Ounce.

On Silver not exceeding *Six Shillings* and *Eight Pence per* Ounce.

On Iron and other unperishable Commodities, as a Pledge for one half, or two thirds, according to the Market.

8. And whereas for the Security of this Partnership or Bank, it is agreed, that there shall be Chosen seven persons in trust of good Interest, known Integrity and Reputation, and that to them or any five of them, and such other persons as shall from time to time be Chosen and Appointed by the major part of the Votes of the Members of this Partnership then present to Use and Exercise the aforesaid Trust : All Estates to be settled, shall be Conveyed for the ends aforesaid, and that the Trustees for the time being, shall have full power by Order in Writing, under the Hands of the major part of the Directors, to Commence any Suit at Law against any of the Mortgagers, and make what Releases and Assignment shall be thought necessary, for the Use of this Partnership ; and that the Trustees for the time being, shall be Obliged to Sign and Execute a general

neral Inftrument, Binding and Obliging Themfelves, their Heirs and Executors unto the Directors for the time being, not to do any thing
by way of Releafe or Affignment; or Commence any Suit at Law againft any of the
Mortgagers, but by Order in Writing, under
the Hands of the Directors, and to the Ufe of
this Partnerfhip : The faid Truftees difclaim-
ing all Right and Property in any Mortgage or
Conveyance to them by virtue of their Tru-
fteefhip.

FURTHERMORE, That the faid Truftees
do from time to time attend and perform all
fuch Orders relating to this Affair, as fhall be
given in Writing at any time by the Directors,
or the major part of them ; and that it fhall
be in the power of this Partnerfhip, by the
major Votes prefent in a General Meeting, to
Remove the faid Truftees if they fhall fee
caufe, and to choofe and place in their ftead
others. And that A.   and B.
    Efqrs.   C.   D.   E.
        F.   and   G.   Mer-
chants, all of *Bofton*, in the County of *Suffalk*,
in the Province of the *Maffachufetts-Bay* in
New-England, be the firft Truftees of this
Partnerfhip or Bank of Credit; and that to
them, or any five of them, and the Truftees for
the time being, all the Eftates to be fettled fhall
be Conveyed in Truft; which Truftees fhall
                                    continue

continue in their Stations until their respective Death, Removal or Resignment.

FURTHERMORE, We do Covenant and Agree, that the said Trustees shall be Indempnified at all times by this Partnership or Bank from all Charges and Damages which they shall sustain, or be put to by reason of their Trust, or the due Execution thereof; & none of them shall be chargeable for the acts or defaults of any other but his faults only. And for their Encouragement and Reward, they shall have Annually paid to them out of the Profits, *Thirty Pounds* each, which Sum may be augmented at the Annual Meeting, if it be found insufficient.

9. That there shall be a General Meeting of the Subscribers in some convenient place in the Town of *Boston* aforesaid, on the first *Tuesday* in *June* Annually, where, by the major part of the Votes present, there shall be Elected to Serve for one year next Ensuing, until others be Chosen in their room ; Officers for managing the Affair of this Partnership or Bank, on such Salaries for their Service, as are, or shall afterwards be agreed on. *That is to say,*

Seven Directors, who shall from time to time Choose one of their Number to preside ; Four of which Number shall have power to act ; & in case of equal Votes, the President to have the Casting.

That these seven Directors shall be Impowred

red to call General Meetings of the Subfcribers on all important Occafions, and fhall be
proper judges of all Securities to be taken into
this Bank, and have power to appoint perfons
to apprize and report the value of all Eftates
to be taken as Securities, to give Directions to
the Truftees for Releafes upon payment of
Mortgages, under fuch Regulations as are or
fhall hereafter be made for the good government thereof; none to be capable of this Office, but fuch as fhall Subfcribe *Five Hundred
Pounds* in this Bank.

One Treafurer, who by Order, and under
the Hands of the Directors, or the major part
of them fhall be impowred to pafs out Bank
Bills, and fhall infpect and regulate the Books
and Accompts of this Partnerfhip, and fhall
have the direction of the Clerks in order thereto; which Treafurer fhall find Security to be
bound with him in the Sum of *Ten Thoufand
Pounds.*

One Head Clerk, and one Under Clerk or
more if need be; each of whom fhall give to
the Truftees of this Partnerfhip, *One Thoufand
Pounds* Security or more if it fhall be hereafter
thought needful, and fhall be Obliged to keep
two fetts of Books for the Affairs of this Partnerfhip, and give their daily attendance at fuch
ftated hours as fhall be appointed, and obferve
fuch Orders as they fhall receive from the Directors or Treafurer: And in cafe of the Death
of

of any of the Clerks, or removal by the Directors for mifmanagement, it fhall be in the power of the Directors to appoint others to Serve in their ftead, until the next Annual Meeting, taking Security as aforefaid.

10. That for the maintaining of the Credit of this Partnerfhip, and preventing Frauds, We oblige our felves, that the Books be always free to the infpection of the Subfcribers and Owners, and that they be pofted up every day if poffible ; Caft up and Ballanced once a year, to be offered to the Annual Meeting on the Firft *Tuefday* in *June* ; That there be a perfect Regifter or Entry made of all Mortgages and Pawns made to this Partnerfhip, of all Affignments and Releafes.

11. For the further eafe of this Partnerfhip, and for preventing of Frauds, we hereby agree, that any perfon interefted in the fame, who doth not fee reafon to take out Bills, he fhall have Credit in the Books, and liberty to tranffer all or any part of his Credit to any perfon not under *Ten Pounds* at an Entry, the Perfon transfering to return his Note if any given, & a new Note given to the perfon tranffered to, under the Hand of the Treafurer, and that the Treafurer at the requeft of any Owners of Notes fo Emitted, fhall exchange the fame for Bills, difcharging the Accompt of Notes, and charging the Accompt of Bills ; and that there fhall be a Committee of fix appointed

pointed to prepare, sign, indent & perfect such a Number of Bills as shall be agreed on by this Partnership, to be put into the hands of the Treasurer, and issued out by Order of the Directors according to the Rules of this Partnership, which Committee shall continue, until the Partnership shall see reason to alter them, and four of them to sign every Bill.

12. That in Case any person or persons shall refuse to pay their Interest for two months after it becomes due, he shall pay after the rate of six *per Cent per Annum* from the time it becomes due, until he make payment ; and if any person Indebted to this Partnership be desirous to lessen his Debt, he shall be allow'd to pay in any even Sum, not under *Twenty Five Pounds*; but if any person shall redeem his Mortgage or Deposuit, or lessen his Debt, in less than three Months time after the making thereof, he shall yet pay three Months Interest for the same ; and in case he can't pay in Bank Bills, he may pay in Province Bills, or Current Silver Mony.

13. If any person shall not redeem his Pawn deposited, the continuance whereof shall be hazardous, or not pay his Interest for the same at the time agreed on, it shall be lawful for the Directors of this Partnership, upon three months notice given, to Dispose and make Sale of such Pledge, at the best Rates they can, rendring the Overplus, if any be, to the Depositor ; or if any Security given, appear to be
doubtful

doubtful in the Judgment of the Directors; it shall be lawful for them to demand a renewal or augmentation of such or other Security, to provide for the safety of this Partnership.

14. When the Bills Emitted shall be much worn, to avoid pasting or covering of them, the Possessors may have them exchang'd, and the old Bills so return'd after they have been Examin'd, and an Accompt taken of them, shall be Burnt by a Committee appointed for that purpose, whose Attestation in Writing that they have been Consum'd into Ashes, shall be the Treasurers discharge for the same.

15. That the neet profits arising from this Partnership, shall be, and belong to the Subscribers and Owners of the same, their Heirs and Assigns, in proportion to ther respective Subscriptions, except what is herein otherwise dispos'd of, and shall be under such Regulations as shall best answer the design in giving a Credit to this Bank, but out of the profits of two first years, the Directors shall have power to purchase or build suitable Conveniencies for the Affairs of this Bank before any Dividend shall be made; such a purchase being first made, the neet Proceeds shall be divided amongst the Subscribers, at the expiration of two years; but afterward the neet Proceed shall be divided at every years Meeting in *June.*

16. That when and so often as by the
Decease

Deceafe or Alienation of any **Eftate** by any Member of this Partnerſhip Mortgaged to the Truſtees for the Uſes aforeſaid, ſhall happen to be inveſted in any other Perſon or Perſons; That ſuch Perſon or Perſons to whom ſuch Eſtate ſhall deſcend or be conveyed, ſhall within three Months next after, give notice to the Directors for the time being, at the Office of this Bank, that ſo Entry of the ſame be made, for the better direction of whom, to demand the Principal and Intereſt of ſaid Eſtate; and ſuch perſon or perſons ſhall be obliged to obſerve the Rules, Covenants and Agreements of this Partnerſhip, and ſhall be eſteem'd a Partner.

17. That the Bills ſhall be of ſeveral Denominations as ſhall be agreed on, and of the tenour following, but alterable, at the diſcretion of this Partnerſhip; the Motto to be, *Creſcit' Eundo.*.

THIS INDENTED BILL OF CREDIT, Obliges Us, and every of Us, and all, and every of our Partners of the Bank of Credit of Boſton *in* New-England, *to accept the ſame in Lieu of* Twenty *Shillings, in all Payments, according to our Articles of Agreement; and that it ſhall be ſo accepted by our Receiver or Treaſurer, for the Redemption of any Pawn or Mortgage in the ſaid Bank.*

Boſton, November Firſt, *One Thouſand Seven Hundred and Fourteen.*

18. That

18. That every Subſcriber, who ſhall Convey his Eſtate to the Truſtees, ſhall enjoy the ſame, the Rents and Profits thereof, until by his default in not paying his Intereſt, his Mortgage be ſued out ; and that every Subſcriber, who ſhall ſettle his Eſtate on the Truſtees, may withdraw the ſame, upon ſettling another Eſtate of like Value in its room, to the ſatisfaction of the Directors ; and ſuch new Eſtate ſo ſettled, ſhall be Entituled to the Profits, ſubject to the Charges and Loſſes of this Bank, as the former Eſtate ſo withdrawn was.

19. And for a further benefit to the Publick, when there ſhall be Emitted and Continued at Intereſt *One Hundred and Fifty Thouſand Pounds*, We give out of the Neet Profits of this Partnerſhip, the Sums following, *Viz.*

Four Hundred Pounds per Annum *to the Uſe of an Hoſpital or Charity School, for the Support and Education of the poor Children in the Town* of Boſton, *at the diſcretion of ſuch Perſons as ſhall be Choſen Overſeers of ſuch Schools and Hoſpitals when Erected :* Provided *the Inhabitants and Freeholders of the Town of* Boſton, *do, at or before their General Meeting in* March, One Thouſand Seven Hundred and

and Fifteen, *order the Treafurer to accept the faid Bank Bills in payment of Town Taxes and Affefsments.*

Two Hundred Pounds per Annum *to be paid to the Treafurer of* Harvard *Colledge in* Cambridge, *for the Ufes following.* Viz.

Twenty Pounds per Annum *for a Mathematical Profeffor Refiding there, provided he Read a Publick Lecture once a Month on that Subject.*

Forty Pounds per Annum *for the Encouragement of three Graduates Refiding there, until they take their Mafters Degree, to be equally divided amongft them ; the faid Graduates to refund and pay back fo far as they have received, if they depart the Colledge before that time.*

One Hundred Pounds per Annum *for the Support of fix Minifters Sons, to be equally divided amongft them ; and in Cafe there be not fix Minifters Sons, then the remainder to be given to any other who may ftand in moft need thereof ; the whole* Two Hundred Pounds *to be at the difpofe of the Corporation.*

Forty Pounds per Annum *to a Profeffor of Phyfick and Anatomy, Refiding there provided*
ded

ded he *Read* a *Lecture* once a *month*, on *that* *Subject*.

Twenty Pounds per Annum, *towards the further support of a Publick Grammar School in each County, now in the Province* of the Maffachufetts-Bay *in* New-England, *provided fuch a Grammar School, be Erected and Maintained by every fuch County, with an Addition of* Forty Pounds per Annum, *to every fuch School-Mafter.* Provided Neverthelefs, and it's to be underftood, *that the N̄eet Profits of this Bank or Partnerfhip amount to fo much as the Donations herein Exprefs'd, and that the Donations firft mentioned, be firft paid, in cafe the N̄eet Profits fall fhort.*

'20. That the Office for managing the Affair of this Partnerfhip be always kept in *Bofton* aforefaid, and that every Subfcriber on taking out by virtue of his Mortgage the Sum belonging to him, fhall pay in to the Treafurer for the time being; one quarter of a years Intereft for defraying the neceffary Charges that may arife, in managing the Affair of this Partnerfhip; and every Subfcriber fhall within three months after his Subfcription take out his one fourth part as abovefaid

21. That at any Annual Meeting of the Subfcribers, they may by the major Votes then
present,

prefent, make any Alterations or Additions to this Settlement for the better managing the Affairs thereof, not inconfiftent with the foundation.

22. That in Cafe any of the Poffeffors of the Bills happen to be damnified through default by, or Non-obfervance of the foregoing Covenants and Agreements, or by any other defect of this Partnerfhip, or of any of the Members or Officers thereof; the Perfon or Perfons fo damnify'd, fhall have remedy by Action and Suit at Law againft the Directors of this Bank for the time being, who do hereby fubject themfelves to fuch Suit and Actions.

And we further Covenant and Agree, that there fhall be a Duplicate of thefe Articles duly Executed, and lodged in the hands of the Treafurer of the Town of Bofton *for the time being, that fo perfons injur'd may be in a Capacity to bring their Suit.*

23. That the Directors, Truftees, and all other Officers fhall be indemnify'd by this Bank from all Charges and Damages which they may fuftain by reafon of their Truft and Office in the due Execution thereof, and none of them fhall be chargeable for the neglects or defaults of any but his own.

24. That if any Officer or Officers, Member

ber or Members of this Bank or Partnerſhip, by reaſon of his Office or Partnerſhip, be Sued in any Action of Debt or Damage, ſuch Perſon or Perſons ſhall immeditately give notice thereof, to the Directors for the time being, that they may prepare to defend the ſame ; and that upon neglect of giving ſuch ſeaſonable notice, the Partnerſhip ſhall not be oblig'd to indemnify ſuch perſon or perſons againſt whom ſuch Suit is brought, nor from the Coſt and Damage that may enſue thereon.

25. Whereas the Affairs of this Partnerſhip cannot be effectually carried on without the Election and Conſtitution of the ſeveral Officers before nam'd ; We have therefore appointed *Monday* the Firſt day of *November* next, the day for ſuch Election of ſeven Directors, a Treaſurer, one Head Clerk, and one Under-Clerk, and more if need be, who ſhall have the power to Exerciſe their Reſpective Offices and Truſts, and continue the ſame till the Firſt *Tueſday* in *June, Seventeen Hundred & Fifteen*, and until others be Choſen in their room and ſtead in ſuch manner as in theſe Preſents is Expreſs'd ; Provided there be Subſcribed the Sum of *Fifty Thouſand Pounds* on or before the ſaid Day. And that no Bills ſhall be Emitted from this Bank or Partnerſhip, until further Subſcriptions make up the Sum of *One Hundred Thouſand Pounds.*

26. To

26. To the true and faithful performanc of all and singular the Clauses, Articles, Covenants and Agreements, Forfeitures and Penalties herein before Expressed : We the Subscribers, Parties to these Presents, Do mutually Bind and Oblige our selves, and each and every of us, each and every of our Heirs, Executors, Administrators and Assigns, severally and respectively, each one unto the other, and to the Possessor or Possessors of the Bills of Credit, that shall from time to time, or any time here-after be Emitted by this Bank or Partner-ship in the full Value of the Sums by us, and each of us Subscribed hereto.

Dated the Thirtieth of *October, Anno Domini, Seventeen Hundred and fourteen, Annoque Regni Georgii Magnæ Britaniæ, Franciæ et Hiberniæ, Regis Primo.*

SOME CONSIDERATIONS ON THE BILLS OF CREDIT, NOW PASSING IN NEW ENGLAND

[Cotton Mather], *Some Considerations on the Bills of Credit, Now Passing in New England. Addressed unto the Worshipful, John Philips Esq. Published for the Information of the Inhabitants* (Boston, 1691), pp. 1–9.

This text, which has been attributed to Cotton Mather, defends the use of paper currency by arguing that money is merely a measure of value and a medium of exchange. The use of paper currency would facilitate trade and the paying of taxes. The main problem in Boston was that the nonpayment of taxes had led Massachusetts Bay Colony into significant debt, as without the circulation of specie from tax the government was unable to pay the wages of those employed in the public service. In many cases, individuals had no access to specie and were thus unable to pay their taxes, or were forced to take jobs at undervalued wage rates where they would be paid specie. Paying taxes in paper money would be better than the alternative suggestion of paying in corn, which would require high transportation and storage costs. In addition, paper currency would help maintain the circulation of wealth in the colonies, since paper money could not leave the country as easily as specie. Since paper money had to be secured by land or assets at a bank in the colony, the paper money could only be converted into specie at that particular bank. Colonial paper currency was therefore unlikely to be accepted as payment by other countries as it could only be converted to currency in that particular country, and it would then be unfamiliar and unable to be traded in the new location. Bank notes that could be cashed at any bank were a significant development in the English banking system and did not develop until much later.

Some Considerations on the BILLS
OF
CREDIT,

Now passing in NEW-ENGLAND.
Addressed unto the Worshipful,
JOHN PHILIPS Esq.

Published for the Information of the
INHABITANTS.

Mr. Treasurer,

I Am told, and am apt to believe it, That the Exchequer in *Silver* Runs very Low; Nor can *I* think that the Country in General is much better furnished. 'Twas an honest and good method you took, to pay by *Bonds* what you could not by *Ready Cash.* I therefore cannot a little wonder at the great indiscretion of our Countrymen who Refuse to accept that, which they call *Paper-mony*, as pay of equal value with the best *Spanish* Silver. What? is the word *Paper* a scandal to them? Is a *Bond* or *Bill-of Exchange* for 1000*l*, other than *Paper*? and yet is it not as valuable as so much Silver or Gold, supposing the Security of payment be sufficient? Now what is the *Security* of your Paper-mony less then the *Credit of the whole Country.* If the Countries *Debts* must be paid (as I believe they must, and *I* am sure in justice they ought) whatever change of Government shall come, then the *Country* must make good the *Credit*, or *more Taxes* must be still Raised, till the publick Debts be Answered. *I* say, the Country, and not the *Gentlemen* who *Administer* the Government, who are but the *Countries Agents* in this Affair. *All the Inhabitants* of the Land, taken as one Body are the *Principals*, who Reap the *Benefits*, and must bear the *Burdens*, and are the Security in their *Publick Bonds.* What do the Gentlemen get, but their labour for their pains, and perhaps not a little Obloquie into the bargain? can all their *Estates* (with all their *Gains*, if there were any) bear the *Charge of Government* for the whole Land? no, no, it cannot be supposed. If any murmur at their management as ill, and that they have needlesly drawn the Charges upon us; pray tell them, as long as they enjoy the *Choice of Administrators*, they must bear what's *past*, and right themselves for the *future*, by chusing better next, if they know where to find them. So Merchants do with their Factors, and 'tis their only Remedy.

You know Sir you and *I* have had some former Discourse about the *Nature of Mony* That (as such) it is but a *Counter* or *Measure* of mens Proprieties, and Instituted *mean* of permutation. As *metal* indeed it is a commodity, Like all other things, that are Merchantable. But as *Mony* it is no more than what was said, And had it's *Original* from a general ignorance of Writing and Arithmetick; But now these Arts being commonly known may well Discharge *mony* from the conceited Necessity thereof in Humane Traffick. Is not *Discount* in Accounts current good pay? Do not *Bills* Transmit to Remote Parts, vast summs without the intervention of *Silver*? Are not *Taxes* paid and received by *mutual Credit* between the Government and the People, The Government requiring the Country to give them Credit where-with to pay the Countries Debts, and then again receive the same Credit of the Country as good pay? 'Tis strange that in the mean while between the *Governments* paying the People, and the *Peoples* paying the Government: The Governments (or rather the *Countries*) *Bills* should not pass between *Man and Man.* 'Tis strange that one Gentlemans Bills at *Port-Royal* for divers years, and that among Forreigners; or another Gentlemans *Bills* in the Western Parts for as many or more years should gain so much Credit as to be current pay, among the Traders in those places; yea, that the Bill (as *I* have heard) of any *one Magistrate* in the *Western English Plantation*, shall buy any Commodities of any of the Planters; and yet our people (in this pure air) be so sottish as to deny Credit to the Government, when 'tis of their own *Chusing*: Had the *single Gentlemen* (above named) a good bottom for their Credit in their *Ware-houses*, and are not the whole *Estates* of the *Massachusets* as good? Is the Security of one Plantation-Magistrate, better than that of *All* the *Massachusets Representatives*? can that one *Magistrate* give force to the Contracts, and cannot *All our Government* do the same.

Certainly Sir were not peoples Heads Idly bewhizled with Conceits that we have no *Magistrates*, no *Government*, And by Consequence that we have no *Security* for any thing, which we call our own (a *Consequence* they will be Loth to allow, though they cannot help it, If once we are Reduced to *Hobs* his state of *Nature*, which (says he) is a *state of War*, and then the *strongest* must *take all*) I say if such foolish conceits were not Entertained, there would not be the least Scruple in accepting your Bills as Currant Pay.

If you should require the Country to pay their *Taxes in Silver*, that so you might be enabled to bear the Charges of the Government by Silver, when such quantity of it as is needful for that purpose cannot be had in the Country, or at least not in any proportion to be procured, unless men (according to the Proverb) should *Buy Gold too Dear*, and so Ruinously undervalue the fruits of their Labours and their Lands. This were to require men to *Make Bricks without Straw*.

If you Require the Taxes in *Corn* at an *overvalue*, with I know not what odd *Abatements* if they bring in Mony; which is to set up (in my Understanding) a *Measure* and a *Measure* (a thing which God allows not) And then if the Government pay the Charges of *Conveyance* from *Remoter-parts*, and bear all Damages afterwards, what will it amount to when all Charges and Damages are allowed; perhaps scarce two shillings to the Government, of five shillings from the Country; and when will the publick Debts be paid? or when will be an end of Taxing? Certainly (what-ever were intended by the Proposers of this way of Tax) the Tendency of it is only to render the *Government odious* by a great noise of *Taxes*, when little comes thereby; a great cry of Hog-sheering, when there is no Wool.

If neither *Silver* can be had, nor *Corn* brought in without loss both to the Government and People, what remains but *Accounts*, *Bills*, or such like *Paper-pay*? and certainly this necessity may (if *I* mistake not) bring to the whole Country no small advantage; for

1. Is there not hereby 40000*l Running Cash* in the Country more than *ever was*, If mens folly hinder not its Currency? yea and more than they are *ever like* to have, so long as they cannot keep Silver In the Country, which they will never do while the *European Trade* continues, and that is like to be as long as we are a people. *Silver* in *New-England* is like the water of a *swift Running River*, always coming, and as fast going away; one (in its passage) dips a Bucket-full, another a Dish or Cup-full for his occasions; but if the *Influx* of plate from the *West-Indies* be stopt but for a little while, and the *Efflux* in Returns for *England* continue; will not the Mill-pond be quickly drained, so as neither Bucket nor Cup can dip its fill? Whereas on the contrary,

2. This our *Running* Cash is an *abiding Cash*: for no man will carry it to another Country, where it will not pass; but rather use it here, where it will (or at least) *ought*: and then only the *Growths of the Country* will be carried off, and that will be no Damage but rather an Advantage to us,

3. If this be made Currant, the *Credit* of the Colony will *rise* to the utmost height of it's ability on all Extraordinary Emergencies; whereas otherwise you may be quickly Distressed; for if the Soldiers cannot put off their Pay to Supply their necessities, who will hereafter serve the Country in their greatest Dangers, and if the Merchants cannot Buy as well as Sell for Credit, how shall they carry on their Trades? and how shall they'l end upon great occassions if the Countries Bill lie dead on their hands? surely they'l no more trust the Country, whatever sud-

dain need we should have, unless on the bare consideration of their own Security.

There is indeed a way found out by poor mens Necessities to make the Bills passant; namely by *Selling* them at *Under-rates*. Thus the poor *Soldier* is horribly *injured*, who have adventured their Lives in the publick Service, and the *Government* made *contemptible* as not worthy to be trusted. *I* remember many years since, there was such a prank plaid in *England* and *Ireland* after the War. Some bought up the *Soldiers Debenters* at very low Rates, and then with half Debenters and half Mony purchased great Estates in Kings and Bishops Lands, (a fine Trade they made of it if it had held) but God shook his Lap at this dishonest and interloping gain; and a great unexpected Revolution made them lose both their Lands and Mony. Thus the woman shook her Dog by the Collar, till she made him Disgorge again all her Puddings.

A better way (in my opinion) to make the *Credit passable* without Interruption, is,

1. To Raise the Rates of those above the *common Standard*, whom you catch Tardy in Debasing the Credit of your bills either by purchasing them with little mony; or selling commodities for them at Excessive dearer Rates.

2. Let all refusers to receive them have forthwith their *Taxes* demanded in *Silver*, nor let them have the benefit of paying *them*, who will not also Receive them. And in like manner several such, as shall at any time reproach them as a *Grand Cheat*. Who is it but *They*, that makes 'em so.

3. What if the *General Court* Declare by a Law, that if any man tender these Bills for payment of his Debts, to be accepted at their full value, which the Country has put upon them; If any private person will not receive them so, That then the Government will not concern themselves for the recovery of those Debts, till all the *Publick Debts* are discharged. It is a known Maxim of Law in *England* (and *I* think in all other Countrys) that *of Debts, The Kings must be first paid*. And great reason for it; for why shall the Government secure *others* Debts by Law; and not *their own*? now if these refusers stay for their Debts till the Country be first serv'd they may stay till they are weary. And if hereafter they resolve to make no more *Debts* (for fear of this Law) I believe their Trading will be very dull. Whereas (on the Contrary) If they shall accept the *Bills*, 'tis probable their Debts will come in apace; their Trading will revive, and the Countries Credit become Currant.

To Conclude [*Fas est et ab Hoste Doceri*] The *French* (I hear) *at Canada* pass such *Paper mony* without the least scruple; whereby the Government is greatly Fortified, since they can at all times make what they need. Now if we account our selves to Transcend the *French* in *Courage*,

'Tis a shame for us to come so far short of them in *Wit* and *Understanding*.

These are my present thoughts, which you may communicate as you see cause; mean while please to accept them as Really intended for the Publick good. By A well wisher to New-England & your Humble Servant. &c.

A WORD OF COMFORT TO A MELANCHOLY COUNTRY

John Wise, *A Word of Comfort to a Melancholy Country, or the Bank of Credit Erected in The Massachusetts-Bay, Fairly Defended by a Discovery of a Great Benefit, accruing by it to the Whole Province; With a Remedy for Recovering a Civil State when Sinking under Desperation by Defeat on their Bank of Credit* (Boston, 1721), pp. 1–58.

John Wise (1652–1725) was educated at Harvard, and became a congressional minister. He was deeply interested in colonial relations with England and issues of money and taxation. Taking sometimes unpopular stands on issues – such as defending those accused of witchcraft in Salem, or those who recommended smallpox vaccines – Wise became one of the many early voices supporting American independence.

Wise combines American morality and economics in his *Word of Comfort to a Melancholy Country*. He argues that it is not through the accumulation of specie that a country becomes rich, but through frugality and hard work (which is his articulation of the Puritan work ethic). Wise also argues that money facilitates both internal and external trade, leading to an advancement of the colonies. This advancement would eventually encourage the establishment of craftsmen and manufacturers in the cities that could then compete with those in Great Britain. This piece demonstrates Wise's support of the proposal for a bank of credit. His writing was a major source of inspiration for later writers, particularly Hugh Vans, who is also included in this volume.

A
Word of Comfort

TO A

Melancholy Country

OR THE

Bank of Credit.

Erected in the
Maſſachuſetts-Bay,
Fairly Defended by a Diſcovery of
Great Benefit, accruing by it to
the Whole PROVINCE; With a Re
medy for Recovering a Civil State
when Sinking under Deſperation by
Defeat on their *Bank of Credit.*

By AMICUS PATRIÆ,

Maximus in Republica nodus eſt, et ad Res Præcl...
Gerendas Impedimentum, Inopia Rei Pecuniariæ...

The Want of Money (or a Sufficient Medium of ...)
is the greateſt of all Interruptions in a Common-
Wealth; and puts by, or Obſtracts the carrying on
of Buſineſs in a Flouriſhing Manner.

BOSTON: Printed in the Year,

Maſſachuſetts-Bay

IN

New-England.

TO Conſider This People, ſo Enobled in their Government ; Religon, Trade, Produce, and Properties in Soyle ; with their Manly Genius, and Wiſdom, being ſo manny Great and Royal Gifts of Heaven ; And what they are in a fair Proſpect, with the Bleſſing of GOD, like to Arrive to, in their External, affairs, in a few Ages more ; It would grieve a Man's Heart who is either a *true Lover of his Country*, or of *Mankind*, to ſee them Intangled [as once *Abraham's* Miraculous Victim was caught in a Thicket] in a Labyrinth of perplexing Thoughts, in ſo plain a Caſe, as they are now Labouring under, *Scil.* In that Matter, and Affair, Relating to their *Medium of Trade, and Bills of Publick Credit.* I muſt acknowledge

knowledge [upon a Presumption that a fair, *Medium of Trade*, or Commerce can no ways be upheld, or continued in this Great Province] our Destiny is very Apparent, and will come upon us like an *Armed Man*; for there will be no Evading, most Rueful Circumstances in a Little Time; for that without a *Medium*, all things will Jumble, Run Retrograde, and Tumble into Caos ; and this must needs fill us with many Evils both of Sin, and Misery ; as Murmurings, Revilings of Governments, Injustice, Oppressions, Discouragements; and possibly desperation it self in a very great Degree in our Temporal Affairs: For what will most Men care for, in such a Confounded Condition, more than just to shuffle along thro' an Unfortunate World ; and let them that come after e'en shift for themselves ? for what will despair, in Outward Affairs, Suggest less to any Man, *Then when he is Dead the World is at an End.* But to be brought to such a Disposition of Mind is a great Imperfection in the state of Man : If it prevails in Religion it Damns him ; and in Naturals it Undoes him, for that it Cuts the Throat of all Endeavours, That for my own part, I must therefore needs Reverence the wise Premonitions of those who begin to feel the Stroke, who are nextly Exposed ; and where the Woes will fall first and Heaviest, when things are Come to Extremity, and that is our Capital : Where Possibly Ten Thousand Lives are housed, and must be Supported by Trade, according to the Method they have been always Trained up in : Therefore if you Suppress, or let fall the *Current Medium*, they are absolutely Undone, as to any thing that looks like a Flourishing Condition : And when our Head is sp●●ed, the Members of the Body will soon Languish. But yet I cannot see any Just Reason for them, or us [from any Symptoms we yet feel] to infer Conclusively, that our Case is in the least Degree Desperate :

For

For that the Means of our Relief are in our own Hands; and we can save our selves, as Easily, as to lay the Word. Indeed if we should be so Corrupt, or Silly as to abandon our selves to Ruin, rather than use a plain Means for our Support we must then lye down and Dye. Or if when we are Cripled, we will sullenly sink down under the Sroke rather then use Crutches, we may then spend the Rest of our Days in self Condolence over our Miseries, but who will Pity us? and not rather Brand us for *Self-Murderers*; in that we have very Laudable Means, Honourable among Wise Men, and Justifiable before GOD, for our help; and that is a Bank of Credit, either under the Management of the Government, or in the Hands of Particular Gentlemen of Known Integrity and Estates.

This may be Considered under a few heads, *Scil.* Propositions and Questions.

I. PROPOSITIONS.

I. PROP. [Not to meddle with our **Morals.**] *We are Defective in Nothing, or in Nothing so much as in the want of a Sufficient Medium of Trade.*

These are some of the Happiest Days we have seen for this Fifty or Sixty Years last past. We have now, with full Satisfaction found Protection, and Umbrage under the Wings of a Protestant Prince, who holds the Ballance of *Europe*: And Desires to be in nothing Greater, then in the Happiness of His People. There be now no *Machiavilian Councils* held near the Throne how to Inflave the Nation; But all is Contrived how to Render it Free, Rich, Great and Powerful. So that things are very Happy at Home. And this Province also is under Halcion, and very Joyful Circumstances, being Headed by a GOVERNOUR who imitates his Master in his Royal Vertues, his Courage, Justice, Clemency, and other Enobling Qualifications which Adorn a Prince. And to perfect our happiness we enjoy the Gospel Liberties, without Infringment; together with Health, Peace and Plenty.   And

And yet our *Medium of Trade* is fo exceeding fhort; and infufficient that Bufinefs begins to Clogg ; or does not go on fo roundly as it might do, were it more redundant and full. As for the Money Medium we have none at all, its quite Exhaufted ; and the Bills which have fupplyed its Place, they are grown very fcarce, which is evident by the Loud Complaints of Town and Country.

II. PROP. *Temporal Commerce and Trade, is as neceffary for the Conveniency, Comfort and Outward Profit of Man, whilft he holds his Tenure on Earth, as Civil Alliance and Cohabitation.* For that it may be faid of Single Perfons and Families, as well as of Countries. • *Non Omnis fert Omnia Tellus.* All Men as all Nations dont raife all things that are for their Benefit & Comfort ; therefore Trade is very needful. Tho' it be certain, That Trade & Commerce may be managed or carryed on, efpecially by diftant Parts of the World ; and in fome Cafes by Perfons of the fame Country by Exchange and Trucking one Commodity for another ; let them be what they will. Yet we muft note, That this Method in Bufinefs, is fitter for fuch a People, who (to indulge themfelves in great Idlenefs & Sloath,) Dwell in the Clefts of the Valleys, in Caves of the Earth, and in the Rocks, and digg *Juniper Roots* for their Meat, or can Live upon *Acorns :* But it is not at all agreable with a Wife and Bufling People, that would fpend their Life, to the heigth of Religion, and right Reafon. For that to Exchange all forts of Commodities without a fuitable Medium will deftroy Trade, and render it impracticable, as to any great Good, or Clear Profit that will infue upon it to fuch a People. For that the Inconveniencies that will attend a Common Barter without a Medium are innumerable and intollerable. As to mention but one. In this way, unlefs both the

Parties

Parties dealing (which rarely happens) have the like occasion, of each others Commodities ; he that has least neceffity will over-reach the other, by impofing the Price of both ; and always to his own Advantage and the others Detriment ; which is not any ways juft or equal. And indeed its hardly poffible to uphold Equality where there is no Common Medium known and allowed of to be as a Rule or Meafure between them.   Therefore,

III. PROP. *All Prudent Men and Civil Nations, upon long Experience, find that a Convenient Medium muft be had, and made ufe of to Support Trade and Commerce with due Advantage.* Two Things may be obferved under this Propofition,

1. *A Medium of Trade need not be Coftly, if it be but Convenient and Safe.*

2. *The more Coft and Intrinfick Worth a Medium carries with it, or the more Valuable it is in it felf, the lefs ufeful it will be in fupporting an Univerfal Trade and Commerce.* Which will be evident by a Comparifon fairly Run between the Money and Paper Medium , upon a Prefumption the latter is upon good Security, and found at Bottom.

1. *The Money Medium from its coftly and valuable nature, is very inconftant, unfixt and volatile.* Few Governments can Lock their own Doors fo clofe, but that it is apt to Steal away and make its efcape : whenas the other is conftant, abiding, & keeps within its own Circuits. The Money is a ftaple Commodity, and univerfally acceptable in all ports of Trade ; and then being fhuffling and always lyable to Exportation, there is no Depending upon it tor carrying on any Bufinefs in a fteady way ; for if Men enter into fome Wife and Great Ingagements with a confidence in the Money Medium, away it flips ; leaves them in the lurtch ; to folve, unfolvable Obligations, and
                                        poffibly

possibly to their undoing. But now on the other hand whatever valuable Designs Men set forward upon the Reputation of the Paper Medium, being always at home, they may in their prudent Conduct, acquiesce and depend upon it, with the greatest assurance.

2. *The Money Medium is not only Good Merchandize; but being of so durable and rich a nature, it is a very fine Estate for the Wise and Fortunate to secure amongst their intended Bequestments for the next Age.* To lay up Gold as the Dust, and the Gold of *Ophir* as the Stones of the Brook, seems a Promise annexed to that Rule of Duty whereby Parents are obliged to lay up for their Children; That when Men are in Possession, either from Avarice, Prudence, Duty, or good Nature to their own, are very loth to part with this charming Specie. And tho' it may go from them with less pain then when their Skin is stript from their Fingers, yet it comes away with much aversion. For of this Specie it may be said, *Sui Nimium Tenax.* So that it cannot rationally be supposed so convenient a Medium to support a common Barter and Commutation amongst all Men, as that which is less valuable in its own Nature; and so Persons are more apt to part with it.

3. *The Money Medium inclines Men more to Extortion, Dissembling, and other Moral Evils in Trade,* then One which has no Intrinsick Value in it. They are the Moneyed-Men that hide and stand high upon their Terms; and usually undervalue every Commodity exposed to Sale. *Its naught! Its naught, says the Buyer;* tho' he knows better when he says so: And its Money you expect, and therefore you must lower your Price, or I shall not be your Chapman, &c. yet dissembles all the while. And thus under the influence of such a high tempered Medium, Men of Trade are fain many times to Sell with little or no profit, or at half price, or how they can. And how

often

often are Men in compaſſing the Money Medium impelled to prevaricate with Truth. For. have not ſome (poſſibly in Jeſt-Earneſt) ſaid, *What pity it is that Lying was a Sin, it being ſo neceſſary in our Trade?* That of this Medium we may but too ſadly complain, and argue as once the Poet,

Auri Sacra fames, Quid non Mortalia cogis Pectora?
    The Love of Money is the Root of all Evil.

But the Paper Medium is eaſy of Exchange, and not ſo apt to corrupt the Mind.   So that,

PROP, IV. *This Province can create for them-ſelves, a Sufficient Medium, that ſhall anſwer all Points of Buſineſs and Profit, better then Money's. And that by a Publick or Private Bank of Credit; and either of them will do under the Influence, Patronage, Sanctions, & Awe of the Goverment.*

A few Things under this Head,

1. *As to the Money Medium* [to what has been fairly ſaid, I may here further add] *It ſeems altogether in vain for us to expect it, or make any Projections Concerning it.* Were it a better Medium of Trade then really it is, we have not the matter of it in our own Country and our preſent Capacity denies us of it. And moreover, all Countries Generally complain of the ſcarcity of this Specie ; as *Sweedland, Germany, France,* &c. nay *Spain* it ſelf, who is the Proprietor of the Mines in *Mexico*, and *Peru?* That what can we expect will fall to our Share ? Indeed we have no Reaſon to be overfond of it ; for, when we had it, it was never ſufficient in a due Degree, to Support the Government, and carry on the buſineſs of the Country, but at a very Poor and Pitiful Rate. That it ſeems to me as tho' we had loſt one half of our time for want of a ſufficient Medium : For where Men have Done Well, they might have Done much Better, and where as we have been fain to Creep, we
                                                                    might

might have Run in Bufinefs, and advanced our Country double in the time to what it is ; had we had but
a full Medium. And as for what we had it was rather the means of our Oppreffion, then of our Prof-
perity, when it was in ufe and Fafhion : But however,
and Finally, when we have been Mafters of a fmall
Stock, not near a fufficiency to fupply our Trade, &c.
as has been faid ; yet then, the Trading part of Men,
have made it Merchandize and Shipt it off : And we
find it like the Animals going into the Lyons Den,
Veftigia nulla retrorfum : there's none comes back,
&c. That after fuch a long and Clear Experience, can
we be fo dull and ftupid, as to think that if we can
get it again we can keep it ? No ! by no Means !
unlefs you will burn our Ships, and knock all our Merchants on the Head ; and make fuch a Wall as may
keep all Men who know the value and intrinfick worth
of Money, from Trading with us : For that if it
comes back, & does us any good as a Medium of Trade,
it muft be Current ; and always upon the Run, that
there will be no ftopping of it, but away it goes, by
Sea, or Land. And if any Laggs behind, a Thoufand
to one, but it's Clapt up clofe prifoner for after Ages,
or expofed to buy Bills at Cent, per Cent, and fo away
that goes after the reft, like the helve after the Hat-
chet. Efpecially confidering how at prefent it is with
us. Therefore,

    1. *If there be any Help for us, our Relief is by a
Bank of Credit.* The Paper Medium, is the Medium
which we muft depend upon. And if this had been
Projected and wifely ufed Twenty or Fourty Years before it was ; it feems to me as tho' Thoufands of Lives,
and more Thoufands in Temporal profits would have
been faved. We might have fo Built and Fortified our
Country, and decoyed fuch Numbers of Inhabitants
to us. that a parcel of poor Naked Indians, had never
attempted our Ruin, or prevailed as they have. But
how ever,

however, it feems for the future we fhall not much mend the matter in the next Century if our very next bufinefs in order to our moft flourifhing State, is to call in all our out-ftanding Bills with all Expedition, break up our Bank of Credit, and all Men fet their Mouths wide open, and keep gaping for the return of the Money Medium, before we can do any more great feats. But I hope our Eyes will be opened wider than our Mouths, that fo we may fee that the happinefs of our State, as to our Outward wellbeing, is under G O D, involved in a Bank of Credit, as being the beft Method in bufinefs for us, and not to wait upon *Chy- meras,* or fuch frightful uncertainties.

I fhall proceed and open my affertion under two heads, *Scil.* By fetting in a fair Light what this Medium has done : And, What it can do for us ; if we fhall fee Caufe to be fo careful of, and kind to our felves, as to make further ufe of it.

1. *What it has done. fince it has been Projected, by the Wifdom of our Legiflature.* I am very well affured, and think I have very good Authority for it ; that our State, and Outward Condition, had been very horrid, and Defperate ; long before now, if the Bills had not been Emitted ; But they have fupported us, and done every thing for us that has been needful in our Civil and Secular Affairs fince their Authorization.

Yea they have been the Means of our Support in all our great Works we have fo Comfortably carried on, for now well near Thirty Years laft paft.   And here I fhall inftance, but in a very few particulars,

I. Part. *By our Bills we have Supported and Maintained a Chargeable Government in Church and State, without Grumbling.*

In our moft happy Times [as in our fondnefs we call them] We allowed our Governour an Hundred per Annum, &c. and when the Salary was changed, from the Corn Specie to Money, there was fuch a mutter- ing

ing and grumbling in the Country, as tho' they were going into a mutiny. What I to Pay such a Salary, and pay it in Money! Oh! these Impolitick Statesmen of Deputies will quite undoe us! But now since the Bills have taken Place, we have given our Governour a Thousand Pounds per Annum; and every Man crys, G O D bless him with it, as far as I know; I see no Scowling Faces, nor hear of any Discontent. And Gentlemen! Is this a Dull Illustration? At the lowest rate, Men value our Bills at, I suppose it may be equivolent to five Hundred Pounds Sterling. And this we have done frankly; but it has been done by our Bills. And what do you think it is the way quite to undoe us to Emit more! Certainly it cannot be! Our Government in Church and State; in Schools and College possib'y has not stood us in less then Thirty if not Forty Thousand Pounds Annually for many Years, and all this we have done with Cheerfulness, but it has been mainly done by our Bills; for we must have sunk under our Load without these Crutches. I would speak of one particular Example further in our carryings on, and that is with respect to our College. Oh what Begging, and Contributing was there; even from every poor Girl and Boy, that had but a Penny to part with to a Beggar, to bring Venerable *Harvard* into its first Brick? But now Alas! at a words speaking up goes an other Parallel with that, and we hear nothing of Begging, or of any Groans in its Birth. Oh Dear Country! These Bills are of a very impregnating Nature, they will beget and bring forth whatsoever you shall please to fancy. For do but Fancy or wish a Noble Fort in any of your Frontiers; set the Bills to work and up it goes in a Trice. Or if you have a Mind to Cultivate your Vast Woods to the North, or North-West, the Bills will do it as Effectually, as ever King of England, subdued the Old *Britains* by chopping down theirs.

R. A

· But in one Word more, as to our *College*, Do but compute the Classes of that Famous Society, for the last Thirty Years, which is the Run of our Bills ; And our *Alma Mater*, (if we infer from her fair, and numerous Offspring) seems apparently to have renewed her Youth, and grown Younger and Younger. Sometimes we were wont to have One, and sometimes Two, or Three at a Birth, with abundance of groans to bring them forth; and in some Years nothing but Dead Embrio's, or Abortions ; So poor and insufficient was the Seminal Matter and Flames of our State, *viz.* Our Medium. For indeed proportionably to our Number, we had more Corn and other Produce, then we have had in those late Years, but in those Times had no sufficient Medium at all. But of late our Dear Mother brings forth Thirty or Forty at a Birth; And escapes not a Season, but makes a great Addition Yearly to her Numbers ; That if you crush our Medium, you will Abate her strength, and thereby suppress her fertile, and noble Conception ; for Apparently this is the means that has awakened her Genial Powers.

One Instance more shall issue this Head ; And that is as to Ecclesiastical Affairs : I do presume we have not set at much less that *Twenty Thousand Pounds* per Annum, for the Support of the Gospel for many Years.

Object. But some may take me up very short, and say, *Never plead this Example ; here's the soar place ; these are the Men who have been injured by the Bills.* All Men say, there has been much Unrighteousness committed by them, and it has in a special manner fallen upon these and other Salary Men ; that there's no reason to Admire the projection under this head : For of all Men, Salary Men have been the only Sufferers ; others could help themselves and keep up an equivalent to Money, when Money grew

grew scarce and Dear, and Bills Cheap and Plenty.

Answer 1. Gentlemen ! I hope the Wise, and Judicious will not be affrighted, from a Noble design at one piece of Bad Fortune.   For,

2. Could not the Government easily have Traced the motion of the Bills, and helpt themselves by making some Just Addition to their own Salaries ? Surely they might, and none could have blamed their Care, Justice, and Prudence. And could they not also have made a small Precept, in favour of their Gospel Ministry, to encourage their People to Regard Justice, and make an equivalent ? Indeed many good People were so wise and Just, as to do it without one: And possibly most Places took it into Consideration, and did something; that there has not been near so much Unrighteousness in the Country as some Men speak of. But however there is no blame owing to the Medium; but if any is Due it is a Debt to them that had the Management of these things.   But,

3. When we had a little Silver Money, it was always high Prized ; and other things were in great subjection to it : And it held such a sway, and to such a degree of Tyranny, from the rate it was kept at, and from the continual escape it was making, it had brought us into a pitiful heap of Circumstances, and especially, as to our Ministry in Church order, for before the Bills came into use , it would make one sick to tell over the Story of these things ; Oh the Repineing, higling, complaining of Poverty ; with bad and poor payments ; Criminal and Dreadful Behindments, as tho' Sacriledge were no Sin, or but a very venial one ; and not only in this or that poor village but too Epidemically. But since the Bills have been in Force, these Annuities have not only been Augmented, but Frankly and Seasonably payed, and I believe it has been so through the Country. And do we think these Reverend Men, dont find that they can

make

make as good a Dinner on the Bills of Credit, as on Gold, and Silver? Yes! Every whit; and where due Additions have been made, the seasonableness and round Payments have made their lives much more easy, and comfortable, then when Silver Ruled the Roft, And thus our Bills have been one, of the best of all Temporal Blessings in the Management, and for the support of a Chargeable Government, both in Church and State.

2. Benefit. *We have maintained, carryed on, and almost gotten thro' the Charge of a Bloody, Long and Expensive War.* The Wars since they began in this Country, have Exhausted, Wasted, and Confounded, besides Lives, more (I do imagine,) than *Two Millions of Pounds*, within the Vicissitudes of about *Forty Years*. For how many fair Towns have they demolished? And many more have they prevented of a Being? And what an immense Treasure have we been defeated of; as well as what we have consumed, to save what we have yet left? And had not these Bills been Projected, within the last *Thirty Years*, it seems to me, we had been in danger of a Mutiny from their irresistible Oppressions, we must have fallen under one from another; and if so, our Enemies might have stood still and breathed, till we had done their Work for them. But the Bills so soon as Projected, gave ease. The *Canada Voyage* under Sir *Wm. Phips*, which stood us at *Thirty Thousand Pounds* was Solved by the Bills. And since the *Eastern* & *French Wars*, have hardly been felt, only now and then in the smart of a Spear or Bullet, or in the Death of a particular Friend, &c. But as to the Civil and Publick Charge, it has by the Bills been carryed along with so much Ease and Alacrity, as tho' we had had the Riches of an Empire to Command.

Object. But some Men may say, *Indeed for carrying on of a War, the Bills of Publick Credit, are a*
very

very proper Means. Sir Edward Cook *that great Statesman and Oracle, allows the Bills to be very proper in a time of War.*

Anf. *If they are proper in War, why not in Peace?* Indeed, it is an old Saying and a true one, Scil. *Money is the Sinews of War.* And if it be why not alfo in Peace ? For I dont fee how a People or BodyPolitick can well hang together without fuch Sinews in Peace any more than in War. For the meaning is, that Money which Anfwers all things, is to Support, Carry on and Defray all Charges; and if a People have a full Supply of it, then they are ftrong, and have good Sinews, Ligaments, Bones and what not to carry their Load, and go on with their Duty. And certainly, that Medium which will enable them in their Duty in War, will be of Equal Advantage in time of Peace. Which may be more evident if we diftinguifh between a Country that has a Sufficient Stock of Money as a Medium of Trade in time of Peace, (Sir *Edward Cokes* Cafe) but not fo plentiful as to fupply all the Emergencies of War; therefore the Bills may be prudently made ufe of in fuch a Cafe to enlarge their Stock. Now we muft underftand, that the Cafe is very different with a Country which has no Money at all : for if the Bills will fuit and relieve the former in a time of War, they muft needs be a very good Medium for the latter, both in the time of Peace as well as in War. Unlefs you will be fo Rafh as to fuppofe a Country may do without any Medium at all in time of Peace; if they can have one in War : which to fuppofe is contrary to the Suffrage of Mankind. Therefore as the Bills have Relieved us, fo eminently in War, we may rationally depend upon them in times of Peace, feeing our *Money* is all gone, and not likely to return, unlefs our Merchants will fetch it back for us.

3. Benefit,

3. Benefit, *By our Bills, is the flourishing State that our Country is now in.* For that within this Twenty or Thirty Years, notwithstanding, all our Grand expences, vast Consumptions, horrid Wastes and Depredations : We have kept a great part of our Country in very good Repair, and are sensibly grown in our Outward Affairs. For is there not Apparently, thro' the heart of our Country, a greater aspect of Wealth, and good Fortune, to be seen, as we pass along, than ever ? Are not our Lands finely built, and fenced, with noble Stocks of Cattle feeding, and coming to a good Market ? How many new Precincts have been set off within this Time, for Promoting Vertue and Religion ; with Costly Houses for God's Worship Erected ; fair Salaries Settled, and all these great Charges carryed on, if not without groaning, yet without grudging or grumbling ? Now Gentlemen ! These things in an eminent degree, are all under God and Nature, owing to our Bills. Nay ! Look but into *Boston*, (if you knew it but Twenty Years ago) you will find an invincible Plea under this Head. Pray now ! How came that Famous Emporium, the Mistress of our Towns, to rise as a Phænix, out of her own Ashes, so suddenly, and in greater Glory than ever ? And Rear up such an *Exchange* for the Seat of Government and Congress of Merchants ; so costly and so fair, as it need not blush to shew its Face with most in *Europe* of that kind ? These things with a Thousand others of Moment, are peculiarly owing to our Bills. For again, was it our *Gold and Silver* that has created such a stupendous Appearance of useful and costly *Store-Houses* on the *Long-Wharffe* in *Boston* ? Consider the Foundation and Superstructure; and also how stocked with all Valuable and Useful Commodities, from all parts of the World from Year to Year ? Why as to Means, next to the Wisdom, good Husbandry, Courage, Brave and Prudent

Conduct

Conduct of our venturefome Merchants, all is to be attributed to our *Bills of Credit.* For without them in fome degree, according to my fenfe, you could no more have Lived thus long, and done thefe things, and kept up your Outward Eftate in fuch a Plight; and Capacity, than you could have pretended to have made a Moon and Starrs. What! and now in a great Fright to throw away the means of our Salvation! But let Divine Goodnefs Divert fuch an Infatuation.

2. Thus after a fhort view of what the Bills have done, I fhall Confider, *What they can ftill do. Or what Benefits we may yet Reap in the Continuation of them.*

1. *The Bills can fupport, maintain and preferve our Merchandize with great advantage and clear profit.* Indeed the Store-Houfes of our *Corn, Flower, Flax, Pork, Lumber, &c.* are many of them in other Colonies, but our Bills will fetch them all home, and fully anfwer their Value and Importation, and not in a much inferiour degree than Silver it felf, when in its beft Capacity; as will appear fomething more clear in the following Competition.

In the Prefent Year, 1720. Goods Sold for Bills,	Formerly Goods Sold for Money.
Barbad.Sugar,30s.to50s.C	Barbad.Sugar25s.to45s.p.C.
Bever-Skins,3s. 10d.p.Po.	Bever-Skins,5s.to25s6d.p.Po
FrenchSalt,18s.p.Hoggfh.	FrenchSalt,20s.to16s.Hog.
Bees Wax, 2s. *per* Pound.	Bees-Wax 22d.to18d.Poun.
Hopps 5d. *per* Pound.	Hops,11d.to 9d.to4d.Poun.
WheatVirginia,6s.p.Bufh	Wheat Virginia,5s6d.Bufh
IndianCorn,3s.*per*Bufhel.	Indian,18d. to3s. to6s.Bufh.
Hay 3s. 6d.per C.	Hay,2s6dopen.to5sScrew'd

That

That furely our Bills by this Comparifon are not without Value, neither are they under fo fatal Eclipfe, as to deferve quite and clean to be made Extinct in Darknefs, as fome Men pretend to ; but by this Account, will fairly do our bufinefs; and all things Confidered, [notwithftanding fome odds in the Terms] may be efteemed by us par with Money. And as for our Province, the Produce of it, which poffibly amounts to near a Million, [or fay half the Money] *per Annum* ; and a great Part ftands for the Market. *viz.* in *Milk, Eggs, Butter, Cheefe, Poultry, Fruit, Cyder, Hay, Corn, Flax, Hemp, Fat Cattle, Horfe, Tar, Pitch,* the Royal *Whale* with his *Bone* and *Oyle,* the *Codd Fifh, Cufk,* &c. dryed, which laft mentioned poffibly yields us half one Hundred Thoufand Pounds in a Year; and out of the whole premifes we furnifh out feveral Staples for other Countries, and for fome of the beft of *Ports ;* Alfo with our Lumber, and the Ships we build &c. All thefe things our Bills will Anfwer for, to the Profit of the Merchant in fupporting a Foreign Trade. This is Fact : When Money was going, and the Bills firft Commenc'd ; the owner of the Fifh, when the Merchant has made the offer *Scil. Muft I pay you in Money, or in Bills* ? *In Bills, fays the owner, they are moft accommodable, and beft for difpatch :* And tho' there is no fuch Competitinow, the Money being rooted out and fupplanted by the Bills ; Yet the Bills Retain their Honour ; and are in fuch Demand with all Men, that they are a valuable Confideration, for all other Species, upon which our whole Trade, and Merchandize Circulates, and as Current as Money it felf. It muft hence be Conclufive, that they will do us Immenfe Service, and Serve as a Medium, for increafe of our Wealth, and Flourifhing State if we are pleafed, not to be fo indifcreet as to throw them away.

I

It is to be obferved that all Beneficial things add something to the common Pile. Every Spoonful adds to the Ciftern. Every frugal Family, and Induftrious Man, who earns and lays up any thing more then he has Occafion to confume, is a good to the Common-Wealth: But it is to be allowed of as a great Truth, that amongft good Husbands, it is the Wife Merchant that is the great Benefactor to the Publick: For that it is very Apparent to any difcerning Perfons, that [notwithftanding what ever fome Men are pleafed whimfically to fay about Merchants over Trading; whenas amongft the Wife and Skilful in thofe Myfteries there can be no fuch thing amongft them; no more then there is amongft Men, whom G O D teaches to Threfh out the Corn, of their over Threfhing themfelves; for that Wifdom is profitable to direct in all Affairs] I fay it is the Merchandize of any Country, Wifely, and vigoruſly managed, this is the king of bufinefs, for increafing the Wealth, the civil Strength, and Temporal glory of a People. Merchandize was an early Projection, for the Convenience of Nations; and for the increaſe of Wealth and Profit amongft Men. A company of *Iſhmaelites* [Traders] from *Gilead*, with their *Camels*, bringing Spicery, and Balm, and Myrrh, going to carry it down to *Æ-gypt.* [To make their Market] *Gen.* 37. *Tyrus* that was but a Naked Rock, at the upper end of the *Mediterranean*; Yet by Merchandize became the queen of the Seas, the *Metropolis* of the World, and Admiration of all Countries. Says the *Prophet, Thefe were thy Merchants in all forts of things, in blue cloths, &c. The Ships of Tarſhiſh did fing of thee in thy Markets, and thou waſt repleniſhed, and made very glorious in the midſt cf the Seas.* Ezek. 27.

That certainly if a great Rock fpread out in the Sea may be thus cultivated, and brought to fuch perfection, by making it a Place for the World to meet at

and

and to Buy and Sell on ; and a Rock which never Rolls, if in a few Ages may be over run with such a Moss, as the *Prophet* cloths the Rock of *Tyrus* with. Then what a perfection may *Cape-Ann*, or *Glocester*, a Promontory thrust so far into the Sea ; Or in a peculiar manner *Boston* so spacious an *Isthmus* at the head of a noble *Bay*, with a bold and spacious *Harbour*, the Center of a vast Continent, spread over with Industrious Colonies ; I say what a Capacity, may this Place be brought to, by Commerce and Merchandize, in a few Ages more, unless they are Mortifyed, and Slain for want of a Suitable Medium, to support their Trade ? And to this Purpose says the Learned *Molloy*, All Mankind are Traders by themselves, or others; and the ends designed by Trade, Commerce and Merchandize, are the Strength, Wealth, and Imployment, of all Sorts of People ; and where it doth most Flourish, the end of it tends to the Advancement, Opulency, and Greatness of such a Kingdom and State. We need not Run into the History of Earlier Times, to give an Account of the many Kingdoms, and States that have Risen by Industry, and Commerce : It is enough if we cast our Eye on our Neighbour the *Hollander*, a Place by Relation of *Ortelius*, not much bigger then *Yorkshire* ; & such a spot as tho' GOD had reserved it a as place only to digg *Turff* out of, for the accommodating those Countries, wherein he hoards up the Miseries of the *Winter*, it affording naturally not any one Commodity of use ; yet by Merchandize and Trade (the Daughters of Industry) it is now become the Store-house of all those Merchandizes that may be Collected from the Rising to the Setting of the Sun: And gives those People a Name as large, and high as the Greatest Monarch this day on Earth. Hence it is that Trade, Merchandize and Commerce, are become the only Object and Care of the Great Princes and Potentates of the Earth, as knowing that

the

the Return and Effects of Commerce, is Riches, and the Plenty of all things conducing to the Benefit of Humane Life, and for the Supporting their Crowns and Grandeur, and Fortifying their Countries and Kingdoms with Reputation and Strength.   *Mol. Præf. De Jure Maritifno.*

Now if the Cafe be fo, and this tho' a Brief, yet a true Reprefentation of the Great Benefit of Merchandize, which to Supprefs, Defert or Weaken ; or not fupport with all imaginable incouragement, is to darken the Crown, weaken the Strength, and make the Glory of a Nation, or Country, to Ierifh.

That Gentlemen ! If a Bank carried on by Bills of Credit, will Bonafide, fecure fo noble a Trade as belongs to this Province, and will keep it up on all fides to the height, and in a vigorous Circulation [as it is moft Apparent that it will] then let the Merchandize be accommodated, which will be for the Interest of the Crown; and fill our Country with Joyful Songs and Fraifes to G O D for His Goodnefs.   An! me-thinks, the Merchant and Farmer will continually Charm us [by inter.changing their Friendly Salutations in managing their Commerce] upon a full Settlement of fo proper a Medium for each Man's Intereft.   For can we expect lefs from the venturefome Merchant, than that [when having Collected his valuable Cargo for a Foreign Port, by the Credit of the Bills] he fhould with cheerful hopes hoift his fore-Courfe, and bid his Country thus Farewel, &c.

Tityre, tu Patula Recubans fub Tegmine fagi
Tenui meditaris avena
Nos Patriam fugimus.
Farewel dear Country, whiftle to your Teams !
 We for your fake, now leave the quiet Shoar.
But if the Wind will ftand behind our Beams
 We hope again [with double ftock or more]
  To hear your Oaten Pipes.

And

And from the Laborious Farmer, in hopes these Foreign Enterprizes will enliven the Markets, for his own Productions; and that the Bills will maintain a quick Circulation; secretly blesseth himself, (in Saluting his Departing Brother) with,

Oh ! Meliboe ! Deus nobis hac Ocia fecit.

Brave Boys go your ways ! We love the Beech's shade,
   Here we will stay this is our Element ;
That is your's : And thus has God wisely made
   Spirits to vary ; Riches to Cement.

I shall conclude the Paragraph, with that Excellent Saying of Sir *Edward Coke*, Scil.

Trade & Traffick, is the Life of a Common Wealth.

2. The *Bills will maintain a numerous Set of Mechanicks, who are the inseperable Adjutants of Merchandize*, &c. The Black-Smith who makes the Anchors, and does the rest of the Ship-Work ; tho' he moyles in a dangerous Element, for such a Medium of Trade ; yet makes no scruple, but rather than miss of so rich a Prize, takes the Bills ; tho' the Sparks fly. They suit his Profit; Purchase his Stock, Iron, Coal, &c. Support his Family, &c. And so officious they will be to all others of such like Mysteries and Labour.

3. The *Bills will Sustain the whole Ministry, and all Charges in Church, and State.* What would Men have then ?

Object. Oh ! say some, we will try a *Corn* and *Provision Medium*, till the Money comes.

Ans. This at first hearing was very surprizing, for there appeared such a numerous Set of Oddities and Chymæras in it, that I found it hard keeping in due Bounds. For besides infinite other Improprieties, thought I, how is it possible, That *Judicatory* should be be, carryed on, and Supported. For how fhall Mr; *Sheriff* be anfwered for laying the Writ? Will it not be extream odd to tender *Codled Apples*, or *Eggs*, or any fuch fmall Species? As for Money there is none left. And when the *Plantiff* enters his Action, Things will be ftill at the fame Flunge. And as for *Councellours at Law*, they generally allow themfelves very plump Fees, that in attending on our Country Seffions, they muft expect to come with large Wallets, and Load home with *Corn, Poultry*, or what other Convenient Chattels their Clients have, &c. That to think a Country fo full of Bufinefs of greateft Moment; and pretend to fupprefs a Medium fo accommodated to all Affairs, and every Man may carry it in his Pocket, I fay, to throw away this; and take up with one that is a heap of Luggage, and requires all the Waggons, Carts, and Sumpter-Horfes in our Country to carry it from Town to Town. Thought I, this is Ridiculous mus all over.

4. *The Bills of Credit will Reinforce our neceffary and painful Husbandry.* Nay they are better to the Farmer far away then the Gold or Silver Medium, for there is fo much of a fecret Charm attending that, and carrying fo much a Tyranny fin its nature, that Men who have it feem infatuated by it, and are inclined thereby to violate the Rights of other Men, without Regard to Reafon or Juftice, for how will Moneyed Men higgle down every thing; and ufe many unfair Artifices to fink and lower the Price of what comes to the Market. For one he crys, *Heus Amice ! What have you to Sell? Indian Corn. At what a Bufhel? Three Shillings. What not under that? No, Crops are very fhort, and I can't afford it under? Hab! Country! that wont do, for I'll Sell you Forty Bufhels at One & Twenty-pence*; tho' it may be, has not had a Peck in his Houfe for thefe Three Weeks. Now we muft note, there is Money in the Cafe,

Cafe, and many Temptations attending it.

But the Bills have another look and influence with them; and more readily yield to Mens Equal Demands in what they have to Sell. And by this means, the innocent Farmer (who is ufually more fimply honeft and plain hearted, (than with Fraud and Diffembling to beat long upon a Bargain) has better Markets opened for his Effects throughout the Year. There is indeed fcarce any thing comes amifs to the City out of the Country, and the Bills make a ready and full Penny for it. The Farmers little Crops, or firft Fruits, his *Milk, Eggs, Cherries, Chickens, Green Pees,* and what not! hereby he reaps a fine Income in the firft of the Year, before his greater Effects come in, as his *Firkns of Butter, Cheefe, Cyder, Fat Cattle, &c.* And the Bills will Circulate all, and at a very good Rate. And thus it ought to be in all wife and well Regulated Countries. The Farmer muft be duly, and fufficiently incouraged or you ruin all. Keep him in a thread-bare Coat, and ftarve him of his Profits, by Pinching, and Penurious Markets, and Prices, you will then much dif-animate one of the beft Servants to the Crown, and the means of your Plenty, your Safety, and Flourifhing Co: dition. But Trade with him upon free and reafonable Terms, and the Bills in their very nature admit of it; for they allow of a quicker difpatch, and fuller Price, and with more Equity, and thus it ought to be; and this animates the Farmer; keeps him to his Plough; Brightens and inlivens all his Rurall Schemes; Reconciles him to all his hard Labour, and makes him look Fat and Chearful. And I muft note unto you, you muft keep up your Farmers heart; for if he fails, you are in danger to ftarve all; and alfo he is the beft Wall to his Conntry; the King and all Men muft be maintained out of his Field; and defended too; for from hence Mufter-Rolls are filled up, and Armies are Reinforc'd with the Beft Souldiers, and

and moſt Effective Men. Therefore Judge *Littleton,* (in his Twelve ſorts of Services ; or manner of holding Lands, or Tenements,) having placed Socage, or the Service of the Plough, next following to Knights Service, ſays *Coke,* ' It is done very aptly, or moſt properly; for that the Ploughman makes the Beſt Souldier. That let Knights Service lead the Van, and ' Socage will with a Dareing Reſolution bring up the ' Rear. And this *Coke,* more fully Explains, in opening ' the Tenure of Socage. For there he ſays, ' Agriculture, and Tillage is of a great Account in the Law, ' as being very profitable to the Common-Wealth. ' For by the Failure of Husbandry, and Tillage, many ' great diſadvantages inſue; and in a peculiar manner the Defence of the Kingdom will hereby be ' much infeebled and impaired; for that the Body's of ' Husbandmen being more ſtrong, and able, and patient ' of Cold, Heat and Hunger, than of any other Men, ' they therefore make the Beſt Soldiers. He inforces his Obſervation from a like ſaying of the wiſe *Seneca,* Scil. *Nullum Laborem Recuſant Manus, Qua ab Arato ad Arma Transferuntur, &c. Fortier autem Miles ex Confragoſo venit, ſed ille unctus, et Nitidus in Primo Pulvere Deficit.* Or thus,

Thoſe Blades who are Detach't from rugged grounds ;
  And then drawn up into Battle array,
Will ſtand the hardeſt Brunts ; Bear the deepeſt Wounds
  When Neat, and Oyled Heads will run away.

Now all theſe Great and Noble Deſigns will our Bills maintain, if we have but the Wiſdom and Senſe to improve them.

  5. There is one great Benefit more, which I imagine will iſſue from the Bills : *To me it ſeems as tho' they might be inſtrumental for the Increaſe of the Number of our Towns and People.* It's very grievous to think, what Rich Tracts, and Vaſt Territories we have deſerted ſo many Ages to Owls and Satyrs, which might be Subdued and made noble Seats ; Brightned

with the Worship of God, and of Immense Benefit to the Crown. In our present Settlements, we are but like the Lift on the Cloth; whenas in an Age of Two more (with an ordinary Blessing) we might more than double our Country, in Number of Towns, and People; and the incouragement which may be given by the Bills of Credit (in the present Juncture of Affairs in the Christian World) will certainly forward the Design abundantly.

For suppose we admit of this Projection. That a Range of Townships, from River to River, Four Mile Square (according to the view of our late Gentlemen) and 50 or 60 Heads of Families joyning for a Society, &c. to settle within three Years, &c. and that every Master of a Family Adventuring to support him in his Undertaking, in Building, Clearing of Ground, Buying Servants, Stock, or other ways, &c. they and each one so Chusing shall take one Hundred, or one Hundred and Fifty Pound out of the Bank, upon Reasonable Security; and shall have it Ten Years Rent free, and then Repay it, &c. I do presume by these means we may Subdue and Settle those Desolate Lands with very good and Effective Men : and if done each Town would be Worth more than *Ten Thousand Pounds* to the Publick, at the Expiration of the Term. And on other Considerations it would much Advance our Country.

For then those Woods and Swamps which are now Impregnable Forts and Ramparts for a Naked Skulking Euemy, and renders them invincible, when once brought under Culture (and now or never) will be somewhat like the Wall of *China*, which is a Barrier to that Empire, against the *Tartars*; or that in *Britain*, Erected by the Romans, to cover their Conquest, against the *Picts*. So would this be to us in some measure, against a like Enemy.

And then we may go on with great Encouragement.

Bottom.

Boldnels, and Dispatch to fill up such Vacancies as will still remain, between the Old and New Settlements, which will add greatly to our Strength. And if we can prevent the Approach and sudden Slaughters of War by such Precaution; or only make our selves strong and powerful, it must needs administer much to our well-being; and also to our Security upon any Rupture.

Obj: ct. But possibly you will say, *Where be the Men, That's the main Point ?*

An w. *Do you prevail with the Government to settle the Terms, &c. and leave me to find the Men, &c. which I doubt not of, both out of our own, and other Countries.* For this will invite our good Brethren out of *North Britain,* and *Ireland,* who will bring with them equal Religion with us ; but a Superior Ingenuity and Skill in Manufactures. We have also a great many likely Men, who will be accomodated, and also suit the design : For, that many of our Old Towns are too full of Inhabitants for Husbandry ; many of them living upon small Shares of Land, and generally all are Husbandmen ; or if they are any of them Tradesmen ; their Husbandry hinders their Trade : And also many of our People are slow in Marrying for want of Settlements : whereas in old Countries they generally Marry without such Precaution, and so increase infinitely, &c. We have Old Batchelours, with Dames to Match them, to settle several Towns, &c. And when we have accomplished this Projection,

6. *We may expect that Manufactures will go on amain in our Country.* And when we once come to such Perfection, we seem to presume our Capacity will be such, that we may fetch back the Money ; but nothing of that nature in the ordinary course of Business can be done, before this comes about. And to pretend to Manufactures, without a great Overplus

(to

(to our Husbandry) in our Number of People, is but to talk Chymæras. And tho' now in our prefent Capacity, all good Houfholders do what they can, for Ordinary wear for a Family, to rub along with thro' much hard Labour, and Cold Winters; and fo in the Run of the Year we, after a Fafhion, make up our Produce of Wool, &c. But this is nothing like Manufacturing the Effects of a large Country for a Foreign Vend. But when our Country is fill'd with People; and we can afford fome Towns fully ftock'd with Artificers, Combers, and Weavers, &c. And Farmers fhall keep large Walks for Sheep, and every Man fhall keep clofe to his own Calling, then we may do fomething to purpofe in Manufactures, but not before. This feems plain, from the Examples of Old Countries, where being over-crowded with Inhabitants, they are fain to Beg, Steal or Fight for their Living, or Work for Six-pence or a Groat a Day, great Numbers of them. Therefore our Bufinefs is to incourage Settlements, with all Difpatch, that we may put things into fome good Forwardnefs, and leave a Wife Model for the next Age to go by. And the BILLS will do it all.

This is very obvious, our Country, tho' of a pretty Aultere Climate, yet if well and effectually managed, is capable of a Self-Subfiltence, as fully as moft Countries in the World. If I am not mifinformed, or miftaken, the Juice of many of our Sweet Trees, and the Fruit of others, will yield a Generous Sugar. And if we cant well do with our Cyder, or without Wine, why may we not Cultivate the French Grape; we being many Degrees nearer the Sun than they. But if not, our Bees can ldo great Feats, if rightly managed, in producing a Generous Nectar, equal with the beft of Wines in ftrength and healthfulnefs. Alfo our Soil yields plenty of Corn, &c. Feeds and Breeds all forts of Cattle, &c. and is very natural in its productions

to maintain an Excellent, Vaſt and Profitable Manufacture both of Woolen and Linnen.   Wool, Flax,
Hemp, are very natural to our Climate.   And alſo the
Iron Mine, but this does uſually eat up its Owners
for want of Hands; and ſo will all the Reſt of our
Manufactures do, as has been ſaid.   Therefore the
Buſineſs of our preſent Age is to incourage a Foreign
Trade; and give it all the Support and Advantage we
are Capable of ; for moſt certainly with the help of
ſuch a Medium, and in ſuch Plenty, as by it we can
eaſily Vend and Circulate our own preſent Produce
and Effects ; we can then Buy of our Merchants many
neceſſary as well as convenient Things, cheaper than
we can poſſible make them, and ſo ſave our Time by
the Bargain, for other and more profitable Buſineſs.

    Alſo it is, and will be much for our Service to Rein-
force our preſent Husbandry, ſo far as it ſpreads; Let
the Farmer have all Due Incouragement, as before, &c.
But in a peculiar manner, it is our Wiſdom to promote
the increaſe of our Plantations, and Multiplying the
Number of our People,   Our Bills will Support us in
all theſe Affairs, if the Almighty will give us the Wiſdom and Vertue to improve them.

    It is moſt Certain G O D gives us many wiſe cauti-
ons to correct Inordinacy, and all Sinful diſtruſt concerning the Things of this Life : But he has left it
as a Charge upon our Nature, to Propagate our Species : And alſo has denounced many a heavy Penalty
to conſtrain us Faithfully to preſerve and uphold His
Kingdom; And Civil Government, and good Order
in His Empire.   And by no Means to ſlight the Comfort, and Outward felicity of our Lives and Families ;
If we do he marks us in the muſter Rolls of his Hoſts,
to be worſe than Infidels ; Therefore all due Means
muſt be uſed ; and your Bills of Credit are a Compli-
cation of all Profitable meaſures, for bringing about, and
accompliſhing theſe great Ends.   Therefore in Obedi-
ence

ence to G O D and Nature they ought to be kept up, and Improved as the Means of our Wellbeing, unless we are funk into a Lower Capacity, as to all fenfe of Intereft, Religion, and Honour, than Men who have never been ufed to either.

I I. The Queftions, Now follow, and Principally we may Confider how to Preferve the Value, and Dignity of our Bills ? And then by whom a Bank of Credit may be beft managed in this Province ? And Finally how a Bank may be Qualified for the beft good of the whole ? I fhall at this time Confine my Difcourfe to the two firft.   Then,

I. Queftion. *How fhall we keep up the Value of our Bills of Publick Credit ?* There be many good Gentlemen, that profefs they would join their fuffrage for their Eftablifhment, if there was any way to keep them Par with Money.   Therefore this is the great *Queftion,* How it fhall be done ?

Anfwer. To this puzling Queftion, I fhall Anfwer under a few heads, or thus Cut the Gordian Knot.

1. *Gentlemen* ! You muft do by your Bills, as all Wife Men do by their Wives; Make the beft of them. It is an acknowledged Theorem, that there is no doing without Wives. The Lonefome and fower Phylofopher would frankly contefs, that Women, were neceffary Evils : For without their Affiftance the whole Humane Race muft vanifh ; And unlefs they are Metamorphifed into things called Wives, the whole Species would foon Laps into an heard-of Brutified Animals. The great Skill is to cultivate the neceffity and make it a Happinefs ; for that end. Wife Men Love their Wives ; and what ill-conveniences they find in them they bury ; and what Vertues they are inrich't with they Admire and Magnifie. And thus you muft do by your Bills for there is no doing without them ; if you Divorce or Diffeize your felves of them

you

you are undone ; Therefore you muſt ſet them high in your Eſtimation ; and be no ways Prodigal of their Reputation, ſo as to vilify or run them down; as tho' they had more miſchief than Good in them.   You muſt not Preſage any terrible Deſtinies deſcending from them, as tho' you thought the Publick Faith was To Debauch'd as not to be truſted ; or that they were ſent by the creating Power of Government like Birds of Prey to rob our Corn Fields or Ravige our Country. All manner of Aſperſions caſt upon them by Fear or Jealouſies muſt be wip't off, and they be look'd upon as the Beſt of Pawns, and better than Money in hand ; This muſt be our Rule , becauſe the Fund is firm at Bottom ; and the Government which has the manage-ment, will do that which is Good, Right and Equal to all Men.   And alſo for the ſake of our own private and Publick Good.   Such a temper of Mind will for ever, not only ſecure the Currency of our Bills ; but will moſt certainly keep up their Value equal with Money ; or to ſuch a Degree, as by juſt proportion ought to be : and this is Left of all.   For,

2. *We muſt not judge we have loſt in the value of our Bills, from ſome experience we have had in improving of them, when they have ſeemed to ſink below their due Eſtimation.*   For at their beginning they were (generally ſpeaking) par with Money, and many times preferable to it, for at times Men would allow 25s. or 50s. per Cent. in Money for the Bills. And tho' it is alſo certain when Men had Clipt the Money down to Fifteen-penny weight, Bills fell alſo to that value in ordinary Trade ; yet this informs us that the Bills were ſtill held equal with Money : but after the Money and Bills had with equal Currency paſt at that rate for ſome Years ; ſome particular Men who had Bonds for Lawful Money againſt their Neigh-bours would refuſe the Bills unleſs Two & eight pence upon the Bills were added to make them full, Seven-

teen

teen penny; yet in thefe Times fome Men made no odds either in Ufe or in their Principal. And again, When the Money was more drained out of the Country, and grown more fcarce, then fome particular Creditors (tho' not all) demanded Two Shillings more to be added to the Bills to make them compleatly the Silver Specie. Yet under all thefe Alterations, it is to be obferved that the Bills paft, with as great a Currency as the Money.

But moreover, the Bills feem to have loft a Point in their Reputation by certain Emergencies, that have not been fo well obferved; or fome Cafualties which happened, before or about the time when they grew more plentiful. As for Inftance, The Britifh Fleet was fome Means of Raifing the Price of our live Stock, there was alfo in fome of the late Years, a confiderable fcarcity of falt Provifions, for the fupport of the Fifhery, and of Shipping, for that Pork was not imported fo plentifully as at other Times. And alfo there was a great refort of Foreign Ships of Trade, that whilft here, mainly Victualled with our frefh provifions: And our Fifhery alfo fupplied it felf from a Weekly Slaughter in a great Meafure: So that all Provfions grew to a great height, to what they had been, and made it feem as tho' the fault had been in the Bills; whenas under fuch Circumftances, if we had had our Silver in equal Proportions, as ordinarily; there would have been poffibly no great odds in Prices; and that becaufe of the prefent Scarcity & large Vend. Whence it muft needs be great Weaknefs in any to infer the infufficiency of the Bills from what has paft hitherto; for if they do they are very weak Logicians, or elfe have mift of the True Premifes, as has been now, Recited.

3. This One Particular may further be obferved, which may rationally prefage their rifing and keeping High Enough in all our Affairs: *For that however Times*

Times have been, yet the Bills have done all the Bufineß of our Country, they were Ordained for. And alfo tho' many hard Demands were made upon them on the account of Money Obligations, yet it was far better to the Debtor, than to have paid the Specie Indented for; becaufe the Bills were to be had upon Reafonable Terms, but the Money was not; it being almoft quite gone out of the Country; and had left many Men under heavy Bonds, (fo fickle is it in its own nature) which the Bills by their Currency Relieved, tho' with fuch an Allowance. So that at that Rate they were really and truly better to us than Money. Indeed if their Currency had been Blank'd or Baffled in any of our Great Affairs, either as to Private Debts and Obligations; or more Publick Duties, we might have fome fair Plea againft them.

As fuppofe the Publick Miniftry in Church or State had flighted them.

Or, if the Merchants had demurred, or frowned, and faid, Gentlemen! Thefe Paper Tickets; we will have nothing to do with them; they won't fo much as pay Ware and Tare; much lefs Reimburft our Coftly Cargo's; No! We can't part with our Brafs, Copper, Pewter, with our Broad-Cloths, Silks and Scarlet, upon thefe Terms.

Or if the Farmer had fhockt up his Shoulders, and faid, Thefe Tickets will not Anfwer for Fine Horfes; nor pay for Raifing, Grafing and Staling Fat Oxen. Therefore for our Parts, we will neither meddle nor make with them. Such Affronts and Checks had been an effectual Eftoppel to them; and might have funk all Men into defpair of their rifing to an equal Value with Money; but there is nothing of this Nature has appeared; but all forts of Men have taken them in fupporting all their Affairs; and they have been fo Convenient, Good and Acceptable, that we have now I fuppofe iffued all Specialties; and have Settled tied all Trade, Debts and Obligations upon their Credit, and a presumption of their continuance ; which signifies the high Esteem and Value which we have for them ; and in that we have no other Medium to depend upon, this will be as high in Estimation, as Men in Justice and Reason can expect.   For,

4. *All Men of Sense and Humanity (but such who Love themselves more than all Mankind besides) will allow, That it is too hard a Fate for Men of* good *Conduct to spend their Days in Rolling the Stone of Sisyphus : But that by their Frugality and* Painful *Improvement of the Means of their Subsistence, they ought to make a clear Gain, as being* most *agreeable with the Law of God and Nature.* And if our Bills will admit of this, as a Medium of Trade, as well or Better than Money : And when they are at such a Pitch and Degree, as to accomplish this end : We may then justly affirm, that they are in our Case equal or Superiour to Money. For if they will do all the Business, and keep us thriving, will not this be as good as Money ? Yea, I am very sure it will, and better too : For that the Money Medium has been the Means of our Oppression, rather than of our Flourishing State, as has been said. It is not a little Sprinkling of Money, which is always upon the Wing, or Bobbing up and down like *Tantalus* his Apples, that will make a Country Rich.   But it is Diligence, Frugality; and the Circulation of the Produce, with a clear Gain and Profit to every Man, whereby he is fully Recompenced for the use of his Prime Stock ; for his Labour, and the Risque which he runs : But I am very well perswaded, Money has never done this as a Medium in *New-England* ; nor nothing near it : Especially as to Farmers, and Husbandmen, which is the great Studd & Strength of our Country : Therefore abundance if not gone behind hand, have stood at a stay ; or with all their hard Labour,

bour, and hard Fare, have turned like the Door on the Hinge, as tho' Sluggards, whenas the Fault has been in the Medium of Trade, on which they have depended, Scil. *In the Money Times.* This feems very plain in many, but I fhall confider it but in one Example, viz. *In Neat Cattle.*

And here let us imagine, how long, and cold our Winters are ; and what care, time, houfing and fodder muft be imployed, and fpent upon a Stock of Cattle, to Raife, Feed, and fit them for the Market, &c. Now can any Rational Man [that knows any thing of this Affair] Judge it agreeable with any Points of Equity, the Rules of Fellowfhip, and profit ; for Men to fell their Cattle, as they have been Conftrained to do, in the Money Times. *Scil.* Five or Six Pounds for a Yoke of Oxen when Lean ; or for Six or Seven Pounds when Fat ? And as for thofe which have always Lay'n upon charge till they have come to the Market, *viz.* young Cattle coming four ; thefe have commonly been Sold at Thirty or Forty Shillings per Head , which has not made out near the Prime Coft. And if fo this is but little better then taking their Labour, for their Pains ; which is Certainly a very poor Method for Farmers to grow Rich by.

Now, *Gentlemen* ! If the Bills have been the Farmers Refcue by eafing fuch Points, &c. then tho' they dont come up to the Rigorous Value, and Price of Money, when it was a meer Etxtortioner, or but little better than a common Robber : Yet if they bring things nearer to the Rule of Equity ; and Adjuft matters in Commerce fo fairly, that all Men may live and thrive, upon their Labour and Profits ; this is to bring the Bills to fuch a Level, as the Money ought to be at in a Country of Trade, and Religion, whete Men fhould love their Neighbours as themfelves ; and do as they would be done by ; and therefore fhould be Willing, that others fhould live Profperoufly upon
their

their Means, their Incomes, Labour, and Profits, as well as themselves. And when it is thus in a Country; and thro' Mercy it has thus happened with us under the Government of our Bills: Now from what has been said, the Consequence is not that the Bills are fallen below the just value of Money; but the meaning of it is, that our Native produce is Risen, and brought up to a due Value, or Estimation, by the Improvement of the Bills; which ought to be approved by all good Christians, and Common Wealthsmen. And this may be further supported by the Judicious. Opinion of Sir *Edward Coke* in his Tenure by Rents, [and indeed in some sense all our Lands are Rent Tenure-Lands; as we owe and must pay for them an Annual Income to Church and State] Therefore [according to Sir *Edward*] If Trade and Commerce be maintained, so that our Native Commodities, and Produce of our Country, which are Rich, Necessary, and Costly Things; without which we cannot possibly subsist; If these be holden up at a good Rate; and be kept salable at such a Value, that the Labourer and Farmer may make a clear Profit by them, then may Tenants do their Duty to their Landlords the better; and they themselves live like Men.

Object. *But does not this hurt all Salary Men by keeping up the Prices of our own Produce?*

Answer 1. *The Country has by the Money Medium, and the Indians, been kept, near Fourty Years in low Circumstances, to what they might have attained to, if they had had better Neighbours, and a better Medium of Trade.* And many Precincts have been set off, &c. Such Things have without Doubt kept the Salary at a lower Ebb, &c. But howsoever,

2. *As the Money was to blame for setting the Salaries so low in the time of its Government; so let the Salaries now Rise proportionably by the good Fortune of the Bills; then none can complain of ill Usage*

Usage, from any Baulk on the first Terms of Settlement.

5. As we are in this present attempt, trying whether we cant find that the Bills are truly and justly par with Money ; so we set the Scales even, and weigh Right without doubt we shall. And for this end, or in computing the true Value of the Bills we must distinguish. (1) Between a full Stock of Money, and noMoney at all, or that which is next to none. And this you will find to make a great odds in theCase. For if there be noMoney, or that which is next to none in our Country ; & we infer that the Bills are of no Value, because they wont purchase Money ; or really are of no more Value, but only of so much as they will in Fact procure in Money ; this is a very corrupt and fallacious Method, in adjusting between Money & the Bills. Yet so far as I can perceive, this is accounted, the Crime, and Ground of Process against the Bills. That is to say, because the Bills will not now purchase Shilling for Shilling, and Pound for Pound, in good Dry Money, Pieces of Eight, at Seventeen-penny-half-penny-weight, *Therefore the Sentence is past, that they must be Burnt, as tho' they were State Hereticks* ; whenas there is not a Shilling to be seen or heard of in ordinary Commerce or Conversation.

But, *Gentlemen !* By this kind of Judicature you may Indict Gold and Silver for Insignificant Fools ; or empty Cyphers, in the Affairs of Mankind ; and affirm that this Silver Money has quite lost its Value, and is become good for nothing. For that the time was a Man may say, that I could have bought good Wheat at *Four Shillings* in Money per Bushel, and now its all gone out of Town and Country ; that if I would give *Forty Shillings* for a Peck I can't get it. Oh this Silver Money is worth nothing at all. Now, *Gentlemen!* This is the great, meritorious, and

strongest

ftrongeft Plea, as you fuppofe for the Condemnation, and Execution of the Bills. i. e. They muft go to Pot, and be all Burnt, becaufe forfooth, the Money is all Run away. This is the true State of our Prefent Cafe. But it is a very Corrupt Judgment [by fuch Pleas] is drawn up againft the Bills. For in our own Experience when the Money was moft plentiful the Bills were equal, and in many Inftances fuperiour to the Money, as has been faid. And do but Reduce your Money again, bring it on to the Spot; and I will hold you a wager of *Five Hundred Pounds*, the Bills fhall in our ordinary Way of Trade and Commerce be of higher Value and Eftimation then the Money; Only you fhall be Bound, to oblige the Money to keep at home as honeftly and conftantly as the Bills do. Thus it is in *Holland* and in *Venice*, Examples which I fhall make farther ufe of by and by.

Therefore Good Sirs] Dont be rafh againft your Bills, leaft you Kill the beft Servant you ever had, without fufficient and legal Evidence, for if you do, it will be a kind of Murder; and may be, will be repented of when it is too late.

(2.) *We muft alfo in the Decifion of this Queftion diftinguifh upon the Qualifications of Communities and Governments, and what follows upon the Difference between them.* And *Imprimis*, we muft Confider in our own Cafe; that we are not only a Dependent Government in our civil Relation to the Crown of *England*; But alfo in fome Degree we are a Dependent Merchandize on the fame Kingdom; neither as to our Trade can we be other wayes till we are come to a greater perfection in our Manufactures. Therefore Men may Talk of Shortning our *Britifh* Trade whilft they are Weary; and upbraid us with our Finery,&c. which are Theams more proper for Pulpits then Statefmen to Talk of [for what were Ingenious Myfteries,&Inventions dignified for with Lawrells For

working

working Wood, Iron, Brass, Leather, &c., into Fine
Coaches and Chariots, and Horses as Fine and Proud
as they, suited to them; why were these made, &c?
And turning glittering Earth, and glutinous matter
of Worms into Embroderies, &c. But to furnish a
Generous People, that would Banish sordidness, and
live Bright and Civil, with fine Accomplishments a-
bout them?] Therefore I say, if we will Live upon
Ground-Nuts and Clams, and Cloath our Backs with
the Exuviæ, or Pelts of Wild Beasts, we may then
lower our Expences a great Pace; and renounce this
Branch of our Merchandize; but if we intend to Live
in any Garb, or Port, as becomes a People of Religion,
Civility, Trade and Industry, then we must still supply our selves from the Great Fountain; but yet the
pressing necessity under this head, always has and always will keep us short of Money; for there is nothing
better for Returns, nor more pleasing (not only to our
Correspondents, but to our Superintendants rather;
and so to our Great and Kingly Owners at home) than
our Money as it comes to hand; and therefore away
it has and must go; yet this Defect in our State of
Being is well enough supplyed by our Bills; but
only as to those who are Enemies to them, they take
some seeming Advantage against them by our want of
Money; as under the Antecedent Illustrations, and also under this present head; It makes way for them
to keep up many small Scandals against our Bills;
for upon every odd and unlucky accident in Commerce, all must be attributed to the Bills, they must
bear the blame; and especially where the Prices are
higher then usual. For if one ask's [tho' it be in a
time of great Drought] something more for the Butter and Cheese; presently the Buyer, [if a Back-friend
to the Bills] flies out against the Bills, as tho' there
would never be good Days till they are all Burnt. Or
if we Sell our Pumpions, Squashes, or Apples a little
                                                    dearer

dearer, [tho' the Grand reason may be from the Worms and Buggs that Devour our Trees and Vines, &c. Yet] it must be all attributed to the deficiency of the Bills : Oh these Bills will quite undoo us by hoisting up the Markets! &c. Whenas if our Money was in our Country in equal proportions with our Bills, it would be the same in all our Trade : Nay the Bills would be preferable to the Money; for thus it is in *Holland*, and *Venice*, where they have as much nay more Money than they have Bills. And the Reason of it is as bright as the light at noon Day. For that they are altogether Independent as in their Government; so in their Merchandize, that when in their Trade Gold and Silver comes to them as the chance may be; they are under no awe or Obligation to any Foreign and Kingly Merchants to drain them [from any necessity] of that Specie; therefore their Money is Colleague with their Bills, and Dwells as intirely at home as tho' a Prisoner; and yet is in all Mens hands, &c. and equal in Commonness with the Bills; and yet the Bills in *Holland* are *Three Pounds per Cent* better than Money, and in *Venice,* 20 l. But the Case is quite otherways with us, as has been fairly Distinguished, and that is because, we have no Money at all; and if we get it we can't keep it, in our present Capacity.

Therefore Good *Gentlemen*! Out of Love to your Country, and the Civil Well-being of it, Ponder these things Wisely; and be perswaded to keep up your noble Fund; keep it full; and full enough, which so suits your Climate, and your Circumstances; And abate all Prejudice against so noble and wise a Projection, as your Bills comprehend, and then your Bills will be as good as Money.

6. *In favour to our Bills, we must not Compute their Destiny from any silly Instances, of such a Nature, which we may chance to pick up in the World.*

World. As why need we fret and plague our felves, with the Recitation, or by Objections raifed from *South-Carolina*'s Fate orFolly ? as tho' it was to be an infallibleRule o Prediction,for us to foretell what would happen to our Bills and Commerce becaufe it has happened to theirs. For altho' the People or Government of that Colony, have made theinfelves Ridiculous by Emitting of Bills of Credit ; and had neither Prudence nor Courage enough amongft them to fecure their Coftly Projection, from being more then a *Fools-Bauble ?* What's that to us ? Ours at the worft of Times ; and under their greateft Misfortunes, they have been reduced to ; have done, not only the Bufinefs they came about ; but a World more ; and have gone beyond the Expectations of our Wife Projectors ; and have all along kept a very good Port, Currency and Eftimation among all Men. And tho' the Produce of our Country has rifen under their influence, to the incouragement of the Oppreffed Farmer, yet have not been fo proftituted by the Folly or Knavery of any, but that they have kept up a great Credit, and Currency to this Day. And therefore notwithftanding any fuch' debauch'd Example in the World, any Rational Man, from what has been, and what is, may eafily infer what will be. *viz.* That our Bills will be the Beft Medium we can have ; and finally to gain our Conclufion, without leaving any room to Doubt.

7. *Let us look upon our Publick Bills thro' fuch Bright and Manly Examples as we have derived to us (not from Fools) but from the Wife & Prudent, in the Management of the Affairs of this Life.*

1. Init. *New-York Colony has kept up the Value of their Bank Bills, equal with their Money.* This has been done by their Prudence ; and not from any intrinfick Value, either in their Bills or in their Bank: Ours are as Valuable in themfelves as theirs. For tho'
our

our Bills are not Founded in Money ; yet are supported by the Publick Faith ; and derive from a Land Security, which is better then Money, from its certainty, or immutability. So that the Credit of their Bills is owing to their wife Conduct ; for they all know the formal Diftinctions between Silver and Bills as thofe at *Carolina*, or as we do, tho' poffibly they had fome advantage above us, in not much altering the Prices of their own Produce ; from their Climate, Soyle, Intervale River Lands, and Indian Labourers, &c. whence they Raife all forts of the Provifion Species cheaper then we can : for we being crowded fo much nearer the Pole ; and our Indians being moft of them killed off, that would work for 9 *d.* or 10 *d.* per Day, our Farmers muft be indulged fome grains of allowance upon a Crefis to rife in their Prices, which poffibly the other Colony has not done, &c.

2. Inft. *The Banks in Europe, with the Bills of Credit for the fupport of Commerce have been very Profitable.* I fhall in a fpecial manner infift upon the Bank of the Republick of *Venice.* Under Divine Providence the *Venetians* owe their prefent good Fortune, Strength and Gory in a peculiar Degree, to their Bank Bills. They are a People, who have ruifed themfelves, from a Company of Unfortunate Mortals, who to efcape from the extremity of their Condition purfuing them on the Continent, fell upon the broken Banks, or Iflets, at the upper end of the Adriatick Sea, many Ages ago ; where they Built their Town, now become the Famous City of *Venice.*

And after fome time they Projected a *Bank of Credit*, to Support them in their Settlements of Trade. And in a peculiar fenfe by this means, &c. are become one of the moft Splendid People on Earth ; And are able both by Sea and Land to vie it with the Great Turk ; and now ftand on that fide of the World, a firm Barrier to Chriftendom, againft that haughty Infidel.
Their

Their Bills of Publick Credit have been exceeding serviceable in supporting their Worldly Affairs : And yet possibly, for some scores, if not for some hundreds of Years, have not kept one Ducket in their Publick Treasury to keep up the Credit of them.

Take the following account from a Credible Author relating to this Affair, viz.

Bills wherever Banks have been erected (tho' Money Banks) always have been of better Value than Money in Specie.

Whereof three Reasons may be given.

1. Reason. *For the ease of Compting, and Carriage; and preventing Damage to the receiver by Counterfeit, Clipped, Light or Base Coin, (which is obvious to all.*)

2. Reason. *For Safety in Travelling, Laying up, &c. as visible as the other.*

3. Reason. *For the Advantage that is to be made by the Exchange, on the account of such conveniencies.* - Whereof take two Examples, viz.

1. Example. *The Bank Bills of Holland, are ordinarily better than Money, by at least Three Pounds per Cent.* And,

2. Examp. *Those in Venice by Twenty Pounds per Cent.* And Laws are made there to keep them from rising higher ; for they were once at 28*l.* per Cent. and not without some difficulty reduced to Twenty. So that Each Bill of 100 *l.* is now Current at 120 *l.*

Object. *But how is that possible or Credible ?*

Ans. There is this Account rendered of it (which has confirmation by many other Instances that might be given concerning the current Prices of many Commodities, which have not so much of intrinsick Value in them)' viz. The State of *Venice* Propounded the Erecting a Bank to consist of *Two Millions of Duckets* (comprehending *Six Hundred Thousand Pounds*) accordingly Monies were brought in ; and Bills given
out

out for the fame Value ; and a ftop put to the receiving in, or giving out any more of either.   The ufefulnefs of thefe Bills was fuddenly found to be fuch in the practice, and employment of them, upon the three forementioned Accounts, that every Man at one time or another, found his Affairs required them ; fo that at firft fuch Bills would not be parted with for Money, under *Ten Shillings* per *Hundred Pounds :* And no fooner was that become the Current Rate ; but they were fucceffively raifed, by *Ten Shillings* at a time, till they came to be in every ones Eftimation 28 *l.* per Cent. better than Money in Specie ; and fo paffed accordingly.   Whereupon the State of *Venice* Enacted feveral Laws againft their paffing fo high, which failing to accomplifh what was Required ; at length they conceived it neceffary,   in order to the bringing down the Price, to propofe the giving forth Bills, for *Three Hundred Thoufand Duckets* more, By which, means they brought it back to *Twenty Pounds* per Cent. (which pleafed the People) And then fixt it, from rifing higher afterwards by a fevere Law. Since when, it ftands fo to this day : and this is no more than what is familiar in the Price of other things, *viz.* Diamonds, Rubies, Pearls, Horfes, Pictures, &c. which have their Eftimation from the various Pleafures and Fancies of Men, &c.

And if it be demanded, *What induced that State to allow it fo high ?*

The Anfwer is eafy : *viz.* The State of *Venice* had male ufe of the Monies Depofited, in their Publick Occafions, (where obferve the Hazard of a Money Bank,) and having promifed for Satisfaction of Creditors, to raife the like Sum, if they fhould have occafion for it, they Reap this Advantage of their Peoples high Opinion of the Bills, that they are thereby affured, that never will any Creditor come to ask them a 100 *l.* for a Bill of a 100 *l.* when he may have a 120 *l.* from
                                                           another

another hand. A notable way to pay a Vast Debt. But by means hereof, the Creditor has no other Fund, or Security but the States Word: for there is not one Ducket for them in the Bank.

Now *Gentlemen!* Let me Pray you, with Sedateness of Thought to peruse and think over these Noble and Famous Examples, in the Affairs and Wise Managements of Civil States.

Consider the Men, the Means, and Concommitants, Consequents and Eff. cts which follow, &c. and distinguish well, and like true lovers of your Country, and I am ready peremptorily to conclude, you will discern, that these Examples now laid before you, carry in their Aspect Good and Happy Omens towards us; And that if we are not under invincible Prejudice, or sunk into Despair: but are yet capable of receiving influence for our Civil and Temporal Good; we must needs by such Examples, and from the deep Wisdom, State-Reason, and Policy in them, be raised to a Masculine Resolution, to make use of the like Means, for the vast Benefit of us, and ours: And why not from Generation to Generation, (and that without Foggling) as the Renowned *Venice* has done ? Unless we suspect we shall grow too Rich, too Great and Powerful !

1. Confider *Persons*; *And I cannot think, but you will allow, so far as Imagination is necessary in raising the Glory, and value of a thing, the People of this Province are as capable as any other* : For that certainly we carry as much of the *Lapis Aurificus*, or *Philosophers Stone* in our heads, and can turn other matter into Silver or Gold by the Power of thought as soon as any other People, or else I must own I have not yet Learnt the Character of my Country. And you may observe the *Venetians* did a great deal, in this Important Business, by the power of a wise Imagination.   But,

2. *As*

2. *As to Means, & the Reality of things; we have as good a Medium, & as well adjusted as theirs.* For we are upon as sure a Bottom, and (as our Author suggests) much surer, than they. For that our Bills are upon a Land fund, or security, and the Publick faith to Defend it; and the Government to manage it, to regulate, and see that every thing shall be done in the issue and termination, as becomes a wise Government. Then where is there any room left for Baffling, Doubting or Hesitation, where Men have any Love for their Country, and a Publick Spirit in them.

3. *As to Effects, Consequents, Concomitants, &c.* They are very numerous, in every State relating to this Subject; and in Times, Places and Examples very Differing, &c.

As to our own Concerns, to pass all other Remarks, this is an attendant on our State, &c. viz. A Medium of Trade it must be had, its indispensibly necessary; our Money, that little we had is gone; we have had long Experience of the usefulness and profit of the Paper Medium; as has been said: It does all our Business, hurts no Man, but blesses all Men (but what is purely Accidental, &c.) The whole Country in this Projection have been Owners (by their own Creation) of a Better, and more valuable Treasure, and of clearer Profit in the use and management of their Bills: than the Mines of *Mexico* are to the *Spaniards*, were these last obliged to make good all out-sets.

We have possibly from the first Projection Exhibited half a Million in Bills of Credit: It is a mighty Estate, and acquired with little or no Cost. Whereas if those who work upon the Mines in *Peru* & *Mexico*, were allowed but a Bisket-Cake for Provisions, and a Penny a Day for Wages, they would run the Crown and Owners deeply in Debt, as is Reported. That certainly Our Mine, which we work upon is Richer than theirs: for that we can cleanse Ours from the Oar,
and

Run it into Coin, at about *Fifty Shillings* per Thoufand Pound.   And if so, suppose we cannot bring our
Bills up so high as *Venice* has theirs, nor reach to the
rigorous Value which our own Money has ftood at ?
Yet notwithftanding we may venture by the Power of
Thought to conclude them in our own Concerns, to
be as good yea better than Money.   For we muft
confider, our Med um is our own ; it coft us little or
nothing : And yet will keep us Loyal and Obedient to
our PRINCE. by (cheartully) Supporting Church and
State.   And alfo Juft and Equal in our Trade and
Dealings one with another ; And make us Great, Rich
and Flourifhing in our Outward Affairs : And what
can any Medium do more tor any People ?

II. QUESTION.

WE now come to Examine into the Second Grand
Queftion. Scil. By whom may a BANK OF
CREDIT be managed, moft to the Advantage of this
Province ?

Anfwer, The Anfwer is in Two Parts.

1 Part, *Relates to the Publick.* It is very apparent, that thofe who have had the Management of
the Bank hitherto, have done it well; They have in
their great Wifdom faved and fupported their Country ; and why fhould any Men meditate a new Miniftry, for this Great Truft ? For that there be very
forcible Reafons why the Country and Government,
fhould keep it in their own Hands.   As, (1) It is
agreable with the Examples of other Wife Governments ; who for their Wifdom, Conduct, and Succefs
are worthy of our Imitation; as *Holland, Venice,
New-York, &c.* Tho' its true, (*Exempla Illuftrant,
Quamvis non Reftringunt,*) fuch things informs us,
but do not always bind us,' &c. (2) The Profit accruing by a Loan Bank feems moft reafonable it fhould
                                                          be

be to the Publick; thereby every one has a proportionable fhare of the Income. (3) Where Money (as in our Cafe) is not to be had, to Support the Government; the Government muft of neceffity, Annually Emit fuch a Number of Bills, as will Anfwer the Publick Charge, both in Peace and War. For to do it by the Corn, and Provifion Specie, it will foon be found intollerable: For that when the Bills are Emitted and Circulate, it will be an eafe to Officers, and alfo to the People, &c. for every Man may pay his Affefsment, as he fits in his Chair; he need never Tackel up his Team to tranfport his Burthenfome Loads to the Seat of Government; and when it comes there, poffibly it muft lye, and fat the Rats and Mice, whilft it waits for a Market, &c. Now under this Prefumption that the Government will think it beft to keep our Bills in their own proper Bufinefs; if a Bank be Erected by Private Gentlemen, this will occafion various forts of Money in our Country, and this may be as the Cholick in our Bowels; or occafion many Inconveniencies in ours Affairs: And therefore it feems far Beft for the Publick to hold all in their own hands. (4) A Loan Bank Erected by the Country, as ours at prefent is; it muft always be founded and Supported by the Lands of particular Gentlemen, and in this fenfe, it is really and truly a Private Bank, both as to the Matter, and the Perfons involved. And thofe Men who run that venture, and thereby difperfe the whole Fund, for the Advance of the Publick Trade, as well as for their own Profit, muft needs be efteemed great Benefactors to the Publick; and to treat them with any thing that looks like Surprize, or Tricking, will not be Honourable, nor agreeable with Wifdom, if any mifchance fhould happen, &c. This is to fignify that thefe are the Men that lye at Stake, and are only in hazard. For thofe who take the Bills in the Circulation of them, have the Publick Faith to reft upon, and the Authority of the Government ; which have taken sufficient Pawns for Security in the Lands Depofited, &c. So that the Poffeffors of the Bills are fecure and out of Danger. Yet alfo in the management of the Projection in this way, confidering the Temper, Wifdom and Power of the Miniftry which has the Care of the Bank, yiz. *The Government :* they will better Umpire all Cafes, and do every thing that is Equal, Right, and full of Clemency to the Bankers, who are moft in danger, as well as fee Juftice done to other Men, &c. Whenas poffibly a Private Bank (properly fo confidered) may not be fo fafe on all fides : There may be more danger of Partiality, Collufions, Fraud, and thereby plunging or fnapping Mens Eftates, put into a Private Bank, upon fome Innuendo's, Niceties, or Punctilio's in Law, at leaft it may feem fo to fome, &c. That upon a Prefumption that the Publick fhall think meet to continue the Bank under their own Management ; it muft needs be allowed by all to be, and remain in very Good, nay in the Beft of Hands.   But yet,

II. Part.

AS to a Private Bank (peculiarly fo confidered) there be very good reafons to be given why a particular Company of fuitable Gentlemen, fhould be Intrufted with fuch a Grand Affair for the fervice of a Country. (*Scil.* Under the Infpection of the Government, &c.) That is to fay, In our Cafe, if our Country and Government find their own Bank (as to their Apprehenfion, &c.) is fateagued, with fome fuch incumberments, and inconfiftences, that they neither can, nor will difpence with. As to Inftance, firft in the lofs of the Money, they cant bear it, but will try for the Recovering of it, &c. And alfo, as to the value of the Bills ; they will not be contented to

fet

set down with the decision that common Trade, and Commerce has hitherto made on this Point. For says abundance of Men (and may be very wise Men too!) let every Body say what they will, and with their fine flourishes Palliate the matter : Yet its Plain enough, the Money has been two hard for the Bills, and apparently has made a Fool of them : And tho' the Bills have kept the House ; and the Money is gone from home ; as tho' it had been turned out of Doors for a wrangler ; yet the Bills have not done their Office fully, or played their part as was intended : And they are so qualified in their own Nature ; and so soft and apt to warp, that no Government can so stiffen them, but when all is said and done as can be, they will remain, but a leaden rule in measuring Exchanges, &c. And therefore the Country is resolved to call in all out-standing Bills, and in convenient time dissolve their Bank ; and try for the Money Medium ; for that there be abundance of Men, that have these Idea's, *Scil*. Let the Bills be all Burnt ; and the Money will come. Now, if we are reduced to such a notion of things ; and to such a Resolution ; there is then, apparently very great, and strong Pleas, why a particular Company of Gentlemen should erect a Bank of Credit ; for that it is very plain, upon the foresaid Hypothesis, such a Projection will no ways hinder, but help and bring to Birth the foresaid Resolutions and hopes ; but to throw up the present Fund, and leave all our Affairs open to chance and hap-hazzard ; without substituting another for the sake of a Medium, will be to murder our Temporal Business ; and at once undo our selves. So that if the Country is quite heart sick with their own measures ; I am very well assured, upon a very good Argument, that a Private Bank shall cure them, and do every thing to their Satisfaction. I shall with all convenient Brevity, offer a few Preliminary Thoughts Relating to the present

fent Subject ; and then point at Perfons proper to be
intrufted with the Affair ; and the Reafons of it.

1. A Few preliminary Thoughts, wherein I fhall
diftinguifh between a Publick and Private Bank. Viz.
*Imprimis, A Publick Bank of Credit, is fomewhat
Precarious ; yet it carries a vaft Bounty with it to
thofe Countries who have the Wifdom to give it an
Honourable Reception : But to others it is but a
Common Plague.* There be Two Principles abfolutely
needful to preferve it in a Country, viz. Prudence,
and a Publick Spirit in Head Men of Eftates ; if fuch
Men will but wifely govern their Private Interefts in
favour of it ; they will foon fhackle other Mens ;
and Bridle their Reculancy, and bring them to conformity. A Wife Government may Project, but it is
Wife and Great Men under Government, that muft
Cultivate fuch a Projection, for a Publick Good.
Therefore where the Principal Men of Eftates and
Trade will become Patrons, (tho' not perfonally involved) this will fupport it. I do imagine the formal Reafon not of the Being, but of the Profperous
and Flourifhing State, of thofe Famous Banks (that
have been mentioned) owe for their Glory, to this
Temper of Mind, in the Principal Gentlemen of the
feveral Countries, where they were Erected.

That is thus. At the firft Commencement and O-
pening of thofe Funds, we muft imagine, thefe Men
payed a great Veneration to the Bills : And there being a Trade going forward, peculiarly under their
Management ; and alfo many Credits, and Bonds for
Lawful Money, againft other Men, &c. It was after
this manner, &c. [1] As to their Trade, when Men
come to buy a Supply with the Bills ; they accommo-
date them at the Old Money Price, and take the Bills
without Higling or making any diftinction, &c. And
(2.) As to their Bonds, and Obligations for Specialties

ties, when the Debtor comes ; poſſibly he inquires. Sir ! there is a Bond of *One Thouſand Duckats* in your hands againſt me, will you take Bank Bills ? Reply, *Bank Bills Man* ! There's nothing will ſuit me better than Bank Bills : For I muſt tell you, I have that high Opinion of the Bills, that I will abate part of my Intereſt, if you will clear thereſt, and the whole Principal by the Bills. I do aſſure you my good Friend, and you may tell it to all your Neighbours, that we in the Merchandize do prefer the Bills above the Money, &c. Now ſuch a prudent Temper Circulating, and Inſluencing the Principal Members of ſuch a Grand Community, will ſoon become a Law for all other Men, &c. Thus it has been in *Holland, Venice, New-York, &c.*

But on the other hand, Where the Bills have gone up and down and been Ridiculed. Its owing to head Men and Men of Fortune, *Avice Verſâ*, &c. In *France, Sweedland, and South-Carolina,* &c. Now, it ſeems to me plain that if thoſe Civil powers or States that have ſtood and look't on and ſeen their Noble Projections for the Advance of Trade trampled upon, and could not poſſibly prevent the Proſtitution, if they had (I ſay) when they diſcerned things lapſing into ſuch Confuſion, Reſigned the Management of the Bank to principle & ſuitable Gentlemen, or turned their publick into a private Bank ; they might have eaſily Recovered the Glory and Sufficiency of their Bank, &c. Eſpecially if ſupporting and Reinforcing the Bequeſtment with due Sanctions. As, (1.) That the profit, ſhall be fixed in the Truſtees, &c. (2.) That the Government inſpect, &c. (3.) That the Bills ſhall be held as Current and Lawful Money, in anſwering all Aſſeſments, and alſo in diſcharging all Creditors, to the Publick, as their own Bills, &c. And tho' in this Method, the ſenſible prcfit ſeems a Booty

to

to some, particular Men ; but the General Good by keeping up a valuable Medium for all Business, is as equally beneficial to all Men in common, as tho' done by the Government. So it will hold in any Example in the World; as I imagine, and so in our own Case; where there is found, such defects as cannot be Remedied otherways, &c.

2. *The Persons to be Intrusted, must be Men of known Integrity, of Real Estates, Good influence, and Considerable Trade.*

A Convenient Company of such Men imbodied by a Charter from the Government, &c. may Manage a Bank of Credit, as matters may be Circumstanced, better than the Publick Government ; *viz.* when things are out of Joynt, as in *France*, &c. and as some think in our own Case in some degree; as has been said, &c. I say such Men by their Example, and wise Management can do more to bring things right, and keep them so ; then all the Menaces, Penal Laws, or Wisdom of a Government. I have not yet understood that the King of *Sweeden*, with all his bigg and Majestick Looks, or Imperial Orders, could ever Rescue his Bank Bills from the Contempt they met with in his Common Markets. Now I say, it appears to me, that there may be such Gentlemen involved in this Affair, who can (upon the aforesaid Presumptions) do more than the Government, or any regular Monarch on Earth. I shall just point at such Men as are proper in this Case. Scil. Landed Men, &c. Great Merchants, who (tho' worth many Thousands) keep the main of their Personal Estate, stirring in a way of Trade, & Merchandize, both in their own and other Countries. Also such other Gentlemen, Men of great Estates, and of great Wisdom, who tho' they keep up a very Considerable Trade, and Merchandize, yet let out much at Interest ; and as their Gains this way, is less,

fo

ſo alſo is their Riſque: There is a ſort of Wiſe and very Prudent Men, that are a kind of *Amphibious* beings who live in both Elements, Land and Water, theſe are Eminently Qualified, as Members for a Private Bank. And alſo Rich Farmers, and Mechannicks, Men of Character, and Influence (according to their Sphere) in the Places where they live. The main of theſe Men muſt belong to our *Metropolis*, and other Sea-Ports and Towns of Trade, and others to be diſperſed thro' the Province. A Convenient Company of ſuch Perſons ſo Qualified, and Incorporated, I do Imagine, ſhall be capable to carry on a Bank of Credit with greateſt Advantage, with an Immenſe good and Benefit to the Publick. For now being intruſted by the Government with the Outward happineſs, well-being, and flouriſhing State of their Country ; being alſo inſtituted, not meerly for their own Private Intereſt ; but to promote the Publick Good, they muſt needs act in ſuch a Sphere in ſome proportion like the Government it ſelf ; as being now become Publick Benefactors, and Common Fathers to their Country ; and being Men of Noble and Great minds ; muſt and will conſult the Good of other Men, as well as their own. And that ſuch a Community are capable of doing great Service in this Affair, is obvious from the following Reaſons.

3. *The Reaſons are,*

1. *Reaſon.* For that this Company of Gentlemen can Regulate the Prices of all Things Yearly in the common courſe of Trade, and Commerce. The wild and inſulting Prices of Things have ruined the Foreign Banks, &c. And poſſibly ſomething of this Nature has been a Deminution to our own, &c. Now there is a ſovereign Remedy provided in this Projection, againſt ſuch an inconveniency, and miſchief. For by the Wiſdom, Precautions, and Example of theſe Men, they will

will thereby conduct all such Points, as tho' Contro'= lers and absolute Masters of the Market, and yet hurt no Mans Property, or Infringe Liberty; and hereby Equity in Commerce will be better upheld; Excessive Demands suppressed; the Honour and Credit of the Medium maintained; And the Just and Reasonable gains and profits of all Men suited and secured. For we must further note, that they are Men of differing Functions, and their own Interests, as well as Honour, Wisdom and Honesty, will oblige them always to steer right, and do well for other Men; for if they hurt others, they hurt themselves. And no Man need suspect or fear, no not a Knave, much less a wife and honest Man under this head. For that it is a very sure Maxim, viz. *Self Interest will neither Cheat or Lye : For that this is the String in the Nose (thro' the World) which governs the Creature.*

2. *Reason.* For that this Projection will both keep up the Value, and also the Circulation of the Bills; and in a great Measure prevent hoarding for the future, and correct it at the present. I am not so seen into the Capacity, State, Produce, Trade, and Business of my Country, as to be Peremtory; yet do imagine, that our Medium at this Day, as to our outstanding Bills, is not near Sufficient for the whole Trade of this Country, and a great part of them, possibly is confined. Some Men it is very probable, do according to their Usage, their Income, and Trade, Annually yielding a considerable Surplusage, to what they have occasion to pass away (Lay it up) till Opportunity presents to Let it out at Interest, &c. This seems to make some stop, or divert the common stream. But many others (as some Men Jealous) keep close what they can lay Hands on, for a peculiar Market. And its well if more then one Third of our Supply and present Stock is not stopt by this means, like Stagnate Waters, is

in Pits and Mud-holes. And I doubt there be a great
many Men, fubtile in Bufinefs, who by their Politick
Meafures, makeGoods do, when they fhould rather pafs
away Bills, that they may keep Circulating, &c. But
however when the Principal Men of our Country,
fhall be involved in the management abovefaid, fuch
things will in likelihood be folved, &c. and fo the
Common Fountain will, as indeed it fhould, always
move and Circulate, like the Main Ocean. This great
Body was Ordained, to fupply the Earth with
Showers; with Rivers, and fmaller Streams, for the
fatisfying the Thirft, and nourifhment of every living
Thing : Even the Plants, Birds and Worms, are fupported by its Bounty; and then the Tributary Clouds,
and Springs repay themfelves to the Seas. So it fhould
be in our Cafe, and the means propofed, carries fuch
a profpect with it, that the future, and alfo the prefent
State of things for Hoards, will foon diffolve upon
fuch an inftitution, or furrender.

3. *Reafon.* From the Capacity that many Hundreds of the Kings very Good and Loyal Subjects are
reduced to, in their Temporal Affairs, upon a confidence in the Paper Medium, and the Continuation of
it; *That to Supprefs it will be attended with many
Grievances.* Therefore Quære, *Whether the Mouth
of Æolus his Cave, is not here or hereabouts?* And
tho' it be, the Projection offered, will certainly fhut,
and bolt the Door, and Divert all that is portentous
from that Quarter.

4. *Reafon.* Finally, For that this Projection will
be a Remedy, for that which many Men groan under
as our greateftMisfortune; unlefs theCafe is abfolutely Defperate; and if fo, all Men muft be Refigned;
but otherways, this is the only, and proper Method,
to fetch home our Money; and to keep it when we
have

have got it : And this you suppose will help all Cases? I say if it be practicable, or within the Reach of honest Men's Art, and Wisdom to recover the *Silver* for the use of this Province, this is the way to do it. For hereby your Merchants, and most Potent Men in such Business, will come under Obligations to do what is in their Power, in Order to it. And there is none can do it (or so much as pretend to it) But themselves. For as in Domestick Interests, it is a common saying, that a Man must ask his Wife whether he shall be Rich ? So in this Case, we must ask our Merchants, whether we shall have our Money Medium, yea, or no ? It is certain we are happy, in a Celebrated, Wise and Powerful Government ; who can do very Great Things, being Endowed with a Civil Omnipotency, but they cannot help us in this point. When we had our *Money*, they did all they could ; they Enacted frightful and penal Laws ; Erected Walls, and set their Guards to Confine it ; but could not keep it ; and now its gone cannot command it back again.

Or may we imagine, that the Fish will bring us in according as it is computed, *Fifty Thousand Pounds*; and should it do so, and much of it in *Money ?* we must observe, that the Merchants have a peculiar Dominion over this Valuable Staple. And the Outlet is vast, (as Salt, Rigging, &c, Provisions, Sea-Stores Craft, and what not) and all is from the Merchant, &c. that if the Money comes, it must needs fall into the Merchants hands, as the Figgs into the mouth of the Eater, &c.

But you will say, the Merchant must disperse abundance of the Money, he must Live, and Buy Provisions, for the Support of himself & Family. Ah ! Dear Country ! They have so many Subterfuges, and whiprows for a Livelihood that there is no starving them out of their Money, when they have once got it ! may be they will want now and then a few Apples for the Children, or

a

a fat Fowle for the Table, &c. but alafs! they'll often make a Ribbon, or fome fuch pretty thing do, to Coakes the Farmer's Daughter of her Cargo, and fave their Money. And as to the main, of their Cheer, and Maintenance. *Scil.* Their Furniture, their Cloathing, Corn, Flower, Salt Provifion, yea almoft a full fupply, do they know how to fetch by their Merchandize, from other Places and fave their Money, &c. but fuppofe fome confiderable Part, would Circulate; It is always paffing into the Gang way of our Merchants; and they are always upon the Watch, to make their Returns, and this is one of the moft profitable Species to that Purpofe, &c. fo that Money held and Improved upon fuch Terms, is but like a fcramble, catch it who can catch: Or but like a Flock of Wild Fowle much beaten, which is always ready to ftart and be gone, that they are no profitable Game. So I fay fuch a Skittifh parcel of Money, or Money in a Country Improved upon fuch fickle Terms, is moft certainly no Medium to be depended upon, in the Wife management, and fteady carrying on of Bufinefs. So that upon this Suppofition, that the Money may be Recovered and Preferved for our ufe, it muft be done by our Merchants. Thei efore if you are pofitive, and refolved, that you cannot do without the Money, you muft then Oblige your Merchants to fetch it; and when it is comes, they muft keep it for you, and not make Returns with it. But let it go in Copartnerfhip, and as Collea ue with the Bills, for a Medium of Trade, as in *Venice*, &c. And for this end (as things are now ftated) under the fettlement, and Infpeétion of the Government, &c. You muft Refign the Bufinefs of the Bank to them, &c· as has been faid: and this is the moft proper and effeétual Remedy for your help. This will moft certainly Cure us of all difeafes Relating to Trade and Commerce, which we Groan under, and of which we fill the Country with
fuch

such Loud Complaints. Thus I Conclude, wishing any Country all Blessing, and a settled Posture in their Affairs; and that they may fix upon that way and method, in their Temporal Concerns of Trade and Commerce, as will tend most to their Happiness, both for them and theirs, both for the Present and Future Ages.

So GOD Save King GEORGE; Direct His Wise Government, and Bless this Province.

F I N I S.

A MODEST ENQUIRY INTO THE NATURE AND NECESSITY OF A PAPER-CURRENCY

Benjamin Franklin, *A Modest Enquiry into the Nature and Necessity of a Paper-Currency* (Philadelphia, 1729), pp. 1–36.

As the call for paper currency in the colonies was driven by necessity, the primary questions often centred not over whether there should be paper money, but over the organisation of the banks and the provision and protection of paper currency. Most colonies allowed the issue of paper currency with various regulations and degrees of success. In the first non-Massachusetts piece in this volume, Benjamin Franklin addresses the problem from the Pennsylvanian perspective in *A Modest Enquiry into the Nature and Necessity of a Paper-Currency*. Franklin, like many others at this time, argues that paper currency would facilitate trade. Franklin's theory of money draws on William Petty's theory of value and the idea of money as a medium of exchange. Thus, *A Modest Enquiry* provides a good example of an early application of value theory to the practical problems of American economics, raising the contemporary standards of economic analysis in the process. Incidentally, *A Modest Enquiry* proved to be instrumental in Franklin's bid to print the paper currency for Pennsylvania, thus firmly establishing his printing company.

A MODEST

ENQUIRY

INTO THE

Nature and *Neceſſity*

OF A

PAPER-CURRENCY.

―――― *Quid aſper*
Utile Nummus habet ; patriæ, chariſq; propinquis
Quantum elargiri deceat. ―――

Perſ.

PHILADELPHIA
Printed and Sold at the New PRINTING-
OFFICE, near the Market. 1729.

A MODEST

ENQUIRY, &c.

THERE is no Science, the Study of which is more useful and commendable than theKnowledge of the true Interest of one's Country; and perhaps there is no Kind of Learning more abstruse and intricate, more difficult to acquire in any Degree of Perfection than This, and therefore none more generally neglected. Hence it is, that we every Day find Men in Conversation contending warmly on some Point in Politicks, which, altho' it may nearly concern them both, neither of them understand any more than they do each other.

Thus much by way of Apology for this present *Enquiry into the Nature and Necessity of a Paper Currency.* And if any Thing I shall say, may be a Means of fixing a Subject that is now the chief
Concern

Concern of my Countrymen, in a clearer Light, I fhall have the Satisfaction of thinking my Time and Pains well employed.

To proceed, then,

There is a certain proportionate Quantity of Money requifite to carry on the Trade of a Country freely and currently; More than which would be of no Advantage in Trade, and Lefs, if much lefs, exceedingly detrimental to it.

This leads us to the following general Confiderations.

Firft, *A great Want of Money in any Trading Country, occafions Intereft to be at at a very high Rate.* And here it may be obferved, that it is impoffible by any Laws to reftrain Men from giving and receiving exorbitant Intereft, where Money is fuitably fcarce : For he that wants Money will find out Ways to give 10 *per Cent.* when he cannot have it for lefs, altho' the Law forbids to take more than 6 *per Cent.* Now the Intereft of Money being high is prejudicial to a Country feveral Ways : It makes Land bear a low Price, becaufe few Men will lay out their Money in Land, when they can make a much greater Profit by lending it out upon

upon Intereſt : And much leſs will **Men** be inclined to venture their **Money** at Sea, when they can, without **R**iſque or Hazard, have a great and certain **Profit** by keeping it at home ; thus **T**rade is diſcouraged. And if in two Neigbouring Countries the Traders of one, by Reaſon of a greater Plenty of **Money**, can borrow it to trade with at a lower **Rate** than the Traders of the other, they will infallibly have the Advantage, and get the greateſt Part of that **T**rade into their own Hands ; For he that trades with **Money** he hath borrowed at 8 or 10 *per Cent.* cannot hold Market with him that borrows his **Money** at 6 or 4. —— On the contrary, *A plentiful Currency will occaſion Intereſt to be low :* And this will be an Inducement to many to lay out their **Money** in Lands, rather than put it out to Uſe, by which means Land will begin to riſe in Value and bear a better Price : And at the ſame **Time** it will tend to enliven Trade exceedingly, becauſe **P**eople will find more **Profit** in employing their **Money** that Way than in **U**ſury ; and many that underſtand **Buſineſs** very well, but have not a Stock ſufficient of their own, will be encouraged to borrow **Money**

Money to trade with, when they can have it a moderate Intereſt.

Secondly, *Want of Money in a Country reduces the Price of that Part of its Produce which is uſed in Trade:* Becauſe Trade being diſcouraged by it as above, there is a much leſs Demand for that Produce. And this is another Reaſon why Land in ſuch a Caſe will be low, eſpecially where the Staple Commodity of the Country is the immediate Produce of the Land, becauſe that Produce being low, fewer People find an Advantage in Husbandry, or the Improvement of Land. —— On the contrary, *A Plentiful Currency will occaſion the Trading Produce to bear a good Price:* Becauſe Trade being encouraged and advanced by it, there will be a much greater Demand for that Produce; which will be a great Encouragement of Husbandry and Tillage, and conſequently make Land more valuable, fo that many People would apply themſelves to Husbandry, who probably might otherwiſe have ſought ſome more profitable Employment.

As we have already experienced how much the Increaſe of our Currency by what Paper Money has been made, has

encouraged

encouraged our Trade; particularly to inftance only in one Article, *Ship-Building*; it may not be amifs to obferve under this Head, what a great Advantage it muft be to us as a Trading Country, that has Workmen and all the Materials proper for that Bufinefs within itfelf, to have *Ship-Building* as much as poffible advanced: For every Ship that is built here for the *Englifh* Merchants, gains the Province her clear Value in Gold and Silver, which muft otherwife have been fent Home for Returns in her Stead; and likewife, every Ship built in and belonging to the Province, not only faves the Province her firft Coft, but all the Freight, Wages and Provifions fhe ever makes or requires as long as fhe lafts; provided Care is taken to make This her *Pay Port*, and that fhe always takes Provifions with her for the whole Voyage, which may eafily be done. And how confiderable an Article this is yearly in our Favour, every one, the leaft acquainted with mercantile Affairs, muft needs be fenfible; for if we could not Build our felves, we muft either purchafe fo many Veffels as we want from other Countries, or elfe Hire them to carry our Produce to Market, which would

would be more expenfive than Purchafing; and on many other Accounts exceedingly to our Lofs. Now as Trade in general will decline where there is not a plentiful Currency, fo *Ship-Building* muft certainly of Confequence decline where Trade is declining.

Thirdly, *Want of Money in a Country difcourages Labouring and Handicrafts Men (which are the chief Strength and Support of a People) from coming to fettle in it, and induces many that were fettled to leave the Country, and feek Entertainment and Employment in other Places, where they can be better paid.* For what can be more difheartning to an induftrious labouring Man, than this, that after he hath earned his Bread with the Sweat of his Brows, he muft fpend as much Time, and have near as much Fatigue in getting it, as he had to earn it. *And nothing makes more bad Paymafters than a general Scarcity of Money.* And here again is a Third Reafon for Land's bearing a low Price in fuch a Country, becaufe Land always increafes in Value in Proportion with the Increafe of the People fettling on it, there being fo many more Buyers ; and its Value will infallibly be diminifhed, if the Number of of its Inhabitants diminish. —— On the contrary, *A Plentiful Currency will encourage great Numbers of Labouring and Handicrafts Men to come and Settle in the Country,* by the same Reason that a Want of it will discourage and drive them out. Now the more Inhabitants, the greater Demand for Land (as is said above) upon which it must necessarily rise in Value, and bear a better Price. The same may be said of the Value of House-Rent, which will be advanced for the same Reasons; and by the Increase of Trade and Riches People will be enabled to pay greater Rents. Now the Value of House-Rent rising, and Interest becoming low, many that in a Scarcity of Money practised Usury, will probably be more inclined to Building; which will likewise sensibly enliven Business in any Place; it being an Advantage not only to *Brickmakers, Bricklayers, Masons, Carpenters, Joiners, Glaziers,* and several other Trades immediately employ'd by Building, but likewise to *Farmers, Brewers, Bakers, Taylors, Shoemakers, Shop-keepers,* and in short to every one that they lay their Money out with.

Fourthly,

Fourthly, *Want of Money in fuch a Country as ours, occafions a greater Confumption of* Englifh *and* European Goods, *in Proportion to the Number of the People, than there would otherwife be.* Becaufe Merchants and Traders, by whom abundance of Artificers and labouring Men are employed, finding their other Affairs require what Money they can get into their hands, oblige thofe who work for them to take one half, or perhaps two thirds Goods in Pay. By this Means a greater Quantity of Goods are difpofed of, and to a greater Value; becaufe Working Men and their Families are thereby induced to be more profufe and extravagant in fine Apparel and the like, than they would be if they were obliged to pay ready Money for fuch Things after they had eain'd and received it, or if fuch Goods were not impofed upon them, of which they can make no other Ufe : For fuch People cannot fend the Goods they are paid with to a Foreign Market, without lofing confiderably by having them fold for lefs than they ftand 'em in here ; neither can they eafily difpofe of them at Home, becaufe their Neighbours are generally fupplied in the fame Manner ; But how unreafonable would it

be,

be, if fome of thofe very Men who *have been a Means* of thus forcing People into unneceffary Expence, fhould be the firft and moft earneft in accufing them of *Pride and Prodigality.* Now tho' this extraordinary Confumption of Foreign Commodities may be a Profit to particular Men, yet the Country in general grows poorer by it apace. ———— On the contrary, As *A plentiful Currency will occafion a lefs Confumption of* European *Goods, in Proportion to the Number of the People,* fo it will be a means of making the Balance of our Trade more equal than it now is, if it does not give it in our Favour ; becaufe our own Produce will be encouraged at the fame Time. And it is to be obferved, that tho' lefs Foreign Commodities are confumed in Proportion to the Number of People, yet this will be no Difadvantage to the Merchant, becaufe the Number of People increafing, will occafion an increafing Demand of more Foreign Goods in the Whole.

Thus we have feen fome of the many heavy Difadvantages a Country (efpecially. fuch. a Country as ours) muft labour under, when it has not a fufficient Stock of running Cafh to manage its
Trade

Trade currently. And we have likewife feen fome of the Advantages which accrue from having Money fufficient, or a Plentiful Currency.

The foregoing Paragraphs being well confidered, we fhall naturally be led to draw the following Conclufions with Regard to what Perfons will probably be for or againft Emitting a large Additional Sum of Paper Bills in this Province.

1. Since Men will always be powerfully influenced in their Opinions and Actions by what appears to be their particular Intereft: Therefore all thofe, who wanting Courage to venture in Trade, now practife Lending Money on Security for exorbitant Intereft, which in a Scarcity of Money will be done notwithftanding the Law, I fay all fuch will probably be againft a large Addition to our prefent Stock of Paper-Money; becaufe a plentiful Currency will lower Intereft, and make it common to lend on lefs Security.

2. All thofe who are Poffeffors of large Sums of Money, and are difpofed to purchafe Land, which is attended with a great and fure Advantage in a growing Country as this is; I fay, the Intereft of all fuch Men will encline them to oppofe a large

Addition

Addition to our Money. Becaufe their Wealth is now continually increafing by the large Intereft they receive, which will enable them (if they can keep Land from rifing) to purchafe More fome time hence than they can at prefent ; and in the mean time all Trade being difcouraged, not only thofe who borrow of them, but the Common People in general will be impoverifhed, and confequently obliged to fell More Land for lefs Money than they will do at prefent. And yet, after fuch Men are poffeffed of as much Land as they can purchafe, it will then be their Intereft to have Money made Plentiful, becaufe that will immediately make Land rife in Value in *their* Hands. Now it ought not to be wonder'd at, if People from the Knowledge of a Man's Intereft do fometimes make a true Guefs at his Defigns ; for, *Intereft*, they fay, *will not Lie*.

3. Lawyers, and others concerned in Court Bufinefs, will probably many of them be againft a plentiful Currency ; becaufe People in that Cafe will have lefs Occafion to run in Debt, and confequently lefs Occafion to go to Law and Sue one another for their Debts. Tho' I know fome

fome even among thefe Gentlemen, that regard the Publick Good before their own apparent private Intereft.

4. All thofe who are any way Dependants on fuch Perfons as are above mentioned, whether as holding Offices, as Tenants, or as Debtors, muft at leaft *appear* to be againft a large Addition; becaufe if they do not, they muft fenfibly feel their prefent Intereft hurt. And befides thefe, there are, doubtlefs, many well-meaning Gentlemen and Others, who, without any immediate private Intereft of their own in View, are againft making fuch an Addition, thro' an Opinion they may have of the Honefty and found Judgment of fome of their Friends that oppofe it, (perhaps for the Ends aforefaid) without having given it any thorough Confiderarion themfelves. And thus it is no Wonder if there is a *powerful* Party on that Side.

On the other Hand, Thofe who are Lovers of Trade, and delight to fee Manufactures encouraged, will be for having a large Addition to our Currency: For they very well know, that People will have little Heart to advance Money in Trade, when what they can get is fcarce fufficient

fufficient to purchafe Neceffaries, and fupply their Families with Provifion. Much:
lefs will they lay it out in advancing new,
Manufactures ; nor is it poffible new Manufactures fhould turn to any Account,
where there is not Money to pay the
Workmen, who are difcouraged by being
paid in Goods, becaufe it is a great Difadvantage to them.

Again, Thofe who are truly for the
Proprietor's Intereft (and have no feparate Views of their own that are pre-
dominant) will be heartily for a large
Addition : Becaufe, as I have fhewn a-
bove, Plenty of Money will for feveral
Reafons make Land rife in Value exceedingly : And I appeal to thofe immediately concerned for the Proprietor in the
Sale of his Lands, whether Land has not
rifen very much fince the firft Emiffion
of what Paper Currency we now have,
and even by its Means. Now we all
know the Proprietary has great Quantities to fell.

And fince a Plentiful Currency will
be fo great a Caufe of advancing this Province in Trade and Riches, and increafing
the Number of its People ; which, tho' it
will not fenfibly leffen the Inhabitants of
Great

Great Britain, will occasion a much greater Vent and Demand for their Commodities here ; and allowing that the Crown is the more powerful for its Subjects increasing in Wealth and Number, I cannot think it the Interest of *England* to oppose us in making as great a Sum of Paper Money here, as we, who are the best Judges of our own Necessities, find convenient. And if I were not sensible that the Gentlemen of Trade in *England*, to whom we have already parted with our Silver and Gold, are misinformed of our Circumstances, and therefore endeavour to have our Currency stinted to what it now is, I should think the Government at Home had some Reasons for discouraging and impoverishing this Province, which we are not acquainted with.

It remains now that we enquire, *Whether a large Addition to our Paper Currency will not make it sink in Value very much*; And here it will be requisite that we first form just Notions of the Nature and Value of Money in general.

As Providence has so ordered it, that not only different Countries, but even different Parts of the same Country, have their peculiar most suitable Productions ; and

and likewife that different Men have Genius's adapted to Variety of different Arts and Manufactures, Therefore *Commerce*, or the Exchange of one Commodity or Manufacture for another, is highly convenient and beneficial to Mankind. As for Inftance, *A* may be skilful in the Art of making Cloth, and *B* underftand the raifing of Corn ; *A* wants Corn, and *B* Cloth ; upon which they make an Exchange with each other for as much as each has Occafion, to the mutual Advantage and Satisfaction of both.

But as it would be very tedious, if there were no other Way of general Dealing, but by an immediate Exchange of Commodities ; becaufe a Man that had Corn to difpofe of, and wanted Cloth for it, might perhaps in his Search for a Chapman to deal with, meet with twenty People that had Cloth to difpofe of, but wanted no Corn ; and with twenty others that wanted his Corn, but had no Cloth to fuit him with. To remedy fuch Inconveniences, and facilitate Exchange, Men have invented **MONEY**, properly called a *Medium of Exchange*, becaufe through or by its Means Labour is exchanged for Labour, or one Commodity
dity

dity for another. And whatever particular Thing Men have agreed to make this Medium of, whether Gold, Silver, Copper, or Tobacco; it is, to thofe who poffefs it (if they want any Thing) that very Thing which they want, becaufe it will immediately procure it for them, It is Cloth to him that wants Cloth, and Corn to thofe that want Corn; and fo of all other Neceffaries, it *is* whatfoever it will procure. Thus he who had Corn to difpofe of, and wanted to purchafe Cloth with it, might fell his Corn for its Value in this general Medium, to one who wanted Corn but had no Cloth; and with this Medium he might purchafe Cloth of him that wanted no Corn, but perhaps fome other Thing, as Iron it may be, which this Medium will immediately procure, and fo he may be faid to have exchanged his Cloth for Iron; and thus the general Exchange is foon performed, to the Satisfaction of all Parties, with abundance of Facility.

For many Ages, thofe Parts of the World which are engaged in Commerce, have fixed upon Gold and Silver as the chief and moft proper Materials for this Medium; they being in themfelves valuable

luable Metals for their Finenefs, Beauty, and Scarcity. By thefe, particularly by Silver, it has been ufual to value all Things elfe: But as Silver it felf is of no certain permanent Value, being worth more or lefs according to its Scarcity or Plenty, therefore it feems requifite to fix upon Something elfe, more proper to be made a *Meafure of Values*, and this I take to be *Labour*.

By Labour may the Value of Silver be meafured as well as other Things. As, Suppofe one Man employed to raife Corn, while another is digging and refining Silver; at the Year's End, or at any other Period of Time, the compleat Produce of Corn, and that of Silver, are the natural Price of each other; and if one be twenty Bufhels, and the other twenty Ounces, then an Ounce of that Silver is worth the Labour of raifing a Bufhel of that Corn. Now if by the Difcovery of fome nearer, more eafy or plentiful Mines, a Man may get Forty Ounces of Silver as eafily as formerly he did Twenty, and the fame Labour is ftill required to raife Twenty Bufhels of Corn, then Two Ounces of Silver will be worth no more than the fame Labour of raifing One Bufhel of
Corn.

Corn, and that Bufhel of Corn will be as cheap at two Ounces, as it was before at one ; *cæteris paribus.*

Thus the Riches of a Country are to be valued by the Quantity of Labour its Inhabitants are able to purchafe, and not by the Quantity of Silver and Gold they poffefs; which will purchafe more or lefs Labour, and therefore is more or lefs valuable, as is faid before, according to its Scarcity or Plenty. As thofe Metals have grown much more plentiful in *Europe* fince the Difcovery of *America,* fo they have funk in Value exceedingly; for, to inftance in *England,* formerly one Penny of Silver was worth a Days Labour, but now it is hardly worth the fixth Part of a Days Labour ; becaufe not lefs than Six-pence will purchafe the Labour of a Man for a Day in any Part of that Kingdom ; which is wholly to be attributed to the much greater Plenty of Money now in *England* than formerly. And yet perhaps *England* is in Effect no richer now than at that Time ; becaufe as much Labour might be purchas'd, or Work got done of almoft any kind, for 100 *l.* then, as will now require or is now worth 600 *l.*

In

In the next Place let us confider the Nature òf *Banks* emitting *Bills of Credit*, as they are at this Time ufed in *Hamburgh, Amfterdam, London* and *Venice.*

Thofe Places being Seats of vaft Trade, and the Payment of great Sums being for that Reafon frequent, *Bills of Credit* are found very convenient in Bufinefs; becaufe a great Sum is more eafily counted in Them, lighter in Carriage, concealed in lefs Room, and therefore fafer in Travelling or Laying up, and on many other Accounts they are very much valued. The Banks are the general Cafhiers of all Gentlemen, Merchants and great Traders in and about thofe Cities; there they depofite their Money, and may take out Bills to the Value, for which they can be certain to have Money again at the Bank at any Time : This gives the Bills a Credit ; fo that in *England* they are never lefs valuable than Money, and in *Venice* and *Amfterdam* they are generally worth more. And the Bankers always referving Money in hand to anfwer more than the common Run of Demands (and fome People conftantly putting in while others are taking out) are able befides to lend large Sums, on good Security, to
the

the Government or others, for a reasonable Intereſt, by which they are paid for their Care and Trouble; and the Money which otherwiſe would have lain dead in their Hands, is made to circulate again thereby among the People: And thus the Running Caſh of the Nation is as it were doubled; for all great Payments being made in Bills, Money in lower Trade becomes much more plentiful: And this is an exceeding great Advantage to a Trading Country, that is not over-ſtock'd with Gold and Silver.

As thoſe who take Bills out of the Banks in *Europe*, put in Money for Security; ſo here, and in ſome of the neighbouring Provinces, we engage our Land. Which of theſe Methods will moſt effectually ſecure the Bills from actually ſinking in Value, comes next to be conſidered.

Trade in general being nothing elſe but the Exchange of Labour for Labour, the Value of all Things is, as I have ſaid before, moſt juſtly meaſured by Labour. Now ſuppoſe I put my Money into a Bank, and take out a Bill for the Value; if this Bill at the Time of my receiving it, would purchaſe me the Labour of one hundred

hundred Men for twenty Days; but fome
time after will only purchafe the Labour
of the fame Number of Men for fifteen
Days; it is plain the Bill has funk in
Value one fourth Part. Now Silver and
Gold being of no permanent Value; and
as this Bill is founded on Money, and
therefore to be efteemed as fuch, it may
be that the Occafion of this Fall is the
increafing Plenty of Gold and Silver, by
which Money is one fourth Part lefs valuable than before, and therefore one
fourth more is given of it for the fame
Quantity of Labour; and if Land is not
become more plentiful by fome proportionate Decreafe of the People, one fourth
Part more of Money is given for the fame
Quantity of Land, whereby it appears
that it would have been more profitable
to me to have laid that Money out in
Land which I put into the Bank, than to
place it there and take a Bill for it. And
it is certain that the Value of Money has
been continually finking in *England* for
feveral Ages paft, becaufe it has been continually increafing in Quantity. But if
Bills could be taken out of a Bank in
Europe on a Land Security, it is probable
the Value of fuch Bills would be more
certain

certain and steady, because the Number of Inhabitants continue to be near the same in those Countries from Age to Age.

For as Bills issued upon Money Security are Money, so Bills issued upon Land, are in Effect *Coined Land.*

Therefore (to apply the Above to our own Circumstances) If Land in this Province was falling, or any way likely to fall, it would behove the Legislature most carefully to contrive how to prevent the Bills issued upon Land from falling with it. But as our People increase exceedingly, and will be further increased, as I have before shewn, by the Help of a large Addition to our Currency ; and as Land in consequence is continually rising, So, in case no Bills are emitted but what are upon Land Security, the Money-Acts in every Part punctually enforced and executed, the Payments of Principal and Interest being duly and strictly required, and the Principal *bona fide* sunk according to Law, it is absolutely impossible such Bills should ever sink below their first Value, or below the Value of the Land on which they are founded. In short, there is so little Danger of their sinking, that

that they would certainly rife as the Land rifes, if they were not emitted in a proper Manner for preventing it ; That is, by providing in the Act *That Payment may be made, either in thofe Bills, or in any other Bills made current by any Act of the Legiflature of this Province* ; and that the Intereft, as it is received, may be again emitted in Difcharge of Publick Debts; whereby circulating it returns again into the Hands of the Borrowers, and becomes, Part of their future Payments ; and thus as it is likely there will not be any Difficulty for want of Bills to pay the Office, they are hereby kept from rifing above their firft Value : For elfe, fuppofing there fhould be emitted upon mortgaged Land its full prefent Value in Bills; as in the Banks in *Europe* the full Value of the Money depofited is given out in Bills; and fuppofing the Office would take nothing but the fame Sum in thofe Bills in Difcharge of the Land; as in the Banks aforefaid, the fame Sum in their Bills muft be brought in, in order to receive out the Money : In fuch Cafe the Bills would moft furely rife in Value as the Land rifes; as certainly as the Bank-Bills founded on Money would fall if that Mo-

ney

ney was falling. Thus if I were to mort-gage to a Loan-Office, or Bank, a Parcel of Land now valued at 100 *l.* in Silver, and receive for it the like Sum in Bills, to be paid in again at the Expiration of a certain Term of Years ; before which, my Land rising in Value, becomes worth 150 *l.* in Silver : 'Tis plain, that if I have not these Bills in Possession, and the Office will take nothing but these Bills, or else what it is now become worth in Silver, in Discharge of my Land ; I say it appears plain, that those Bills will now be worth 150 *l.* in Silver to the Possessor ; and if I can purchase them for less, in order to redeem my Land, I shall by so much be a Gainer.

I need not say any Thing to convince the Judicious that our Bills have not yet sunk, tho' there is and has been some Difference between them and Silver ; because it is evident that that Difference is occasioned by the Scarcity of the latter, which is now become a Merchandize, rising and falling, like other Commodities, as there is a greater or less Demand for it, or as it is more or less Plenty.

Yet farther, in order to make a true Estimate of the Value of Money, we must
distinguish

diftinguifh between Money as it is Bullion, which is Merchandize, and as by being coin'd it is made a Currency : For its Value as a Merchandize, and its Value as a Currency, are two diftinct Things; and each may poffibly rife and fall in fome Degree independent of the other. Thus if the Quantity of Bullion increafes in a Country, it will proportionably decreafe in Value ; but if at the fame Time the Quantity of current Coin fhould decreafe, (fuppofing Payments may not be made in Bullion) what Coin there is will rife in Value as a Currency, *i. e.* People will give more Labour in Manufactures for a certain Sum of ready Money.

In the fame Manner muft we confider a *Paper Currency* founded on Land; as it is Land, and as it is a Currency

Money as Bullion, or as Land, is valuable by fo much Labour as it cofts to procure that Bullion or Land.

Money, as a Currency, has an Additional Value by fo much Time and Labour as it faves in the Exchange of Commodities.

If, as a Currency, it faves one Fourth Part of the Time and Labour of a Country; it has, on that Account, one Fourth added to its original Value.

When

When there is no Money in a Country, all Commerce muft be by Exchange. Now if it takes one fourth Part of the Time and Labour of a Country, to exchange or get their Commodities exchanged ; then, in computing their Value, that Labour of Exchanging muft be added to the Labour of manufacturing thofe Commodities : But if that Time or Labour is faved by introducing Money fufficient, then the additional Value on Account of the Labour of Exchanging may be abated, and Things fold for only the Value of the Labour in making them ; becaufe the People may now in the fame Time make one Fourth more in Quantity of Manufactures than they could before.

From thefe Confiderations it may be gathered, that in all the Degrees between having no Money in a Country, and Money fufficient for the Trade, it will rife and fall in Value as a Currency, in Proportion to the Decreafe or Increafe of its Quantity : And if there may be at fome Time more than enough, the Overplus will have no Effect towards making the Currency, as a Currency, of lefs Value than when there was but enough ; becaufe
fuch

such Overplus will not be used in Trade, but be some other way disposed of.

If we enquire, *How much* per Cent. *Interest ought to be required upon the Loan of these Bills*; we must consider what is the Natural Standard of Usury : And this appears to be, where the Security is undoubted, at least the Rent of so much Land as the Money lent will buy : For it cannot be expected that any Man will lend his Money for less than it would fetch him in as Rent if he laid it out in Land, which is the most secure Property in the World. But if the Security is casual, then a kind of Ensurance must be enterwoven with the simple natural Interest, which may advance the Usury very conscionably to any height below the Principal it self. Now among us, if the Value of Land is twenty Years Purchase, Five *per Cent.* is the just Rate of Interest for Money lent on undoubted Security. Yet if Money grows scarce in a Country, it becomes more difficult for People to make punctual Payments of what they borrow, Money being hard to be raised; likewise Trade being discouraged, and Business impeded for want of a Currency, abundance of People must be in declining
Circumstances,

Circumftances, and by thefe Means Security is more precarious than where Money is plenty.   On fuch Accounts it is
no wonder if People ask a greater Intereft
for their Money than the natural Intereft ;
and what is above is to be look'd upon as
a kind of *Præmium* for the Enfurance of
thofe Uncertainties, as they are greater
or lefs.   Thus we always fee, that where
Money is fcarce, Intereft is high, and low
where it is plenty.   Now it is certainly
the Advantage of a Country to make Intereft as low as poffible, as I have already fhewn ; and this can be done no other
way than by making Money plentiful.
And fince, in Emitting Paper Money a-
mong us, the Office has the beft of Security, the Titles to the Land being all
skilfully and ftrictly examined and afcer-
tained ; and as it is only permitting the
People by Law to coin their own Land,
which cofts the Government nothing, the
Intereft being more than enough to pay
the Charges of Printing, Officers Fees, *&c.*
I cannot fee any good Reafon why Four
per Cent. to the Loan-Office fhould not
be thought fully fufficient.   As a low Intereft may incline more to take Money
out, it will become more plentiful in
Trade ;

Trade; and this may bring down the common Ufury, in which Security is more dubious, to the Pitch it is determined at by Law.

If it fhould be objected, *That Emitting It at fo low an Intereft, and on fuch eafy Terms, will occafion more to be taken out than the Trade of the Country really requires:* It may be anfwered, That, as has already been fhewn, there can never be fo much of it emitted as to make it fall below the Land it is founded on; becaufe no Man in his Senfes will mortgage his Eftate for what is of no more Value to him than That he has mortgaged, efpecially if the Poffeffion of what he receives is more precarious than of what he mortgages, as that of Paper Money is when compared to Land: And if it fhould ever become fo plenty by indifcreet Perfons continuing to take out a large Overplus, above what is neceffary in Trade, fo as to make People imagine it would become by that Means of lefs Value than their mortgaged Lands, they would immediately of Courfe begin to pay it in again to the Office to redeem their Land, and continue to do fo till there was no more left in Trade than was abfolutely neceffary. And thus the Proportion would

would find it felf, (tho' there were a Million too much in the Office to be let out) without giving any one 'the Trouble of Calculation.

It may perhaps be objected to what I have written concerning the Advantages of a large Addition to our Currency, *That if the People of this Province increafe, and Husbandry is more followed, we fhall over-ftock the Markets with our Produce of Flower*, &c. To this it may be anfwered, that we can never have too many People (nor too much Money) For when one Branch of Trade or Bufinefs is overftocked with Hands, there are the more to fpare to be employed in another. So if raifing Wheat proves dull, more may (if there is Money to fupport and carry on new Manufactures) proceed to the raifing and manufacturing of *Hemp, Silk, Iron,* and many other Things the Country is very capable of, for which we only want People to work, and Money to pay them with.

Upon the Whole it may be obferved, That it is the higheft Intereft of a Trading Country in general to make Money plentiful ; and that it can be a Difadvantage to none that have honeft Defigns.

It

It cannot hurt even the Ufurers, tho' it fhould fink what they receive as Intereft; becaufe they will be proportionably more fecure in what they lend; or they will have an Opportunity of employing their Money to greater Advantage, to themfelves as well as to the Country. Neither can it hurt thofe Merchants who have great Sums out-ftanding in Debts in the Country, and feem on that Account to have the moft plaufible Reafon to fear it; *to wit*, becaufe a large Addition being made to our Currency, will increafe the Demand of our Exporting Produce, and by that Means raife the Price of it, fo that they will not be able to purchafe fo much Bread or Flower with 100 *L* when they fhall receive it after fuch an Addition, as they now can, and may if there is no Addition: I fay it cannot hurt even fuch, becaufe they will get in their Debts juft in exact Proportion fo much the eafier and fooner as the Money becomes plentier; and therefore, confidering the Intereft and Trouble faved, they will not be Lofers; becaufe it only finks in Value as a Currency, proportionally as it becomes more plenty. It cannot hurt the Intereft of *Great Britain*, as has been fhewn; and it

will

will greatly advance the **Intereſt of the** Proprietor. It will be an Advantage to every induſtrious Tradeſman, &c. becauſe his Buſineſs will be carried on more free-ly, and Trade be univerſally enlivened by it. 'And as more Buſineſs in all Manu-factures will be done, by ſo much as the Labour and Time ſpent in Exchange is ſaved, the Country in general will grow ſo much the richer.

It is nothing to the Purpoſe to object the wretched Fall of the Bills in *New-Eng-land* and *South-Carolina*, unleſs it might be made evident that their Currency was emitted with the ſame Prudence, and on ſuch good Security as ours is ; and it cer-tainly was not.

As this Eſſay is wrote and publiſhed in Haſte, and the Subject in it ſelf intri-cate, I hope I ſhall be cenſured with Can-dour, if, for want of Time carefully to reviſe what I have written, in ſome Pla-ces I ſhould appear to have expreſs'd my ſelf too obſcurely, and in others am lia-ble to Objections I did not foreſee. I ſin-cerely deſire to be acquainted with the Truth, and on that Account ſhall think my ſelf obliged to any one, who will
take

take the Pains to fhew me, or the Publick, where I am mistaken in my Conclufions, And as we all know there are
among us feveral Gentlemen of acute Parts
and profound Learning, who are very
much againft any Addition to our Money,
it were to be wifhed that they would favour the Country with their Sentiments
on this Head in Print; which, fupported
with Truth and good Reafoning, may
probably be very convincing. And this
is to be defired the rather, becaufe many
People knowing the Abilities of thofe
Gentlemen to manage a good Caufe, are
apt to conftrue their Silence in This, as
an Argument of a bad One. Had any
Thing of that Kind ever yet appeared,
perhaps I fhould not have given the Publick this Trouble : But as thofe ingenious
Gentlemen have not yet (and I doubt
never will) think it worth their Concern
to enlighten the Minds of their erring
Countrymen in this Particular, I think
it would be highly commendable in every one of us, more fully to bend our
Minds to the Study of *What is the true
Intereft of* P E N N S Y L V A N I A;
whereby we may be enabled, not only
to reafon pertinently with one another;

but

but, if Occasion requires, to transmit Home such clear Representations, as must inevitably convince our Superiors of the Reasonableness and Integrity of our Designs.

B. B.

Philadelphia, Arpil 3. 1729.

F I N I S.

AN INQUIRY INTO THE NATURE AND USES OF MONEY

Hugh Vans, *An Inquiry into the Nature and Uses of Money; More especially of the Bills of Publick Credit, Old Tenor. Together with A Proposal of some proper Relief in the present Exigence. To which is added, A Reply to the Essay on Silver and Paper Currences* (Boston, 1740), pp. 1–78.

Although there is little biographical information about Hugh Vans (or Vance), two of his writings on money have survived: *An Inquiry into the Nature and Uses of Money* and *Some Observations on the Scheme Projected for Emitting 60000 l. in Bills of a New Tenour, to be Redeemed with Silver and Gold* (1738). According to Dorfman,[1] Vans married into the Boston elite. He was a keen reader of accomplished mercantile writers, such as John Locke and John Law, as is evident in his own writings on economics.

In this rather long piece, Vans brings together with great expertise the main strands of monetary theory in the colonies over the previous fifty years, relying mostly on the works of Wise, Franklin and Locke. Vans's unique approach to the study of economics, includes numerous calculations regarding the costs and benefits of different economic policies. In *An Inquiry*, Vans examines the causes of value, the reasons for changes in relative value and market price, and the nature of money, providing a good example of America's 'political arithmetic'.

---

[1] Davis (ed.), *Colonial Currency Reprints* (1964).

An Inquiry

INTO THE

Nature and Ufes of *Money*;

More efpecially of the *Bills* of Publick
Credit, *Old Tenor*.

Together with
A PROPOSAL of fome proper Relief in the
prefent Exigence.

To which is added,
A Reply to the *Effay on Silver and Paper
Currences.*

B O S T O N : Printed andSold by S KNEELAND &T.GREEN,
over againft the Prifon in Queenftreet. 1 7 4 o.

An Inquiry into the Nature and Uſes of *Money,* &c.

HE Title-Page ſufficiently ſhews the Reader the Deſign I have in Hand. To purſue it in the cleareſt Method, I propoſe

First, to treat of the *Value* or *Eſtimation* of Things

Secondly, of the *Changes* in the comparative Value, or Price of Things in the Market.

Thirdly, of *Money*.

Fourthly, of *Banks*, with a Proposal.

Finally, I ſhall make ſome Obſervations on a Piece, intitled, *An Eſſay on Silver and Paper Currencies.*

Of theſe in their Order: And

I. Of the *Value* or *Eſtimation* of Things.

All Things that are in Uſe in the World, have their Value or Eſtimation from two different Cauſes, *viz* either 1ſt from the craving *Neceſſity*, or 2dly from the voluntary *Choice* of Mankind

Thoſe of the *firſt* Sort have a *real* and *intrinſick* Value or Eſtimation, which is unchangeable and cannot be withdrawn: but thoſe of the *ſecond* Sort have only an *accidental* or *circumſtantial* Value or Eſtimation, which is changeable, and not only may be, but often is withdrawn.

Of the firſt ſort of Things the moſt remarkable Articles are Air, Water, neceſſary Proviſions &c. which as they are abſolutely neceſſary to our being and well-being, we muſt value or eſteem them highly, and
readily

readily part with all other Things in our Poſſeſſion *(which have only their accidental Value)* for a preſent Supply of any of them, when it happens to be in the Power and Pleaſure of others to with-hold them from us; or in other Words, we find by Experience that there is a certain Virtue in the Things themſelves, which we cannot but value or eſteem : And this I take to be the true meaning of *intrinſi.k* Value, tho' in common Speech it is often otherwiſe applied; as we ſay, that one Piece of *Silver* has more intrinſick Value than another Piece ; by which we mean no more than that one Piece *weighs* more than another, when they are both of the ſame *fineneſs* ; or that one Piece has more *fine* Silver in it than another, when they are both of the ſame *weight*   We ſay alſo that *South Sea Stock* roſe above its intrinſic Worth, meaning no more than that it roſe higher than its *Dividend* was worth

' We muſt add one Inſtance more, which particularly relates to our preſent Caſe, *viz* in *New England* we commonly ſay, that *Silver* has an *intrinſick* Value, and *Bills* of publickCredit have not : and why? becauſe Silver will paſs generally throughout the tradingWorld, and Bills of Credit only in *New England*.   But that is wrong, for the univerſal Currency of Silver (ſtrictly ſpeaking) gives it no intrinſick Value, and the Value of each is only accidental, as we ſhall ſhew anon

' Of the *ſecond* Sort of Things, *viz*. Thoſe that have only an *accidental* Value or Eſtimation, there are innumerable Articles, as Diamonds and other curious Stones, Jewels of all Sorts, Silver and Gold, alſo every Degree of Finery, in the ſeveral Species of Manufactures, beyond what is abſolutely neceſſary ; and in ſhort, every Article of Proviſion, Cloathing, or Lodging, upon which there is more Coſt beſtowed than is needful.   Theſe have their Value or Eſtimation from the *voluntary Choice* of Mankind, guided either by Reaſon, or meer Humour & Fancy, in chooſing one Thing and neglecting or refuſing another at one Time, and again chooſing what they before neglected or refuſed.

Some of theſe Articles have obtained a very *general* Value in the World, as Silver and Gold, Time immemorial ; others have had it only in *particular* Places in a more changeable Manner ; and a third Sort change with the Faſhion for the Year or a particular Seaſon, and either go into diſuſe, or at leaſt are greatly reduced in their Price
till

till the Return of the Fashion brings them in use again. Thus we may probably suppose, *Silver* was first brought into use as a *Metal*, and in Time it was used as *Money*, passing by Weight (either in unequal *Pieces*, or else in Coins, where the Weight and Fineness of each Piece is ascertained) till it obtained the common Consent of the trading World; and so long as that continues, it will have an accidental Value, but when it is withdrawn (if ever) Silver must go into disuse, and be of no Value.

Under this Head of the second Sort of Commodities, are our *Bills* of publick Credit, of the old Tenor, to be ranked: They have not an intrinsick Value, as *Air* and *Water*; but an accidental Value, as *Silver* & *Gold*, founded partly upon the Promise of this Government, but principally on the common Consent of this and the other Colonies that are pleased to receive them. They are not *universal* Commodities, as Silver, Iron, &c but *local*, or confined to these Provinces which: however makes no material Difference in the present Case, as we shall show in the Sequel.

I am perswaded, that in order to form a right Judgment of the Cause of the present Difficulties in the Trade of this Province, and find out a proper Remedy, nothing can give greater Light, than the right Understanding of this Point; and therefore shall further pursue the Argument, and endeavour to make it plain and obvious to the Understanding of every Body.

And here,

1st. That the Bills are a *Commodity*, will appear by *comparing* their Promise with the Promise of any other Commodity. For Example, the implicit Promise of an Ounce of *Silver* is, that it will be received universally in exchange for Wheat or any other Commodity at the Market Price, so long as common Consent shall continue to value Silver, but the *Bills* have a twofold Promise, *viz.* An *explicit* Promise on the Face of them, and in the Acts by which they were emitted, *That the Government will receive them in all publick Payments, or for any Stock* (as Wheat, &c) *at any Time in the Treasury*, meaning to be disposed of at the Market-Price, and the Bills can never go into disuse, because there is a Demand for every Shilling of them, founded in the Acts of Government, and they must for ever be a lawful Tender for publick Taxes, so long as any of them are extant. And besides this explicit, the Bills have also an *implicit* Promise founded.

ded

ded in the *common Confent* of the Colonies where they pafs.

But great Strefs is laid upon that Part of the Promife, *fhall be in Value equal to Money* ; ——that is (fay fome) fhall be made good to the Poffeffor at the Rate of Silver-Money at *eight Shillings* per *Ounce*, which I reckon might in the Year 1702 be near the Rate Silver paffed at in the Market ; and fo they would put the Bills on the Foot of common *promiffory Notes* in Trade

But that they are not common promiffory Notes, is plain ; for thefe muft exprefs the Thing promifed, as fo many Ounces of Silver, Pounds of Iron, of a certain Finenefs &c. befides the Time when, and the Place where they are to be paid off : neither of which are to be found in the Bills, nor in the Acts of Government ; all which will appear upon Examination. For in the Year 1702, the Government firft began to emit the Bills, now called old Tenor, and the general Reafons affigned in the Act then, and in the fubfequent Acts for and relating to the Emiffions, were *the extreme Scarcity of (* Silver *) Money, and the Want of other Media of Commerce* : And in 1704 they fay, *and the Impoffibility that the Money, Plate and Bullion within this Province, can fupport the Charge of the War :* And in 1716 they fay, *All the Silver-Money which formerly made Payments in Trade eafy, being now fent into* Great Britain, *to make Return for Part of what is owing there ; by Means of all which the Trade of the Province is greatly obftructed, and the Payment of the publick Debts and Taxes retarded, and in a great Meafure rendered impracticable &c.* Thus far for the Defign of the Government ; and next for the Tenor of the Bills themfelves, viz —— *This indented Bill of Twenty Shillings, due from the Province of the Maffachufetts-Bay in New England, to the Poffeffor thereof fhall be in Value equal to Money, and fhall be accordingly accepted by the Treafurer, and Receivers fubordinate to him, in all publick Payments, and for any Stock at any Time in the Treafury* Bofton, *November* 21ft, 1702. *By Order of the Great and General Court 'or Affembly* I R. E H. N E *Committee* —— Now from the foregoing Quotations it is very plain, that 'the Government intend no more than this, viz That inafmuch as there was not Silver-Money fufficient to carry on the Affairs of the Province, they projected thofe Bills, and promifed to give them the fame Credit as they did Silver-Money, i e. where they owed *twenty Shillings* in Silver they paid it by one of their

twenty

twenty Shilling Bills, and where any Person owed them *twenty Shillings* for Taxes, or had bought any Commodity of them to that Value, they received the same *twenty Shilling* Bill back again in Payment. And indeed to have emitted special promissory Notes, as Affairs were thus circumstanced, would have intirely defeated the chief Design of the Government, *viz* That their Bills should be negotiated without Discount, and serve as well for the Trade, as publick Taxes ; and the Consequences of such Bills would have been to introduce *Stock jobbing* and *usurious* Practices, to the Damage both of the political and trading Interests of the Province.

Indeed there is no mention made of their being received as a *Commodity*, but only as Money ; however, that is sufficiently imply'd : for the more general Definition of Money is briefly this, *viz* Any one Commodity (or a Number of Commodities) chosen out of all others, and received either by the trading World in general, or any Community of People in particular, more readily than all other Commodities passing in Trade, and that for which Contracts or Agreements are usually made. The Notion of a Commodity is inseparable from that of Money ; they differ only in Degree, being of the same Kind. All Moneys are Commodities : but all Commodities are not Moneys ; because the latter by common Consent will be more readily received than the former. Thus as the ingenious Mr. *Lock* well observes, " Amongst all other Commodities passing in Trade, Money is truly one ". For Example, Silver, Iron, and Lead, are all Commodities generally in Use, but Silver is used as the Money, or the most general Commodity in the trading World ; and here in *New-England* having no Silver, nor other fit Commodity for Money, our Bills of Credit are received as the most general Commodity, or Money.

2d'y As *other* Commodities are *distinguished* by their *Weight, Fineness, Measure* &c. and have a greater or less Value in Proportion thereto (i. e two Ounces of Silver will purchase double the assigned Quantity of other things in the Market, that one Ounce of the same Fineness will do, and so on) In like manner our *Bills* are distinguished by their *Quantity* or Number, as *twenty* and *forty Shillings* &c. (the last will purchase twice as much as the first) and by their *Impression, Subscriptions,* and other Marks of Distinction , by all which they are as well secured, if not better than any other Commodity, from Counterfeits.

Г

I muſt here obſerve by the Way, that they are not ſuch a Commodity as hath its Value only from the *Uſe-fulneſs* of its *Matter* (which indeed is moſt agreeable to the vulgar Notion of a Commodity) as *Iron*, which is made into a vaſt Variety of uſeful Manufactures : But we have already ſhown, that it is in the Power, and the uſual Practice of Mankind, by common Conſent to give an *accidental Value* to Things for different Reaſons, as to *Diamonds*, and other curious Stones, for the Sake of their Colour ; to *Silver* chiefly as qualify'd for Money ; and to ſet theſe Things at a vaſt D. gree of Value beyond *Iron*, tho' the moſt uſeful of any Thing that comes under the Head of accidental Value.

3dly. They are a Commodity *the beſt qualified for the true Ends and Uſes of Money*, of any other Commodity whatever. But the Proof of this I muſt defer till I come to the Head of Money.

And finally, Without labouring the Point in Hand, the Fact is *ſelf-evident*, and muſt appear ſo to every one in Trade. For ſuppoſing any Man in this Province poſſeſſed of any Quantity of *Wheat, Silver, Iron*, or any other Commodities, and *Bills* of Credit, he cannot be inſenſible that although the firſt three Articles are in general Demand, yet the *Bills* are by far the moſt uſeful, will be vaſtly more readily received, and may be negotiated to much better Advantage, than thoſe or any other Commodities whatever in Trade.

I ſhall only add here, the Bills were in the Year 1702 *received* by the common Conſent of the Province, as a *Commodity*, paſſing among others in the Market, or as *Money*, the moſt general Commodity in Uſe among us. At their firſt Emiſſion *eight Shillings* in *Bills* were made equivalent (ſuppoſe) to one Ounce of *Silver*, thirty two Pound of *Iron*, and ſeven Pecks of *Wheat* ; or in Words more adapted to our common Way of Speaking, equivalent to *Silver* at *eight Shillings* per Ounce, *Iron* at *three Pence* per Pound, and *Wheat* at *four Shillings and ſeven Pence* per Buſhel, and ſo other Things at the then current Market Price. And having been thus eſtabliſhed in Credit, and continued ſo ever ſince, they never could change their Value, but by the *ſame Means* that all other Commodities always have, and ſtill continue to do : which brings me to conſider the *ſecond* Thing propoſed, namely,

The

The CHANGES *in the comparative Value or Price of Things in the Market.*

HAVING finished the Distinction of *real* and *accidental* Value, I have now to do with the *comparative* Value, or (as it is commonly called) the Price of Things in the Market ; this being the common Notion of Value, and understood by every Body, I shall proceed to the Matter in Hand.

All Things in Use in the World, whether they have a real or accidental Value, *change* their comparative Value or Price in the Market, from the *same Causes, viz* either from the *Plenty* or *Scarcity* of the Commodity to be sold, or from the greater or smaller Number of *Buyers* ; but more fully and clearly expressed thus, by Means of any Change in the *Proportion* between the *Quantity* to be *sold*, and the *Demand* for that Quantity

By the *Quantity to be sold*, we must understand the present Quantity of Goods that the *Sellers* are inclined or forced to part with ; and by the *Demand*, the present Quantity of Goods, which the *Buyers* are under Obligations at the same time to purchase. For the deferring the Sale or Purchase of Things till to morrow, or the next Month, or Year, has no Effect upon the present Market.

The true Proportion between Quantity and Demand, as to any Commodity, is rarely known ; because no Man can tell what Obligation or Disposition other People may have to sell or buy. We can only form a general Judgment of the Circumstance of the Market ; but may be fully satisfied that a Change in the Price can proceed from no other Cause, but a Change in the Proportion of the Quantity and Demand : For Example. Suppose a Man went to Market yesterday and bought Wheat at *ten Shillings*, and to day was obliged to give *eleven Shillings*, he might easily discover that there was less Wheat, or more Buyers, at Market to day than yesterday The exact Change in the Proportion, between yesterday and to day, none can tell ; but every one must necessarily conclude, that the Change in the Price was the Effect of the Change in the Proportion of the Quantity and Demand Many Incidents may contribute to raise or lessen the Demand for a Commodity, besides its own natural and common Circumstances. For Instance, the short Crop of *Indian* Corn and R, e may

b3

be fupplied by good Crops of *Wheat*, and confequently the Demand for *Wheat* increafed thereby : As on the other hand, a Plenty of frefh *Fifh* or wild *Pigeons* will have a Tendency to leffen the Demand for *Beef*, and confequently affect the Price of it : But thefe and all other the like Circumftances are included in the Notion of Quantity and Demand

All *exportable* Commodities, common to the World in general, change their Value by Means of any Change in the Proportion between the Quantity and Demand in the whole trading World; but fuch as are *not* exportable, change their Value from the fame Caufe, within any particular Country

Of the *firft* Sort are Wheat and other Grain, falted Provifions, as Beef, Pork, Butter, and Fifh, Metals of all Sorts, and innumerable other Articles. The Price of thefe, when taken for a Number of Years, is comparatively the fame in all Places where there is Freedom of Trade ; as having only this Difference, that thofe Countries that have the Commodities exported to them, muft pay all Charges, befides a reafonable Profit to the Importer, at leaft the Merchant always adventures upon that Suppofition And thus the Price of a Quintal of Cod-Fifh in this Province is governed by the Proportion of the whole Quantity carried every where, to the whole Demand every where within the Compafs of the Fifh-Trade. As we are *Exporters*, we fave the Charge of Tranfportation, as to what is confumed among us, which we fhou'd pay, were it imported to us from other Countries And the Merchant muft make a Judgment from his former Experience, and the beft prefent Advices he can obtain

Of the *fecond* Sort of Things, *viz* Thofe that have only a fpecial or local Value, the moft remarkable Articles are Houfes and other Buildings, Lands under moft Circumftances, Mutton, Fowl wild and tame, frefh Fifh, Roots, Herbage, Fruits &c. thefe being either not exported at all, or but rarely, change their Value in every Country. as the Quantity is greater or lefs within themfelvs in Proportion to the Demand, & many Times with as little Regard to the Prices of the fame Kind of Things in other Countries, as if they were unknown to all the reft of the World The moft remarkable Inftance in This Part of the World is our wild *Pigeons*, which are fold at one Time for *five Shillings* per Dozen, and in two or three Weeks, or perhaps Days, fall down to *five Pence*,

and

and so by Degrees return to *five Shillings* again ; and yet there is no Article in Trade but under the same Circumstances would undergo the same Changes.

There may be some Exceptions to the foregoing general Rules, and particularly in this Province, *viz* Our Beef, Pork, Butter, and many other Articles, which are usually exported, have their Value from the Quantity and Demand within this Province, because we have not yet a Surplusage of them to send abroad to foreign Markets ; our own Demand being equal to the Quantity: and sometimes we are obliged to import Butter in particular from *Ireland*. Whereas if we depended on a foreign Market for the Sale of a Surplusage of Beef, the Price of *fresh* Beef in this Province would be govern'd by the Price of *salt* Beef in the Markets to which we exported it ; which is the present Case of our Cod-Fish And here I cannot but make a short Remark, of what vast Importance our *trading* Interest is to our landed Interest, and how solicitous our Country-Gentlemen ought to be to support it ; for if they depended chiefly upon foreign Markets for the Sale of their Produce, the Prices thereof must fall at least to half, if not a third of the present Money, (*viz.* Silver at *twenty-nine Shillings* per Ounce) and their inexportable Articles to a very trifle (compared with the Prices in the Mother-Country, and other trading Countrys) and the Purchase Value of their *Lands* fall in Proportion to the Fall of their *Produce.*

The Rents of *Houses* and *Lands* are governed by the Proportion of Quantity and Demand, and the Purchase-Value is governed by the Rent : For Example, if a House bring in *one hundred Pounds* a Year neat Rent (supposing the common Rate of Houses twenty Years Purchase) it may sell for *two thousand Pounds* ; but if by a Change in the Quantity, or Demand, it bring in *two hundred Pounds* a Year, it will then sell for *two thousand Pounds* &c.

The same may be said of *Money*. There is one Way of Judging of the Change of its Value, by *comparing* it with other Things in the *Market* , and another Way of Judging of it, by the Change of its yearly *Increase* or *Interest* : For agreable to Mr *Lock*, *Money* is fitly compared to *Land*; Mankind by common Agreement or publick Authority having added a Faculty to it (which naturally it has not) of increasing yearly so much per *Cent* : In the Land it is called Rent, in the Money Use or Interest.

Of

Of thefe in their Order.

1ft. As to the Change in the Value of *Money*, when compared with *Goods* in the *Market*   Mr *Lock* obferves, " That the *natural Value* of Money in *exchanging* for any one *Commodity*, is the *Quantity* of the trading Money of the Kingdom, *defigned* for that Commodity, in *Proportion* to that fingle *Commodity* and its *Vent*". This is certainly true : and therefore it is exceeding difficult to judge when the Change is in the *Money*, and not in the *Commodity* for which it is given

It is equally difficult to judge of the *gen-val* Change of Money in the Market in the trading World   For, tho' it be certain that many Things have *rifen* in Value, in fome Proportion to the Increafe of *Silver* (the common Money) in *Europe*, yet it is equally certain that many Things have *fallen* in Value, more efpecially of later Years, notwithftanding the yearly Increafe of Silver.   For *Money* has this extraordinary Faculty, that altho' it be the Caufe of a *greater Demand* for many*Things, yet (as it circulates vaftly quicker than any other Commodity) it gives a Spring and Encouragement to the *Invention* and *Induftry* of Mankind, and fo becomes alfo the Means of *increafing* the *Quantity* of many Things, equal to, and often vaftly exceeding, the moft extravagant Demand.

A further Reafon for the Difficulty of Judging in this Cafe, take from Mr *Lock* : " For Money (meaning Silver Money) being look'd upon as the *ftanding Meafure* of other Commodities, Men confider and fpeak of it *ftill* as if it were a ftanding Meafure, tho' when it has *alter'd* its *Quantity* (meaning in Proportion to Demand) it's plain it is *not* "

But the beft and cleareft Notion, that we can have of the Change of the Value of *Silver Money*, is by the *Influence* it has on the *Mode of Living* in all Countries where it is in Ufe : For upon a new Acceffion of Money, People require not only a greater Number of Articles, but a greater Degree of Finery in the fame Sorts ; fo that the yearly *Expence* is confiderably *increafed*, even tho' fome Articles fhould continue at the *fame*, or even *fall* in their *Price*   Thus in *England*, and more particularly in *London*, the Difference in the Mode of Living, fince the opening of the Spanifh Mines in *America*, to this Day, may probably be as *one* is to *thirty*, if not more, for Men of the fame Rank and Employment : And yet many Articles, more efpecially thofe that are raifed in the *American* Plantations,

Plantations, are fold for a trifle of *Silver* now, to what they were then fold for.

2dly As to the Change in the Value of Money with Regard to its *natural Intereft*, or *yearly Increafe*.

By *natural* Intereft I mean the *Market-Rate* of Intereft, which fubfifts in all Countries, and is fometimes *above*, and fometimes *under* the Rate of Intereft affigned by *Law*. The Law neverthelefs may be founded on Juftice and Equity, and a neceffary Rule where Bonds and Specialties, upon which Intereft becomes due, are fued for in the Law: But tho' that forbids a Tranfgreffion of the Rule 'by *Excefs*, when it is in the Power of the *Lenders* to have more (as in this Province) it neverthelefs eftablifhes Contracts for *lefs* than the Rule, where the Parties have agreed it fhould be fo : The Reafon of this is becaufe Money is an abfolutely neceffary Inftrument for carrying on Trade ; and the lower the Rate of Intereft, the better the Inftrument   Therefore all Countries ftrenuoufly endeavour to have it as low or lower than any of their Neighbours, becaufe of the fuperior Advantages it gives them in Trade.

The Change of the natural Rate of *Intereft*, is an undeniable Evidence of the Change in the *Proportion* of the Quantity & Demand of Money, and therefore of the Change in the Value of Money from time to time.   For if a Houfe changes its Purchafe Value from a Change in its yearly Rent, undoubtedly Money muft be allowed to have a Change in its Value upon any Change in its natural Intereft : And therefore if (agreeable to Mr *Lock*) in the Year 1691 the natural Intereft of Silver Money in *England* was eight to ten per *Cent* (fay nine at a Medium) and now as I am informed but about three per *Cent* (the Government have it fo, and the Stocks in general produce thereabouts, in proportion to the Purchafe-Money given for them) then upon this Suppofition we may truly fay that an *Ounce* of *Silver* of the fame Finenefs now as it was in 1691, is worth but one *third* of an *Ounce* at that Time, when compared with the great Capital Stock, *viz* the Lands and other real Eftate of *England*, befides what other Changes it may have undergone for the worfe, by Means of the Change in the Mode of Living, uncertain, yet doubtlefs very confiderable.

But to proceed,

I have but one Change more to fpeak to. and that is not a Change in the natural Proportion of Things, but a
forced

forced Way of *Rating* Things under some Circumstances in Trade, and that chiefly with Regard to a State of private or publick *Bankruptcy*.

For Instance, The Standard for Silver Money in *Great Britain* is *five Shillings and two Pence* per *Ounce*, or three Ounces, seventeen Penniweight, ten Grains assigned to the Money *Pound*: But supposing Silver there (to avoid a Fraction) at *five Shillings* per *Ounce*, or four *Ounces* to the Money Pound, and that *N* owes *one hundred Pounds* Sterling, or four hundred Ounces of *Silver*, but it happens that he has but two hundred *Ounces* of Silver, and can pay no more but half his Debt, by Composition. Now there are two Ways of expressing the Case of *N*, *viz* one Way by keeping to the Standard of *Great Britain*, *five Shillings* per *Ounce*, and saying that *N* pays *ten Shillings* in or for the *Pound*, or that he pays half a Pound instead of a whole one. But there is also another Way of expressing *N*'s Case, commonly in Use in this Province, when we talk of Money, *viz.* that *N*'s Silver is *raised to ten Shillings* per *Ounce,* (instead of *five Shillings*) and therefore *his* Money Pound (agreeable to his Circumstances) is only equal to Silver at *ten Shillings* per *Ounce*, and so his two hundred *Ounces* of Silver at the Rate of *ten Shillings* per *Ounce*, is just equal to *one* hundred of his Composition *Pounds*

Again, suppose *N* owes one hundred Yards of *Cloth*, (the Standard Measure being thirty-six Inches to the Yard) and has but fifty Yards to pay his Debt: In this Case also *N* pays half his Debt according to the Standard Measure ; or in other Words he pays by a Yard (agreeable to his Circumstances) of but eighteen Inches : for fifty Yards of thirty six Inches are just equal to one hundred of *N*'s Yards of but eighteen Inches.

Thus we see that *N*'s Circumstances put a new Rate upon his Money, the Measure of the Value of Things ; and upon his Yard, a Measure of the Quantity of Things : and every Thing he has, must be rated according to the Quantity he is able to pay in Proportion to the Demand. And this, as has been observed, makes no Alteration in the natural Worth of his *Silver* and *Cloth* in the Market, but they continue as they were

This brings me to the chief Thing to be considered under this general Head *viz.* our BILLS of publick Credit, of the *old Tenor* I shall therefore, agreeable to the foregoing Method withRegard to Silver Money, consider them in two different Respects.   1st As

1ft. As to the Change of their Value with Regard to the *Purchase of other Goods in the Market* And in this Regard I shall endeavour to prove that they have not undergone any other Change, than that which is common to all other Commodities For let it be observed,

In 1702 *eight Shillings* in *Bills* was equal to *eight Shillings* in *Silver*, in *Iron*, in *Wheat*, and all other Commodities : And now in 1739, *eight Shillings* in Bills is still equal to *eight Shillings* in these and all other Commodities.

Eight Shillings in *Silver* has now but eight twent-nine Parts of the *Quantity* of Silver it had in it in 1702 *Eight Shillings* in *Iron* has likewise about the same eight twenty-nine Parts, and *eight Shillings* in *Bills* but eight twenty-nine Parts, of the Value they had, when compared with these and other Commodities.

By the Year 1715 Silver at sundry Times by the Scarcity of it in Proportion to Demand, and by no other Means, rose from *eight Shillings* to *nine Shillings* per *Ounce*, and so the Silver Money Pound was reduced from two *Ounces* and half, call it fifty Penniweight, to forty four Penniweight and seventeen Grains. By the Year 1728 it rose to *twenty Shillings* per *Ounce*, and the Money Pound was reduced to twenty Penniweight By this current Year 1739, it has risen to *twenty-nine Shillings* per *Ounce*, or the Money Pound reduced to thirteen Penniweight and nineteen Grains. And this is truly our *natural Silver-Money-Pound*, such a one as our trading Circumstances, or our Market affords; and which must for ever be govern'd by the Market. While that affords a *Quantity equal to Demand*, it will then be *fix'd* in its Quantity, but upon any Variation will contain more or less Silver in Proportion *ad Infinitum*, only with this Reserve, when the Quantity *exceeds* the Demand, it will then be in the Power of the Government and People (and no doubt all would be willing) to agree upon a certain assigned Quantity of Silver that it has fallen to, for the Pound, but otherwise it is impossible for them to fix it.

Or if we take any other Articles of our Exports, shall we not find the same Changes? As supposing (what is absolutely necessary in all Cases of this kind) that *Tarr* had all along kept the same Proportion to its Demand in the trading World, must it not nevertheless have risen *here* in Proportion to the general *Deficiency* in our Returns and kept pace with *Silver*, gradually rising from

eight

eight Shillings to *nine Shillings, twenty Shillings,* and *twenty nine Shillings* per Barrel ?

Or, on the other hand, Can it be imagined that *Britons,* who buy and sell with a Regard to the Rate of *Silver* in all Places, should not be allowed to raise the Rates of their *Goods* by common Consent, in *Proportion* to the Changes in the Rates of Silver ? And accordingly when Silver was *eight Shillings* per *Ounce,* to sell at about one hundred per *Cent* advance (above the Par of *Great Britain, five Shillings and two Pence* per Ounce) and Silver *nine Shillings* per *Ounce,* Goods at one hundred and twenty five per *Cent* ; and so on to this present Year, Silver at *twenty-nine Shillings,* Goods at six hundred per *Cent,* or *seven hundred Pounds* of our Standard for *one hundred Pounds* Sterling Standard, in the Sale of Goods ?

Or finally, Could it possibly otherwise have happened but that the *Bills,* which are a Commodity passing among other Commodities in the Market, should keep pace with all other Commodities, whether common or special ? most certainly it could not be otherwise.

But it will be *objected,* that in 1702, *eight Shillings* in *Bills* were equal to an *Ounce* of *Silver,* but now *eight Shillings* in *Bills* are only equal to five Penniweight twelve Grains and half, of Silver ; therefore the Change must be in the *Bills* and not in the *Ounce* of *Silver.*

I answer, This is all true : But it has *no Relation* at all to the present *Case,* because an *Ounce* of Silver is a *fixed* Measure, but all *our* Measures are *changed,* as in the Case of *N.* For Instance, the old Measure for *eight Shillings* was an *Ounce* of Silver, but the new or forced Measure is but five Penniweight twelve Grains and half of Silver : And this is as truly the common Measure of *eight Shillings,* as if the Government had enacted it, and common Consent concurred in it. So that whether we say, we pay *five Shillings and six Pence half Penny* in the Pound, when we compare the new Measure with the old, or say that we now pay by a new Measure of five Penniweight twelve Grains and half for *eight Shillings* (that is, thirteen Penniweight nineteen Grains to the Pound) it amounts to the same Thing ; and the Change is alike in every Thing in Use among us, as well as in the Bills

This Province has not been obliged to pay *more* to the Mother Country, than its just Debt, but rather *less,* by Means of those *Changes,* for if we *formerly* gave *Great Britain* one *hundred* per *Cent* Advance for Goods, and

paid

paid them in *Silver* at *eight Shillings* per *Ounce*, and other Things in Proportion; and *now* give them *six hundred* per *Cent.* Advance, and pay them in Silver at *twenty-nine Shillings* per *Ounce*, it amounts to near the same Thing And as the Trade of this Province has first caused the Change, and the Mother-Country has follow'd the Course of Trade, so the former has had much the Advantage of the latter in that Regard

The *greatest Loss* has been to those who *agreed for Bills* of Credit, or for Money *indefinitely*, without Regard to the *Rate* of Silver or any other Commodity: For, as we have already shown, *our Measures* are all virtually *changed.* And in this Respect those that have *Salaries*, and *Fees* of Office appointed by the Government, have been great Sufferers, and (where they have not already) ought to be relieved in such a Way as to Equity (all Circumstances considered) appertains: For which I do by no Means think the Change in the Rate of Silver is the best Rule; but rather the different Circumstances of an Office on one Hand, and the Change in the Mode of Living on the other.

But for *all other* Persons, who have been left to their *Liberty*, to make Contracts for a certain Rate of Silver, or other Things, either where Moneys were lent, or Goods were sold, they have an Exception or Reserve made in the *Acts*, for Bills being a lawful Tender, purposely for them (viz. *Specialties and express Contracts in Writing always excepted*) and the Law has ever supported them in such Agreements. Therefore they must blame themselves; and not the Government, who have not yet succeeded in any Methods to stop the Changes in the Rates of Things. *Orphans* must blame their Guardians; *Widows* their Advisers; and *money'd* Men themselves; for they might always have let their Money at a certain fixed Rate, if they had not (its to be feared) been too covetous in expecting, besides 6 per *Cent* (or more) Interest, a further Advantage of the Borrower in the Fall of the Rate of Silver. Upon this Score the *Clergy* have in many Regards been *less free* than other People, and ought to be honourably supported by their Hearers *under all the Changes* of Things.

This Province (simply considered) has so far been a great Loser in Trade, as that all our *Treasure* (Silver and Gold) which is the chief Encouragement and Reward for Industry in all Countries, has been constantly carried off

(and

(and often all too little) for the Payment of our Debts,
due to the Mother-Country. But yet (excepting that
Cafe) at the fame Time our *capital Stock* has prodigiouf-
ly *increafed in Value,* fince the Emiffions of Bills, chiefly
by their Means, and next to impoffible it fhould have
been brought about without them : And we may reafonably fuppofe, that we are now capable of exporting
three times more Produce in Quantity, and the general
Eftate of theProvince is three times more valuable (when
compared with Silver) now than in the Year 1702

On the other Hand, not only the Mother Country, but
the Province has greatly fuffered , the moft laborious and
induftrious among us, Widows and Orphans confider'd as
fuch, and in general every Body, fave the Shopkeepers
and a very few money'd Men, have been greatly *diftreffed*
by Means of the *Want* of a Sufficiency of *Bills* ; by having
their Debts poftponed ; by being obliged to take Goods
(and in a much greater Degree of Quantity and Finenefs
than theirInclinations orCircumftances required)in lieu of
Bills ; by being obliged to purchafe Goods or borrowMo-
ney at a much higher Rate than in otherCountries,where
they have a Competency of Money ; and in fine,by being
put under a Neceffity of purfuing a defpicable Trucking
(and naturally a cheating) Trade.

There is another *Objection* very commonly brought a-
gainft the Bills, *viz.* That on fundry *large Emiffions* Silver
and other Returns have *rifen* in a very extraordinary Manner, which would *not* have happened *without* thofe
Emiffions.

To this I anfwer. That (agreeable to my own Argument) the *fudden & large* Emiffions,as in theLo-n-Money,
might have a *proportionable* Influence on thePrices of Returns to the Mother-Country, and ought for ever to be
induftrioufly *avoided* in the Regulation of Bills. However, ftill I am of Opinion that the Market-Rate of
Things would have *rifen* to the *fame* Height by *flower,*
yet equally *certain* Degrees, *without* the Help of fuch Irregular *Emiffions,*and by the mere *Operation* of our *Trade.*
For confider,

1 *Every trading Country muft at all times have a Sufficiency of Silver to anfwer all Demands,* whether they be
great or fmall, more fudden or more gradual ; elfe upon
Failure thereof, *their Rates* of Silver muft undoubtedly
be *raifed* Now if this Province had been in *fuch* Circumftances, let the *Emiffions* have been never fo large and
fudden,

sudden, *they* would not have affected the Price of *Silver*, the Quantity thereof being still equal to the Demand: But as they have generally been otherwise, we might expect sudden and great Changes at times.

2. Another Reason, to the same Effect, may be this, that *the general Quantity of Bills*, current at any Time in the Province, has been vastly *less than the Demand* (as we shall show anon) so that often *between* the several Emissions a great *Scarcity* has happen'd : And as they were the *chief Money*, for which *Contracts* were made, it was impossible but that many *Debts*, due to the *Mother Country*, must have been *postponed* : so that upon a *new* Emission, obtained with great Difficulty, after long Sollicitations, perhaps *L.* 100000 was immediately applied to the Purchase of *Silver* and *other Returns*; and the Quantity being *unequal* to such Demands, the Prices *rose* Whereas, if there had been a moderate Quantity of *Bills always extant*, the *Demand* would have kept a more *regular Pace* with the *Quantity*.

3. The *Instances* hinted at in the Objection, are vastly *too few* to make a settled *Rule*. For *Changes* in the Price of *Silver* have been *daily*, it has not one Day been *fixed* to an absolutely certain Rate, as in the Mother-Country; since the Year 1702 (and many Years before any Emissions of Bills of any Sort) no two Men hardly selling at the *same* Price for *one* Day. And this was not only obvious to every one all along, but will still admit of Demonstration every Day : that is, we shall find the Sellers and Buyers acting in' the same Manner with Regard to the Sale or Purchase of *Silver*, as they do with Regard to *all other* Commodities, and the Proportion of Quantity and Demand every Day operating on the Price of Silver in the same Manner, as on every other Commodity ; and consequently more or less *Bills, Iron* &c given for the same assigned Quantity of Silver on one Day than another, without the least Regard to the Quantity of Bills extant.

But supposing that the irregular Emissions *had* produced these bad Effects, *this does not at all destroy theScheme of Bills*. There is nothing in the Operation but what is common to all Moneys : for there is not one new*Ounce* of *Silver* added to the old Stock in the trading World, but what has a *natural* Tendency to *increase* the *Demand* for many Things ; as, on the other Hand, the same Tendency to increase the *Quantity* of many Things. The same
Tendency

Tendency muft alfo be allowed to our *Bills*, and indeed in a lower Degree to *all* Commodities whatever For there is not a fingle *Cow* or *Horfe* added to the Capital Stock of this Province, but what has the fame Tendency. As contrariwife, the *Reduction* of Silver-Money in the trading World would have a natural Tendency to *leffen* both the Demand and Quantity of many Things; but ftill *worfe*, when the Quantity of Money is fo reduced, that it is utterly infufficient for the Inftrument of *Trade* (as in this Province) to make Money become the Inftrument of the greateft *Oppreffion*, and to force People upon Contrivances to fupply that Defect by other Commodities, or to run into a general Barter in Trade equally pernicious, and which muft end in a general Ruin. For, what Mr *Lock* fays of Silver, that it is the Meafure of the Quantity or the Extent of Trade in the World, the fame may be truly faid of *Bills* in this Province.

Some will *object*, that according to the general Obfervation of judicious Men, many People upon the *firft Emiffion of Bills* ran into an *extravagant Ufe of Englifh Shop-Goods*, more than the *Exports* of the Province were fufficient to pay for, and confequently *Returns rofe*, and plainly by *their Means*. I anfwer, I have already affigned two different Effects to Money, *viz.* both the Rife and Fall of Things: Which of thefe two were moft prevalent, is difficult to tell, but we are fure, that the Silver from 1702 to 1715 rofe but from about 8 to 9*s*. which is no great Matter, confidering the Benefit the Province might otherwife have by the *Bills*, more efpecially in increafing the Quantity of Returns But by the beft Information I can have from Men of Credit then living, the Fact is truly this, *viz* about the Year 1700, *Silver-Money* became exceeding *fcarce*, and the Trade fo embaraffed, that we begun to go into the Ufe of *Shop-Goods*, as the Money. The *Shopkeepers* told the Tradefmen, who had Draughts upon them from the Merchants for all Money, that they could not pay all in Money (and very truly) and fo by Degrees brought the Tradefmen into the Ufe of taking Part in Shop-Goods, and likewife the *Merchants*, who muft always follow the natural Courfe of Trade, were forced into the Way of agreeing with Tradefmen, Fifhermen, and others; and alfo with the Shopkeepers, to draw Bills for *Part* and fometimes for *all* Shop-Goods; And the Continuance of this pernicious Practice (the unavoidable Confequence of the Want of a Sufficiency of Silver-

Money

Money, or Bills of Credit) has always been, is now in a surprizing Manner, and for ever will be the Bane, and in the End the Ruin of this unhappy Province, by forcing us into a vile Trucking-Trade, or to trading without any other Measure, than such a one as every Man is either willing, or thinks himself obliged by Way of general Reprizal, to try to impose upon his Neighbour, and operates in many Respects as if we had no Laws for the Measures of Justice, no Yards nor Bushels for Measures of Quantity, but every Man left free to do what seemed right in his own Eyes.

The greatest Quantity of Bills extant at one Time was in 1721, and probably fell considerably short of 90 *thousand Pounds* Sterling ; and yet at that Time the general Run of Ship building, the greatest Article of our Returns, was for half Money, half Goods, or more. The Merchant indeed at that Time might have possibly had ready Money for his Goods, and paid the Tradesmen in the same , but every Body knows that even then (and now much more) no Man could live by the Trade, because of the great Abatements in Proportion to the Prices for Money upon them, or for those Notes. And now the Sum of Bills extant may be about *l.* 250000, and equal but to *l.* 45000 Sterling ; and no Ways proportionable to the Demand.

Finally, With Regard to the common Observation of Men in Trade touching the Changes of Commodities in the Market, I may appeal to the Experience of every Body, whether the *Bills* have not always been the *scarcest* Commodity whatever ; whether a Man that wanted ready Money, has not generally been put to great Difficulty, and obliged to sell at a very low Rate ; or when he wanted to buy any Thing upon Credit, for want of ready Money, whether he has not been obliged to purchase his Credit very dear, and at a Rate vastly exceeding the Usage in other Countrys, where they have a Competency of Money.

2 I am to consider the Bills with Regard to the Change of their *yearly Interest*, or *Increase*

The *lawful* Interest in this Province is 6 per *Cent.* No Man since the first Emission had occasion to let his Money *under* : He might always have *that* (which by the Way is comparatively exceeding *high*) with very good Security, none better in the World, than in this growing Province ; and his Bills fixed, as in *Europe*, to an assigned

Rate

Rate of *Silver*: But how much *more* than 6 per *Cent*, the Borrowers and Lenders can beft inform us . it is fo well known that I need fay nothing more upon it. But that the Bills have never exceeded in *Quantity*, even on the greateft Emiffions, is evident; for if they had, their *Intereft* muft undoubtedly have *fallen*; becaufe the *natural* Intereft follows the *Proportion* of the *Quantity* and *Demand*, as the Shadow does the Body   They have a mutual Dependance, naturally lead to, and illuftrate each other

Befides the foregoing, we might offer another Argument, indeed not fo certain, but abundantly fufficient to prove the Point in Hand, and that is from a Comparifon of the fuppofed *Numbers* of People, yearly *Expence*, and Quantity of *Money* in *Great Britain*, with thofe of *this Province*.

Suppofe in *Great Britain* 9 Millions of Souls, the yearly Expence from the higheft to the loweft *l* 8 by the Head, and the current Money (which is fo varioufly reported, that I am at a Lofs what to fay , having found it computed from 30 Million and upwards down to 18 Million) fay at a Medium, 24 Millions Sterling, or *l.* 2. 13s 4d, by the Head; befides immenfe Sums in Bills and Notes paffing in Trade, equal to and on fome Accounts better than Money; that, while they have but a general, tho' fmall Ballance of Trade, and a wife and faithful Adminiftration, might be extended to any Length, even beyond what the Kingdom might at any Time have Occafion for. Befides they have an old Country abounding in all Sorts of Cultivation and Manufacture, in many Refpects beyond the Vent of their Trade. Now, on the other Hand, fuppofe we have in *this Province* 125 thoufand Souls; the yearly expence *l* 40 per Head; and the Money *l* 250000   In that Cafe *they* have a Sum of Money equal to one third of their yearly Expence, and *we* only a Sum equal to one twentieth Part of *ours*; or nearly, but one feventh Part, in Proportion to what they have   The Quantity of our Bills cannot be *enlarged*, as their Silver-Money virtually is, by the Help of *Banks*, they being already a compleat Inftrument of Trade,   And we labour under many other Difadvantages from the yet comparatively Infant-State of the Province; together with the Irregularities in emitting and calling in the Bills, which makes them liable to many and great Stagnations &c.

By

By this Inftance it appears, or even taking the whole *New England* Colonies complexly, and more critically comparing their Circumftances with thofe of the Mother-Country, I doubt not but it might be made appear, that we have not one tenth Part of Money in Proportion to them

Before I leave this Head, it will be needful further to explain what I mean by comparing the trading Condition of the Province to a State of *Bankruptcy*; which I was forced to do out of mere Neceffity: For I know of no other Comparifon, that would have clearly illuftrated the Subject And I would not be underftood to mean a *total* Bankruptcy, as in the Cafe of a private Man when all his Eftate real and perfonal is not equal to the Demands his Creditors may have upon him: For the real and perfonal Eftate (or Capital Stock) of the Province is vaftly more valuable than all the Demands upon it in the prefent Cafe Therefore,

By a State of *partial* Bankruptcy, or Bankruptcy in in our *Trade*, I mean only, that at certain Times the whole exportable Produce, the whole Silver and Gold to be purchafed in the Market, or all exportable Things whatever put together, are *lefs* in *Quantity* than the *Demand* for them, and of Neceffity the Prices of them muft rife in the Market in Proportion to their Scarcity. For Example, Suppofe that laft *February* the Rate of *Silver* in the Market was 27 s. per *Ounce*, and *Tarr* 27 s. per Barrel, and all other Returns in Proportion: And that *N.* had fold *l* 100 worth of *Britifh* Goods to *P.* at an Advance agreeable to the then Rate of Silver, to be paid this *February*; which accordingly is done by *P* and *N.* goes to Market in order to purchafe Silver, but there he finds that by the Scarcity of it in Proportion to Demand it has rifen from 27 to 29 s. per Ounce, and Tarr and all other Returns in Proportion; and that he can no otherwife make Returns than by purchafing Things at the Market-Price. Now in this Cafe *N fold* by a Meafure of 27 s. per Ounce, and *receives* only by a Meafure of 29 s. per Ounce: Or in other Words, receives only *l* 93 for 100, or a Compofition of about 18 s 9 d. in the Pound.

This unhappy and difhonourable State may be called by another Name, *viz* A *Ballance of Compofition*; or to give it the fofteft Name, a *Ballance* (not of Trade, but) of *Debt*, as I formerly called it upon another Occafion; by which I mean, a certain Part of our provincial Debt, due

due to the Mother Country, virtually remitted or forgiven us at Times: As in a moft remarkable Manner in the Year 1734 when Silver rofe from 22 s 6 d. to 27 s. and all that had Debts out when the Change happened, were obligʻd to take their Compofition in Proportion thereto.

The Ballance of *Trade* is only the *Difference* between the Value of the *Produce* and *Manufacture* traded for between two Countrys, which is paid or received in *Silver* or *Gold*, the general Treafure of the World: For Example, if *Great Britain* exports in one Year to *Spain l.* 100000 in Produce and Manufacture, and takes back in Return but *l* 90000 worth of the Produce & Manufacture of *Spain*, fhe muft then receive *l.* 10000 in Silver or Gold, to ballance that Years Account of Trade; and nothing is forgiven *Spain:* But it has happened fome Years in the like Cafe that *we* have had *l.* 10000 forgiven this Province, in the Manner above; which for the Future I fhall call by the Name of a Ballance of *Debt*: which is the one and only Caufe of the Changes in the computative Value or Rate of Things in our Market, and while continued muft ftill have the fame Effect, and that whether we have Bills of Credit extant or not. But it's time to proceed to the next Thing propofed, *viz* to treat

Of MONEY.

THE *Definitions* of Money are very various I fhall collect a few of them, from Mr. *Chambers*, and others.

Money is any Matter, whether Metal, Wood, Leather, Glafs, Horn, Paper, Fruits, Shells, Kernels &c *which hath Courfe as a Medium of Commerce.*

Moft of the Ancients are frequent and exprefs in their Mention of *Leather*-Moneys, *Paper*-Moneys, *Wooden*-Moneys &c.

This is a good general Definition of Money; & agreable not only to the Ufage of ancient Times, but even of the prefent. Look into our *British* Plantations, and you'll fee fuch Money ftill in Ufe As, *Tobacco* in *Virginia*, *Rice* in *South Carolina*, and *Sugars* in the *Iflands*, they are the chief Commodities, ufed as the general Money, Contracts are made for them, Salaries and Fees of Office paid in them, and fometimes they are made a lawful Tender at a yearly affigned Rate by publick Authority, even when

Silver

Silver was promised. And the same may be said of *Shop-Gods* in this Province, in several Respects sufficiently known among us

Paulus the Lawyer defines Money, *a Thing stamped with a publick Coin, and deriving it's Use and Value from it's Impression, rather than it's Substance.*

This Definition must be confined to the Construction, which the *Law* puts upon Money: that is, whatever assigned *Quantity* of Silver, Gold, Copper &c. the publick Authority of any Country have given to the *Pound, Livre,* or *Guilder*, and whatever Changes they shall think fit to make as to *Matter, Weight,* and *Fineness* at any Time; yet the Piece of Matter having the publick Stamp for a *Pound,* shall be a *lawful Tender* for so much. In this Definition he seems to countenance the Custom of reducing the Weight or Fineness of Coins, by Recoinages, which (when made to take in past Contracts) is a publick Fraud.

Or if we take him in a general Sense, he is notoriously wrong : For Money derives both its Use and Value from the *common Consent* of Mankind Neither Silver, Copper, nor Iron have any other Value than what common Consent gives them: nor will they ever give the same Value to *one* Ounce of Metal, which they do to *two* Ounces, or receive one Ounce of *baser* Metal equal to an Ounce of *finer*.

Indeed if a Method could be found to fix an Impression upon any Metal, easily to be distinguished from all other Impressions, next to an Impossibility of counterfeiting, then an assigned Quantity of that Metal might be raised to any Value, and the common Consent of the People (if they stood in good Terms with their Government) might be obtained to such a national or provincial Scheme ; and the Money continue for ever to pass, with as little Variation as all other Commodities have. But this is next to impossible to be done upon Metals : So that an Ounce of Silver or other Metal can never pass for more in Coin, than in Bullion. And therefore those Princes, who have attempted to introduce Copper-Species at a great Disproportion, have been forced to use the most violent Means ; as in the well known Case of the late King of *Sweden,* when a *Farthing's* worth of Copper was ordered to pass for 32 *Pence* of their Money, upon Pain of Death.

Monf. *Boizard* defines Money, *a Piece of Matter to which publick Authority has affixed a certain Value and Weight, to serve as a Medium of Commerce.*

By

By *certain Value*, I suppose, he means a certain *Denomination*, as Pound, Shilling &c and also an *assigned Weight* For the Value of Coins in the Market is equally uncertain with other Things. This is also an Assertion of the Right of publick Authority to make and alter their Coins or Money

Mr. *Lock* says, *Silver is the Instrument and Measure of Commerce*, in all the civilized and trading Parts of the World It is the *Instrument* of Commerce by its *intrinsick Value*. The *intrinsick Value* of Silver, considered as *Money*, is that *Estimate* which *common Consent* has placed on it ; whereby it is made *equivalent* to all other Things, and consequently is the *universal Barter*, or Exchange, which Men give or receive for other Things, that they would purchase or part with for a valuable Consideration: And thus (as the wise Man tells us) *Money answers all Things*. Silver is the *Measure* of Commerce by its *Quantity* , which is the *Measure* also of its *intrinsick Value* : If one Grain of Silver has an intrinsick Value, two Grains have double that intrinsick Value &c.

The Meaning of all this (I humbly conceive) is, that as *Silver* by common Consent is made a *universal Commodity*, so People measure the *Value* of every Thing *by it*, and usually say that Things are dear or cheap in Proportion to the greater or smaller Quantity of Silver they cost in the Market, and for the same Reason they choose Silver, rather than any other Matter, as the *Instrument* for carrying on their Commerce.

The ingenious Author does not by this mean, that *Silver* is either a *fixed Measure* or Standard of the *Value* of all Things bought or sold, as a *Yard* and a *Bushel* are fixed Measures of *Quantity* ; nor that it is the *best Instrument* for expediting Commerce : For as to the *first* he is frequent and express in it, that Silver changes its own Value in a Course of Years, more than almost any other Commodity ; and every one knows that *Bank Bills* and *Transfers* are a much better *Instrument* of Commerce. Therefore he only means that Silver is the *received* Measure or Instrument of Commerce And we must all allow it is one of the best universal Commodities, the general Treasure of the World, the Measure of the Quantity of Trade carried on in the commercial World (as our Author elsewhere observes) and indeed in a great Degree the Measure of the Power and Influence of every Country in the political World.

                                                                    Mr.

Mr. *Law* defines Silver *the Measure by which Goods are valued, the Value by which Goods are exchanged, and in which Contracts are made payable.* By which he Means neither a *fixed Measure* of Value, nor the *best Instrument* of Commerce ; but that Silver is the *received Measure* by which Goods are valued, and the *agreed Value* or universal Commodity (by common Consent) for which Goods are exchanged, and in which Contracts are made payable. For he not only reckons that it *falls in Value,* but that it is in danger of *losing its Use* as Money, and of being reduced to a mere Commodity ; and that it is *far* from being the *best Instrument* of Commerce But to proceed,

Money is a Measure of the Value of all Things bought and sold, and *a necessary Instrument for facilitating Commerce.*

It is a Measure of the *Value* of Things, in some sort as a Yard or a Bushel are Measures of the *Quantities* of Things.

It is an *Instrument* of Commerce ; an Expedient, without which Trade can never be carried on to good Purpose.

In these different Regards Money must be subjected to Rules, as all other Measures are

The *Qualifications* of Money may be reduced to the four following ones , viz.

1. That its own *Value* be *stable*

2. That it be made of *convenient Matter.*

3. That it be received by *common Consent* within the Community for which it is intended.

4. That it have the Sanction of *publick Authority.*

Of these in their Order.

1. *Money must have a stable Value.* Now in Order to have any Commodity a of stable Value in the Market, it must have its own *Quantity* as near as possible always equal to the *Demand* for it , because otherwise it cannot be the *Measure of the Value* of other Things : No more than a *Yard* or a *Bushel,* that by Means of some Imperfection should at Times grow longer or shorter, bigger or less, would be just Measures of *Quantity*

There's no Commodity, left free to its Course in the Market, but what must for ever be liable to change its Value : And no assigned Quantity of any one Thing will long continue just equal to an assigned Quantity of another Thing Even *Silver* and *Gold* are naturally as far from holding an exact Proportion to one another, as any other Commodities : But in asmuch as the *European* Nations have thought fit to receive Gold in Payments in a

certain

certain Proportion to Silver (the Standard) every Kingdom is obliged to be very vigilant in obferving the Proportion that is fixed by the Maritime Nations, or the Majority, to keep to that, and change as they do ; elfe they
run a Rifque of having the lefs valuable Species imported to them, and the more valuable carried off to their
Lofs As for Silver, how can it ever be made a ftable
Meafure of Value ? Since it is introduced without any
Regard to the Proportion there ought always to be kept
up between the Quantity and Demand and lofes its Value every Year by the Influence it has on the Mode of
Living, and on the Rate of Intereft.

Mr *Lock* reckons that *Silver* is reduced to one tenth
Part of the Value it had in the Reign of *Henry* VII (a-
bout the Time of opening the *Spanifh* Mines in *America*)
when compared with *Wheat*, which he reckons a Commodity the leaft liable to change, when taken for a
Number of Years. And Mr. *Law* reckons that *Silver-
Money* is worth but one twentiethPart of the *Goods*,& one
fifty-feventh Part of the *Land*, it was worth about 200
Years ago. But in Mr *Law's*Calculations, Allowance muft
be made for the leffening the Quantity of Silver in the
Coins from time to time There are many ftrange Inftances to this Purpofe, fo well known, that I need not
mention any more.

Some think that the Rate of *Labour* is a Standard-Mea-
fure of the Value of Things : But I am of a different
Opinion. For we find that even this undergoes as many
and as great Changes as other Things do, and from the
common Caufes, *viz* the Changes in the Proportion of
the Number of Labourers to the Demand for them, in
the different Imployments of Life : And it may be faid
to differ in *Great Britain* from a *Groat* to a *Guinea* a
Day Indeed in the firftContrivance of Things, theLabour
to be beftowed on them, muft always be confidered as
one, and often the chief Article of the Coft of them :
Yet notwithftanding, when the Husbandman has produced his Wheat, and the Clothier has perfected his Piece
of Cloth, and both are carried to the Market, they muft
be fold there according to the Proportion of Quantity and
Demand.

A Commodity, that is to be made the Meafure of the
Value of other Things, muft befides its natural Qualifications, have a confiderable deal of Art and Pains added
to them. And I know of no one Thing in Being, that
can

can be so well managed for thatEnd, as our BILLS of pub-lick Credit, put under proper Regulation : They may be made almost a perfect Measure of Value, by being fixed to an assigned Rate of Interest (say 3 to 6 perCent) and may be emitted or called in always in Proportion to the Demand every Day at the assigned Rate ; and whilst they were so managed, they could not be said to *change* their *own*Value, nor to be theCause of the Change in the Value of *other* Things, whether directly or conse-quentially. Nor on the other Hand, could they *fix* the Rate of any Commodity : For this can only be done by the common Consent of a Community, or by special Agreement among private Men. But in one Word, they would be the *Measure* of the Changes in every other Thing, as being fixed themselves

However strange this Doctrine may seem to those, who have either wilfully or ignorantly tantalized this unhap-py Province by calling in Question, whether the *Bills* may be said to have *any* Value at all, contrary to the daily Evidence of their own Senses ; branding them as *Waste-Paper*, - - *Pen, Ink & Paper*, and the like childish Stuff : And however plain we have proved the contrary, yet I shall not desire them to rely on those Evidences, but will call in the Judgment of the great Mr *Lock*, who perhaps was the first, at least in *England*,that ever wrote judiciously on the Subject of Money, which has all along been kept as a great *Mystery*, as he somewhere observes, and (as we have already hinted) supposed to be just what an iniquitous Ministry and a crafty Mint would have it to be, for their own Advantage.

The Author speaking of a Standard-Measure of Value, says, that*Wheat* in *Europe* (& thatGrain which is the gene-ral Food of any Country) is the *fittest* Measure to judge of the *alter'd* Value of Things in any long Tract of Time ; then shews what would be such aMeasure in an*Island* un-known to the rest of the World ; and proceeds to ob-serve, That if in any Country they use for *Money* any last-ing *Material*, whereof there is not any more to be got, and it cannot be increased ; or being of no other Use, the rest of the World does not value it, and so it is not like to be diminished ; *this* also would be the steady standing *Measure* of the *Value* of all *other* Commodities. —— Which is a Case full in Point. *Such a Material* I propose (that need neither be increased nor diminished, will not be exported, and sufficiently lasting, or when
damaged

damaged by any Accident capable, of being eafily renew'd)
for an Inftrument of Commerce. But the ingenious Au
thor prefently ftops his Profecution of this Point, and
gives the Reafon, Becaufe *Silver* and *Gold* have already
obtained in *England*, and the trading World, and he is
not for *altering* (nor fhould I neither if we were on the
fame Footing, becaufe of the great Difficulty of fuch a
Tranfition in moft Countries) but adds, Though it be
certain that that Part of the World, which *bred moft* of
our Gold and Silver, *ufed leaft* of it in Exchange (meaning for other Goods) and ufed it not for *Money* at all.

  Take alfo the Judgment of Mr. *Law*, who wrote ad.
mirably well upon Money in the Year 1705, about 14
Years after Mr. *Lock*, and as many before the fatal *Miffi-
fippi*-Scheme, father'd upon him, but more likely to be
the Device of the then Regent of *France*, I mean the iniquitous Part of it. He fays, If a Money be eftablifhed,
that has no intrinfick Value, and its extrinfick Value fuch
as that it will not be exported, nor will not be lefs than
the Demand for it within the Country, Wealth and Power
will be attained, and 'twill be lefs precarious Money, not
being liable to be leffened directly nor confequentially,
and Trade not liable to decay confequentially ; fo the
Power and Wealth of that Country will only be precarious from what may be directly hurtful to Money. Again,
That a Nation having eftablifhed fuch Money, having
alfo the other Qualities neceffary in Money, they ought
to have no Regard what Value it will have in other Countrys ; on the contrary, as every Country endeavours by
Law to preferve their Money, if that People can contrive
a Money that will not be valued abroad, they will do
what other Countries by Laws (meaning with Regard to
their Silver Money) have endeavoured in vain.

  This is alfo full to the Purpofe : And though we muft
not dream of Wealth and Power in this Province, yet I
am fatisfied that a fufficient Quantity of *Bill-Money* for
the Improvement of the great natural Advantages of the
Province, a moderate Ballance of Trade with all the
World in our Favours, a Competency of Silver and Gold
for common Safety, would all have a direct Tendency to
promote the Intereft of the Mother Country, as well as
our own ; that the Want of either of them would be
vaftly prejudicial ; but that the Want of a Sufficiency of
Money would be the abfolute Ruin of our Trade. We
may alfo learn from this and other Paffages of Mr. *Law*,
                                                    that

that it is better to have *Silver* in any Country paſſing on the Foot of a *Commodity*, than as *Money*. Which brings me to the ſecond Qualification of Money ;

2 *That it be made of convenient Matter.*

As Money is the Inſtrument or Tool of Commerce, convenient Matter is abſolutely neceſſary. It muſt be of little Bulk and Weight, both for the Convenience of Carriage and Keeping: Durable or not liable to waſte or periſh : Capable of being divided, without Loſs, for ſmall Change : Capable of taking a plain laſting and not eaſily counterfeited Impreſſion, that the Receiver may be ſatisfied that the Meaſure offered him is according to the Standard.

In moſt of theſe Regards, *Bills* have much the Advantage of *Silver* For the Imperfection of Silver is the true Cauſe of the Introduction of *Banks* ; which have been of great Service to Trade, by avoiding the Expence & Riſque of Carriage, the Charge of Caſhiers, and the Danger of bad Money, which are conſiderable Articles ; and therefore in all great Places of Trade, the Merchants would rather pay the Bankers for keeping their Money, than be without them.

In this Province we have not one Article of Produce, Manufacture, or imported Commodity, to ſerve as a fit Inſtrument of Commerce. Our *Silver* is all carried off, and ſome particular Years we may want above 50000 Oz. to pay our full and juſt Debt. If we had *Iron, Copper,* or *Lead*, they might be put into Magazines, and Notes taken out promiſing them at a certain Rate and Fineneſs, and they would change their Value asSilver and all other general Commodities do *Wheat* or *Hemp* might be negotiated ſomething after the ſame Manner ; but they are more liable to periſh : Nor have we a Surpluſage of theſe, or any other Things for the Purpoſe, but either export, or conſume all of them. Our *Lands*, and other realEſtate, cannot be exported, and will not commonly be taken for the Payment of a foreign Debt ; tho' they may ſo far as relates to Money, be of Service : Of which more hereafter.

For want of Silver, or Bills of Credit, as an Inſtrument of Commerce, People have in a Manner been forced into a much greater Conſumption of *Shop Goods*, both as to the Kinds and Degrees of Fineneſs, than they would have choſen ; which has introduced all Sorts of Prodigality among us, one Step therein naturally leading to another.

Trading

Trading People, in general, are obliged to purfue this Method, as they cannot make, but muft follow the natural Courfe of Trade. But the *Shopkeepers* have reaped by far the greateft Advantages by it, as being virtually poffeffed of the current Money of the Province, and in that Regard may fitly be compared to the *Bankers* in *Europe*; only that they have greater Advantages than them, by having Goods put into their Shops upon Credit, and without Intereft, and virtually the fame taken back again in Payments, that is, Shop-Goods, or the Produce of them in Provifions, Tradefmen's Work, and the like, with very little Money, and a confiderable Profit allowed them. And in this Regard they ought not to be blamed, fince they act agreable to the Plan of our Trade: For as all People that are concerned in Trade, will unavoidably lay hold of any bad Matter, and ufe it as Money, when they have no better to ufe, fo moft certainly upon the Want of Silver or Bills, even in any Degree of Proporcion to the Demands of Trade, Shop-Goods will be negotiated as Money; tho' in the Main the Hurt and Ruin of all our Trade.

Some few People have traded chiefly for Money; others for a greater or leffer Part in Money, and the Remainder in Goods: But in the End the chief of the Labour of the Province has been paid for in *Shop-Goods*, and the Labourers have been the greateft Sufferers, by fpending a great Part of their Time in attending the Shops; giving great Difcounts for Money in lieu of Goods; and permitting many hurtful Converfions of Money into Goods, which has introduc'd great Extravagance and Idlenefs, to fay no worfe.

In fome particular Places the *Name* of Money has been kept, but a quite *different* Thing intended: For Inftance, *Shop-Notes* that have fpecified half Money, half Goods, have been by iniquitous Cuftom conftrued to fignify half Englifh Goods, half Provifions. I have heard of almoft incredible Difcounts allowed by the poor Tradefmen for ready Money in lieu of fuch Notes.

Another great Inconvenience confequent to the Want of Money is a *Trucking* Trade, which brings with it infurmountable Difficulty. For as a great Number of People depend upon Money to go to Market for their daily Provifions, & other neceffaries, and as that Defect can by no other Means whatever be remedied than by proper Money, fo it will be a Miracle if our Trade do not fink under
the

the Burden, to the vaſt Damage of the landed Intereſt of this Province, and proportionably alſo of the Trade of the Mother-Country.

In fine, The Want of an adequate Inſtrument of Commerce has been the firſt and great Cauſe of all our Extravagance, the Riſe of Silver, and a ſhameful Ballance of Debt, beſides many baſe Practices, bitterly aggravated by our Enemies, and ſufficiently complained of by our Friends.

3 *Money muſt be received by common Conſent, within the Community for which it is intended.*

That Money ſhould have the common Conſent of the People, where it is to paſs, is very obvious to every one; and why I reſtrain it to a particular Community, as a Kingdom, Province, &c. will appear from the following Conſiderations

It is neceſſary in the trading World, that there ſhould be one or more Commodities of univerſal ready Acceptance, in which the different trading Countries might pay or receive their reſpective Ballances of Trade with each other: For it is impoſſible that any two Countries can exchange yearly juſt an equal Value in Produce and Manufactures; and in this Regard Silver and Gold have the natural Advantages of all other Commodities. They are alſo of great Advantage, as being the Commodities, which all Nations have agreed upon to be uſed in the Courſe of Exchange; the Weight and Fineneſs of the Coins of one Country adjuſted to thoſe of another, being the Baſis or Par of Exchange; and the Variation from the exact Standard, called the Riſe or Fall in the Courſe of Exchange; and finally, they are the beſt Commodities to be tranſmitted from one Country to another, whoſe Trade or Policy requires they ſhould.

Again, It would be of conſiderable Advantage to Trade, if all the *European* Kingdoms at leaſt could agree in a fixed Proportion of Alloy to their Silver and Gold, and upon a certain Weight to their Coins; as ſuppoſing the higheſt of Silver to be exactly an Ounce, Troy Weight, and ſubdiviſions by tenth Parts as low as they conveniently could, and that all their Meaſures of Quantity were alſo fixed to one Standard.

Such a general Regulation might poſſibly be brought about: But a Regulation of Money as a juſt Meaſure and fit Inſtrument of Commerce, never could be accompliſhed. No univerſal Commodities, as *Silver, Gold,* &c. can
be

be fo managed.   Every Country muſt chooſe a ſpecial or local one, and ın this Regard *Bılls* of Credit have the Preference of all others

4 The laſt Qualıfication of Money is the *SanЄion of publick Authorıty.*

It is the undoubted Prerogative of the cıvıl Magıſtrate, to appoint all the common Meaſures of Quantity and Va-lue, and to change them as juſt Occaſions requıre, and more eſpecıally to order what ſhall be adjudged Money in the *Law.*   But then it is not the Act of Government, that gıves Value to Silver :   For that depends wholly upon common Conſent, and no one would receıve it of the Government, if ıt had not that Conſent

In lıke manner, ıt ıs not the Act of Government that gives Value to our Bılls of Credit ın the Market , but the common Conſent of the People.   For the Government can and do only ſay, that ſo far as they pay or receıve, the Bılls ſhall be valued, and any one or more Men may emıt Bılls to the ſame Import.   They have (and it is theır undoubted Rıght) ſaid, that the Bills ſhall be a *law-ful Tender* where Money ıs promıſed, but have juſtly ex-cepted *ſpecial Contracts* ; for otherwıſe they would ſtrike at the very Root of Trade.   They may order that the Bills and no other Things ſhall be receıved ın Taxes, and ſo every one would be oblıged to purchaſe ſome of them for that End   But the People might notwıthſtandıng refuſe them as Money ın Trade.   I am next to offer my Thoughts

Of Banks.   *With a Propoſal.*

FOR ſome Yeers paſt People in general among us have run ınto the Notıon of a *Bank,* and ſome Attempts have been made : As the Scheme for the *Merchants Notes,* promıſing *Sılver,* at 19s per *Ounce,* 3 10ths ın 3 Years, 3 10ths ın 6 Years, and 4 10ths ın 10 Years, without Inter-eſt : Alſo a Propoſal for *L* 60000 in Notes promıſing *Sılver* at 20s per *Ounce,* half in 5 Years, and half ın 10 Years, wıthout Intereſt ; not to mention the Provınce-Bılls of the *new Tenor.*   All ſuch Schemes promıſing *Sıl-ver,* at a certaın fixed Rate, and diſtant Tıme, having a dırect Tendency (under our preſent Circumſtances) to to raıſe the Rate of Sılver, and to oppreſs the Debtor, the Succeſs of them has been anſwerable.   However, I am of Opınıon, that a Bank (erected either by one ſufficient
                                                          Man

Man alone, or by a Number of such Men associated together) contrived with a just Regard to our present unhappy Circumstances (for otherwise it would be of hurtful Consequence) might be of great Advantage ; is indeed the first and most necessary Step towards our Relief,
and would contribute, by the Favour of Providence, to
the mutual Benefit of our selves and the Mother-Country. I shall therefore proceed to the Consideration of
Banks, and examine how far they may be *practicable* and
useful in *New-England.*

There are *two Sorts* of Banks in common use in the
trading World, *viz* those that make *effective* Payments of
Silver or *Gold* on Demand, and those that make *no* effective Payments, but only a bare *Transfer* of an assigned
Sum upon the *Bank-Books,* from one Man's Account to
another, as every one has Occasion to pay or receive a
Debt.

Of the *first* Sort are the Banks of *England* and *Scotland,*
established by Acts of Parliament ; the private Bankers
or Goldsmiths *London, Dublin,*&c All founded upon the
Estate, but chiefly the *Credit* of the respective Bankers.

The general *Plan* of such a Bank is —— to begin with,
and always keep in Hand *such a Sum* of Money, as may
answer all reasonable *Demands* ; to lend Money, and
discount Bills and Notes, in the *shortest* and *safest* Way ;
so that if a Run upon them should happen (either by a
Diffidence of their Credit, or the Malice of other Bankers) they may be provided, and have a Supply of Money
equal to all Demands.

They emit Notes *promising Money on Demand* ; and
may be assured, that while their Credit is good, and there
is a competent Proportion of Silver in the Country where
they live, the trading Party will bring them in *more* Money than they carry out. For the *Trader* is greatly benefited by the Bank : as having all the Bills or Notes, due
to him, punctually negotiated by the Bankers without
any Charge ; ready Money advanced upon them occasion-
ally at a moderate Discount ; the Convenience of easier
and quicker Payments, by a Draught on the Bank ; saving the Expence of Cashiers, Baggs and Carriage ; and
having his Money more safely lodg'd, in Cases of Fire or
Robbery, the best Measures being taken for that End.
And besides these Advantages to the private Trader, the
Publick is also greatly benefited : For by Means of the
Bank the *Money* of a Country is virtually much *increased,*

Interest

Interest kept *lower*, the *People* better *imployed*, and consequently under a wise publick Administration, Wealth and Power easier attained, establish'd and promoted.

The Bankers Notes bear *no Interest*, because they pay *upon Sight*, without Delay ; and the Advantage of negociating a Sum greater than their Stock, is the just Privilege of a Trade or Business, of all others one of the most useful.

Mr. *Lock* makes mention of a *private Banker*, that had circulating at one Time *l.* 1100000 Sterling. in Notes signed by his *Clerk :* A Sum equal to *six Million* of our Currency, from which he might draw great Profits (natural Interest being then from 9 to 10 per Cent) and no trading Man in the Kingdom might better deserve them

It is impossible for *us* to have a Bank of this Sort under our present Circumstances : Having no *Silver-Mines*, nor a general *Ballance* of *Trade*, as the Means of importing and keeping it in the Country, but some Years a considerable Ballance of *Debts* against us , so that no Man can either *purchase* a sufficient Sum as a *Fund* for a Bank, nor can he *keep* such a Sum in his Hands, if already purchased, without proportionably *increasing* the *Demand* for *Silver*. If all the *Exports* of the Province were made by its *Inhabitants* only, and they all should agree to make *no Returns* but in *Silver*, yet unless they could prevent the usual *Importations* of *Goods*, there would probably be a *Demand* for *all* the Silver, and *more ;* and so the Price rather rise, than fall : But if one Man, or a Number of Men, should step 10 or 20000 *l* Sterling, as a *Fund* for a Bank, this would *raise* it to a great Degree, and such a Bank would speedily be exhausted, to the Loss, rather than Profit of the Bankers.

It is obvious to even the meanest Capacity, that every *new Demand* must have a Tendency to *raise* the Price of *Silver :* And we have frequent Instances of the Fact. To mention but one. I have known at the yearly Payments of *Impost-Money*, which in the whole was but a small Sum, yet consisting of a greater Number of small Payments (from about one Ounce and upwards) Silver rose *pro Tempore*, from 27 s to 31 s per Ounce, the Purchasers being numerous, the Sums generally very small, and the Sellers knowing the Pinch of the Matter right well.

But tho' our *Trade* cannot supply a *Bank*, yet some think that our *Lands* might easily do it. Suppose then a

Number

Number of Men fhould go upon *this Method* (which would be eafi/ft for the Province, and the Bankers) *viz.* to procure a *Credit* from the Bank of *England*, for *l* 100000 Sterling, at 3 or 4 per Cent Intereft, upon *Land-Security* ; and to draw out the faid Sum *occafi nally* , the *Intereft* to commence from the Payment of their Drafts When they have fo done, then proceed to emit *Bills* for a Currency, promifing a certain Sum *payable* in 3 or 6 Months, to the Poffeffor, in *Sterling-Drafts* (this fhort D.ftance of Time, confidering our Condition, would bring them under little or no Difcount) and let them out upon *Land-Security*, to pay in the *fame* Money, and 6 per Cent. Intereft

This would be the *cheapeft* and *eafieft* Way of *borrowing*, and yet I believe next to *impracticable*. Suppofing the Sum could be had at Home, which is very uncertain (for we have found by Experience, that the Mother-Country will fooner make us an *Abatement* in our Payments for Goods, than take *Lands* without it) the Province would be charged with a *new Debt*, for the Intereft and Principal, and I doubt neither Undertaker nor Borrower here would find their Account in it.

The *neareft* and *fafeft* Method for a *Bank* Circulation of Bills promifing *Silver* at a certain Rate, may be this that follows.

One or more Men having good Credit with the People, to emit Bills promifing *Silver* at a certain Rate (fuppofe 29 s. per Ounce) or an Equivalent in the fame *Bills*, at the End of *one Year* : Then to *call in* all their Bills extant, and make *Allowance* equal to the *Change* in the Rate of *Silver* for the Worfe (if any) for that Year; and this, either according to the *different Changes* it may have undergone from *Week* to *Week* throughout the Year, taking the whole Number of Weeks upon an Average-Computation, or elfe according to the Rate of Silver at the *Time of Payment*, which of the two fhall be thought/ moft equitable : And having fo done, return the *Poffeffor* his *Bills* back again with the *Addition* : And proceed after this Manner from Year to Year. Thus far as to the Poffeffor.

Again, To emit their Bills wholly upon *Loan*, with indifputable *Security*, at the Rate of 4 per Cent. *Intereft*, conditioned to pay *Silver* at 29 s per Ounce, or an *equivalent* at the End of every Year, for the *Difference* of Principal and Intereft, on the fame Foot that the *Bankers* allow to the *Poffeffors*.

I put *Interest* at 4 per Cent, partly becaufe it is the un-doubted *Benefit* of all Countries to have it as *low* as they can, and partly becaufe the *Borrower* makes the *Rate* of Silver *good*, which may poffibly be *coftly* to him.

This Scheme, I confefs, would be very laborious and chargeable to the *Banker*: And how far it would operate upon the *Price* of Silver, is uncertain; the *Payments* not being *effective* as to Silver at the Year's End, and People being forced to do as they can in fome Cafes However I am of Opinion, that fuch a Scheme as I have hinted at, might be put in Execution But I proceed,

2. To confider the *other* Sort of *Banks*: And of thefe the B.nk of *Venice* is the oldeft, and perhaps the beft model'd in the World A fhort Account of it will be en-tertaining to the Inquifitive, and is well worthy of our Attention.

Many Years ago the State or Republick of *Venice*, by a folemn Edict, eftablifhed a Bank, to confift of two Million of *Ducats*. Thofe that had a Mind to encourage it, car-ried in their *Money* to the Bank, and had *Credit* given them for their refpective Sums upon the *Bank Books*: Which *Credit* one might *difpofe of* to any other Perfon, in the Way of *Payment of a Debt*, or by Way of *Sale*; and that by a bare *Transfer* upon the Books from his own Account to the other Perfon's, without any *effective* Pay-ment of Silver or Gold So that the *firft Capital* has been in continual *Circulation* from one Creditor to another, and remains the fame intire Sum of Credit, only belong-ing to different Perfons, to this Day.

They enacted, that all Payments in the *Whole-fale Trade*, and for Bills of *Exchange*, fhould be made in *Banco*, that is, in thefe *Transfers*.

Their fmall or *retail* Payments are in *Silver* and *Gold*, as in other Parts --- He that wants to difpofe of his *Credit* on the Bank Books for *Silver*, muft fell it in the *Market* on the beft Lay he can; and he that wants to purchafe a *Credit*, muft alfo buy it there as he can.

The *Advantages* of this Bank were fo great, that after the firft Subfcription there arofe an *Agio* or *Premium* on Bank-Money, of 28 per Cent. which, doubtlefs, came on gradually, as of 1- 8th, or 1-4th of one perCent at a Time, occafioned by the great Opinion the People had of the Scheme, but chiefly by the Shortnefs of the firft Subfcrip-tion, in Proportion to Demands of Trade. This Ad-vance the State did not like, and it's faid, endeavoured

to

to reſtrain it by *Laws*; but without Effect, till they took in a ſecond Subſcription of 500000 *Ducats* more, which reduced it to 20 per Cent, and it has ſince never exceeded this   But I am of Opinion, that it was *not* the *Effect* of that ſmall Subſcription, nor of a Law reſtraining the Riſe of the Agio, that reduced and kept it under, but ſome *effective Method* to *ſupply* the Perſon that wanted a Credit at 20 per Cent, when he could not purchaſe it ſo in the *Market*. For otherwiſe it might have continued riſing to this Day

Mr. *Chambers* ſays, The State has now five *Million* of the People's Money, and *without Intereſt*; which is a great publick Advantage, and no Body hurt by it : For every Man may let his *Credit*, as he does his Money, to Intereſt.

It is generally believed, there is *little* or *no Money* in the Bank-Treaſury, but that the Government have long ago diſpoſed of it for publick Uſes; and very likely : Yet it does not, nor ought to *leſſen* the Credit of the Bank

Beſides the general Calamities that attend all Countries, by which the Creditors of the Bank might ſuffer in common, I know but *one Caſe* which might affect the Fall in the *Agio*, or make a Run upon the Bank, and that is a Ballance of *Debt* againſt the Republick, or the Want of a ſufficient Quantity of Silver, and other moveable Effects, to pay their *foreign* Debts, (which is the Caſe of our Province) but this is next to impoſſible to happen, while they are a *State* : For as the Evil might eaſily be foreſeen, ſo it might alſo be prevented by regulating their Imports and Exports, making ſumptuary Laws, borrowing Money of other Countries, and even obliging People to part with their ſuperfluous Finery, by ſelling it off to other Countries for the publick Good; and upon a ſudden Diffidence and Fall of the Bank *Agio*, they might engage to pay Intereſt to the Creditor, computing the 100 Ducats at 120, which would probably keep up its Credit, and tax the Subjects for the Payment of the Intereſt.   So that there is not the leaſt Probability of the Fall of their Bank-Money, or that Silver and Gold ſhall be in equal Value with it.

Of later Years they have erected a *Caſh Bank*, for the Advantage of Trade · where the Merchants may keep their running Caſh for domeſtick Occaſions, and they or Foreigners may be ſupplied with ſuch Sums or Species, as they

they want for Exportation ; which has alfo been found beneficial.

Some have faid that they emitted *Bills* : But this is a Fact I muft call in Queftion. However, that makes no effential Difference in the general Plan : Only as it appears to me, the *Transfer* is preferable, and in fome Cafes it would be neceffary to have both Bills and Transfers, as the Creditor pleafed

Now let any Man ferioufly confider this Scheme' of the Bank of *Venice*, and I am perfuaded he will find all the *effential* Parts of it in the Scheme of *our Province-Bills* of the *old Tenor*. Thus, for Inftance, *Their* Foundation was a Depofitum of *Silver* & commonConfent : *Ours* only the *common Confent* of the Government and People, which is *tantam unt*, as being the Foundation of the Value of Silver, and almoft all other Things; and if need were, we could make a greater and better Depofitum in *Lands*, equal to double the Value of our Bank-Circulation. Both their *Transfers* and our *Bills* were made a *lawful* Tender. —— Neither *they* nor *we* make *effective* Payments. *Transfers*, if left free to their natural Courfe in the Market, would be liable to change their Value every Day, as being virtually eftablifhed upon the Footing of a Commodity ; that is according to their Way of Reckoning, would rife or Fall every Day fo much per Cent In like manner, *our Bills*, being (unavoidably) left free to their Courfe in the Market, do change their Value daily. *They* would compute this Change by the Method of fo much per *Cent*. And *we* do it by the different Rates of *Silver*, which amounts to the fame Thing in different Words. Their *Agio* is now fixed : But our Rate of Silver cannot be fo under our prefent Condition *Their Scheme*, which was projected when they were in *flourifhing* Circumftances, in order to the facilitating and further Improvement of Trade, *fucceeded* in producing the defigned Eff & Our Scheme, which was projected when the Government was in very *low* Circumftances, having little or no Silver, and no other fit Matter to ferve as Money, for the Payment of publick Taxes, the Support of the War, and carrying on Trade, *fucceeded* too, and fully anfwered the Ends propofed by it, efpecially the laft mentioned, by the Improvement of the natural Advantages of the Province to a furprizing Degree. —— Their *Transfers* rofe to 28 per Cent, above common Money, till they were effectually reftrained : Our *Bills* indeed after fome Years funk in

Value,

Value, yet not by the Imperfection of our Scheme, but the Ballance of Debt, which it has not been in the Power of our Government (at leaft no effectual Attempts have hitherto been made) to prevent. Otherwife, had our Trade produced a Ballance in our *Favour*, it would have been next a Miracle, if our *Bill-Money* had not been *better* now than at the firft Emiffion, or (in other Words) if *Silver* had not *fallen*, as the Quantity increafed above the Demand.——— Thus, it appears, that the Schemes have virtually both the fameFoundation and the fame Tendency in their own Nature : Tho' theSuccefs has has been very different, owing intirely to the differing *trading* Circumftances of the two Countries, and no other Caufe whatever.

The Bank of *Amflerdam* is nearly built upon the fame Plan. Common Moneys have been and ftill are taken in by the Bank at an affigned *Agio*, generally from 3 to 4 per Cent above *Par* : But the Man that wants a Credit may either purchafe it at the Bank-Rate, or the Market-Rate, as he can make the beft Bargain. They have never made *effective* Payments : But People may lodge particular Species of Money in the Bank, not exceeding fix Months, and have the fame returned to them again, p'ying about 15 d. upon *l.* 100 Sterling, for keeping The Magiftrates and City are made refponfible for the fafe Cuftody of the Moneys depofited, and they are fecured from the fraudulent Practices of Under Officers by fufficient Sureties and capital Punifhments. The Creditor may have a Bill orNote from the Commiffioners, certifying that he ftands Creditor fo many *Guilders* (in a certain Folio) on the Books, upon which he has his future Payments endorfed; or he may keep a running Account with the Bank. All Bills of Exchange (inland and foreign) are by Law made payable in Bank-Money. The Charge of this great Bank is chiefly (if not wholly) fupported by fmall contingent Payments, collected agreeable to the Rules : As 20 Guilders for opening every Man's firft Account, one Penny for every future Entry, 6 d if the Sum be lefs than 500 *Guilders* (about *l.* 27 Sterling) and 6 d. for Bufinefs done out of Office Hours, Forfeitures where a Man over draws his Ballance &c This is alfo a Bank of *pure Credit*, founded upon common Confent ; *no Silver* taken out, nor will it probably ever be the Intereft of any Man to demand it : And for the Subftance it is the *fame* as the Scheme of our Bills of publick Credit. The different

Succefs

Succefs is owing to no other Caufe, but the different tra-ding Circumftances : Which will further appear by the following Confiderations.

Suppofing there could be found in this Province, of wrought Plate and Bullion, to the Value of *L* 50000 Sterling, and that every Man fhould bring in his particu-lar Parcel, and take *Credit* for the fame on the Books of a *Bank* erected for that Purpofe, at the Rate of 29 s per Ounce for Silver &c. and then *difpofe* of that Credit, as already mentioned ; that would be doing the *fame* Thing as they do in *Venice* and *Amfterdam* ; t is in the beft Manner would anfwer the Ends of Money ; and in all Countries where they have a Ballance of Trade in their Favour, this would foon rife above the Rate of common Money, if not reftrained. And thus it would certainly be in this Province, if we had the Ballance of Trade in our Favour : But in the contrary Cafe (as there would be no *effective* Payments) *Silver* might rife to 40 or any other Number of Shillings, in Proportion to the Ballance a-gainft us

Again, Suppofing *Lands* were mortgaged for half their Value in *Silver* at 29 s per *Ounce*, to remain as a perpe-tual Security to the Creditor of the Bank, and to be nego-tiated as above ; yet neither would that, nor any other Security, how great foever, affect the Price of Silver in the Market.

Now as I think thefe Confequences cannot be deny'd, fo this affords us another ftrong Argument, that the Caufe of the Rife or Fall of *Silver* is not from the *Bills*, but wholly from our *trading Circumftances* —— Wherefore I fhall now proceed to offer a few general Hints for

A Scheme.

PErhaps the only Plan, that can be contrived agreable to our prefent Circumftances, and which I am per-fwaded will have the moft direct Tendency to extricate us out of our prefent Difficulties is this.

Let a Number of Men affociate themfelves together, and emit Bills of the following Tenor, viz

WE the Subfcribers, for our felves and Partners, promife to receive this Twenty Shilling Bill of Credit in all Pay-ments for Debts due to us, where Bills of publick Credit of the old Tenor were promifed, and in all our future Dealings as Money : Specialties and exprefs Contracts in Writing al-ways excepted.   Poffibly

Poffibly that Part of the Bill *(in all Payments for Debts due to us, where Bills (of publick Credit of the old Tenor were promised)* may be a Stumbling Block to many among us, who have large Sums due to them upon the Footing of the old Bills, and have hopes that the Government will do fomething in their Favour on that Head ; therefore rather than the Scheme fhould be clogg'd by that Claufe, it might be left out, and the Bills only made to look for-ward.

The Undertakers to give fuffi-ient Security, that they will always receive the Bills according to their Tenor.

The Undertakers to be bound to the Signers of the Bills, as they are to the Poffeffor, in fuch a Manner as may give general Satisfaction.

No Undertaker to take out above 10 *per Cent of the Sum he fubfcribes ; and for that too to give his Bond or Note bearing Intereft, on the fame Footing as other indif-ferent Borrowers : For as he is juftly intitled to his Share of the Profits, and liable to pay his Share of the Charges and Loffes his Depofitum ought for ever to remain intire, as a Security to the Poffeffor.*

The Company to lend out their Bills on good Security at 6 *per Cent Intereft ; and to difcount private Bills or Notes at the Rate of - per Cent, on Conditions to pay in the fame Bills again, or in Silver at the current Market-Rate, when purchafed with the faid Bills   And the Bank to take no other Bills but their own, or Silver as above.*

That they immediately enter into a conftant Courfe of Bu-finefs, which is effential to a Bank   Their Loans to be re-gulated by the affigned Rate of Intereft

As to *Managers, Clerks, Meetings* &c there will be lit-tle Difficulty : So I fhall not detain the Reader on thefe Heads.

Such a Scheme as this I take to be the moft agreable to our prefent Cafe. I am firmly in the Belief, that no other generalPlan than this, can ever take Eff.ct, fo as to anfwer the Ends of Money , and that fooner or later the Diftreffes of the Province, and the woful Effects of fome other Schemes, much talk'd of, will force us into fuch a one as the foregoing, when our Affairs are much worfe than even now : And further that fuch a one, if wifely managed, with an honeft View to the publick Good, would have the moft direct Tendency to promote *Fru-gality* and *Induftry* (without which the beft adjufted Schemes will be of little Significance)to turn the Scale of
Trade

Trade in our Favour, and make us a happy People: Particularly I look upon it the *only Means* to deftroy the moft pernicious Practice of *Shop-Notes*, or rather *Shop-Money*.

We have lately had a Variety of Schemes propos'd. The prevailing one at prefent, promoted by fome particular Gentlemen, is that for *l.* 300000. the *Bills to promife to the Poffeffor Silver at* 20 s (the now current Market-Rate being 29 s) *payable at the End of fifteen Years, without any Intereft*

Now, according to the univerfal Rule, when *thefe Bills* are computed by *lawful* (compound) *Intereft* of 6 per Cent, (not to mention the *natural* Intereft, which is equally the univerfal Practice) they will then be *only* equal to Silver at 47 s 9 d per Ounce on the Day of their firft Emiffion, and would fell for no more in the Mother-Country, if Intereft were at that Rate. —— The *Effects* of fuch an ill judged Scheme may be eafily forefeen by the Succefs of fome of the like among our felves, and other *British* Plantations: For it is next to impoffible that fuch Bills fhould *long circulate* as Money, and but that they fhould be the Means of *raifing* the Rate of *Silver*, promoting ufurious Practices, and bringing this Province into great Difreputation at *Home*, as they who trade hither are like to be none of the leaft Sufferers

Some among us are for *no* Bills of any Sort, but for leaving the Trade to its own natural Courfe; as thinking that the Neceffity of the Thing will naturally oblige us to alter our prefent Mode of Living, and keep our Silver among us to ferve as Money. But this Suppofition is abfurd and intirely groundlefs: For as the next and moft handy Way of carrying on our Trade (in the Default of *Silver* or *Bills*) is that of the *Shop Money*, fo of Confequence this muft prevail (as it has all along) in Proportion to the Scarcity of others, and by this Means Extravagance Increafe, Silver rife, and finally the landed as well as trading Intereft of the Province be hurt to a prodigious Degree.

We have had fome Accounts lately of a Defign on Foot to petition the *British Parliament*, in order to have the Cafe of the Plantations, with Refpect to their *Bills* of Credit, taken into Confideration: And as the Colonies in general, and this Province in particular, are of great Importance to the Mother-Country, doubtlefs they will give great Attention to an Affair of that Kind

Our

Our common Opinion is, that it would be well; if the Parliament fhould *proportion the Quantity of Bills in every Colony* (that are in the Ufe of them) and *fix their Value.*

As to the *firft* of thefe, our common Complaint is, that our neighbouring Colony of *Rhode Ifland,* tho' of fmall Extent, and much lefs Trade than we, yet have made and are ftill allowed to make Emiffions of Bills without Reftriction; while we are reftrained by his Maj fty's Inftructions to his Excellency our Governour; and of Neceffity are obliged to take theirs, which greatly promotes their Trade, and equally difcourages ours. The firft Part of this Complaint I fhall now confider, and the latter Part, *viz.* with Regard to our Reftraint, will naturally follow in the Sequel

I much queftion whether our bringing a Complaint againft the *Rhode-Ifland* Emiffions would not have an Air of Envy and hurt our Caufe ; and whether they might not eafily fet afide all our Arguments on that Head, by fhowing that they have only done what a wife People ought to do, in emitting Bills for the Improvement of their own natural Advantages, and carrying on as great a Part as they can of the Trade of the Plantations, which the Mother-Country has in great Wifdom left equally free to all, whilft all their Neighbours are equally free to their Trade, and at their Liberty to take or refufe their Bills

There are two *Irregularities* in their Emiffions, which yet hitherto have had few or no ill Effects ; thefe may and ought to be remedied for the Future ; *viz* their emitting of *confiderable Sums* (as about *l.* 20000 Sterling*)* at *one Time,* and *immediately difperfing* the Bills ; together with their letting out the Bills on *Loan,* conditioned to repay the whole in 20 Years (as I am inform'd*)* in *certain partial Payments.* For Money ought to be emitted *gradually,* and the general Quantity fo managed that it may be call'd in, or let out, as the *Trade* requires.

However, as to the *Quantity* of Bills now extant there, altho' they are vaftly more in Proportion than in any other Colony, being I fuppofe about *l* 330000: Yet this Sum, only equal to *l* 59000 *Sterling,* may be thought in the Mother-Country but a very *moderate* or *fmall* one to carry on their enterprizing Trade.

I have fpoken with the greater Freedom & in ftronger Terms in Relation to *Rhode-Ifland* Bills, from a firm Perfuafion, that all Attempts to ftop their Currency will

be

be fruitleſs, except that of having a *Sufficiency of our own,* and that Delays in this Caſe may be vaſtly hurtful to us both in our trading and land°d Intereſts

I am now to conſider the *fixing* of the Rate of Silver by *Law*: And this I take to be impoſſible in our preſent Caſe, for we have already a Law of this Province (of old ſtanding) fixing the lawful Tender of Pieces of Eight of 17 *dwt* to 6 s that is neareſt 7 s 3 *f*. per Ounce, and much ater than that, an Eſtabliſhment in Queen *Anne*'s Reign, making Pieces of Eight of 17 *dwt* & half a lawful Tender for 6 s. that is, 6 s. 10 d. two ſevenths per *Ounce,* commonly called *Proclamation-Money* ; which Act or Order came too late : For before the Commencement of it, Silver was got to 8 s. per Ounce   Neither of theſe have been ſufficient to regulate the Price of Silver, for theReaſons already given ; in Effect, that a *Bankrupt's* Pound or Money muſt be according to what he is able to pay : and this is common, at leaſt in private Affairs, to all Countries. For Inſtance in *Great Britain, Silver* being eſtabliſhed by Law at 5 s. 2 d per Ounce, the Man that pays 10 s. in the Pound, his Money is only equal to Silver at 10 s. 4 d. per Ounce. Or if he pays only 3 s 7 d in the Pound, it is but equal (as ours is) to *Silver* at 29 s. per Ounce

The *Remedy* then, that I would humbly propoſe to be apply'd for, is this, in brief : ──

That we might be allowed to emit Bills of Credit, *fixed to aſſigned an Rate of Intereſt* ; agreeable to the foregoing Plan, or in ſuchManner as ſhall be thought moſt proper.

That all Schemes for Bills promiſing Silver, at a certain Rate, and diſtant Time, with ut Intereſt, or other than by Law allowed, be diſcountenanced , & that theCourts of Law be required to regulate their Judgments in Conformity thereto.

That they would be pleaſed to allow us a certain Sum yearly, to be drawn for in Bills of Exchange, for ſuch a Continuance as ſhall be thought needful (or until we can reduce Silver to the Proclamation-Standard, and have a ſufficient Quantity of it paſſing in Trade) at an aſſigned Intereſt   Or elſe that we may be allowed and encouraged to make ſuch Laws *to regulate our Trade, as may effectually bring the Ballance in our Favour, ſo far as to anſwer the aforeſaid Ends.*

Theſe are ſome of the neceſſary Helps, that I would join in requeſting from our indulgent Mother=Country :

And

And the rather becaufe her own Intereft is fo nearly concerned, and probably would be advanced in the End.
But the chief and greateft Favour would be to allow us
a fufficient Quantity of *Bills*, emitted on a well regulated Plan: Without which all other Expedients might
fail of Succefs.

Thus I have finifhed what I had principally in View:
And think I have fufficiently obviated the common Objections as I went along. However, having promifed the
Reader a Reply to a late printed Piece, on the fame Subject, I muft now proceed to

Remarks on the *Effay concerning Silver and Paper Currencies, more-efpecially with Regard to the Britifh Colonies in* New-England.

I Shall not imitate the Author in introducing my Reply
with *farcaflical* Reflections on his Performance. Nor
do I defign any *idle Criticifms* upon it. My Inducement
in taking Notice of it is, chiefly becaufe it feems calculated to promote fuch Meafures with Relation to our *Bills*,
as in my Opinion will be prejudicial to the publick Intereft. Though, I confefs, another Motive is, becaufe
the Author has pretended his Effay is a full Anfwer to a
fmall Piece I had publifh'd, *viz* OBSERVATIONS *on the
Scheme for l.* 60000 *&c* My principal Aim in which was
(as the Occafion led me) honeftly to reprefent the dangerous Tendency of any Scheme for Bills promifing *Silver* at a
cerrain Rate and long Period, and to fhew that *fuch* Bills
would never anfwer the Ends of *Money*. In order to this,
I was obliged to enter a little into the Confideration of
Money in general, and of *Bills* in particular.

I fhall now as briefly as I well can (having already
gone to a Length much exceeding my firft Intentions)
in a *general* Way point out fome material *Differences* between the *Effay* and my *Obfervations*, and then make o-
ther more *particular* Remarks.

I am firft to give the Reader a *general* View of the
material *Differences* between us. The following Inftat-
ces may fuffice

I had in my Obfervations argued, and fufficiently
fhown, that our *Bills* of the old Tenor, were eftablifhed
by Government and common Confent, upon the *fame*
Footing with all other *Commodities*, and *preferable* to all
other

other Commodities, being received as the *moſt general*
Commodity or *Money* of the Province ——— But the
Eſſayer takes no Notice of this neceſſary Diſtinction and
Definition : Only from the Beginning to the End of his
Piece he calls them *Paper Currency*, *Vague*, *Fluctuating*,
Imaginary, *Fallacious*, *Nominal* ; *Bills promiſing a preca-*
rious or no Value ; *a forced provincial Tender , an ill con-*
trived unnatural falſe Medium, and as a Depoſitum no bet-
ter than Waſte-Paper; a Moth of a Currency &c

In my Obſervations (p. 6 &c.) I plainly ſhow'd,
the *ſpecial Cauſe* of the *Riſe* of the Rate of Silver and
other Things in the Market to be from the Operation of
the Ballance of Debt againſt us : And *not* at all from any
Operation of the *Bills*, they having *never exceeded* the
due Proportion in Quantity ——— But the *Eſſayer* on the
contrary, imputes the *Riſe* of the Market to *a Glut of this*
provincial conſuſed Paper Currency, and gives it as his O-
pinion, *that we ought not to have Recourſe to any other*
Conceit (as Ballance of Trade) for its Cauſe, but only to
the Operation of theſe Bills.

My *general Cauſe* aſſigned throughout the whole
Letter, for the *Changes* of the *Value* of all Things in the
Market, is the *Change* in the *Proportion* of their *Quantity*
to *Demand.* And I ſhewed that any *Commodity* or *Money*
when *fixed* in that Proportion, would be an *unerring Mea-*
ſure or *Standard*, by which to judge of the Changes of
all other Things, not fixed after that Manner.

This only and unerring Rule he ſeems to be an utter
Stranger to, and inceſſantly talks of the *Exceſs* of the
Quantity of Bills in the N. E Colonies, without conſider-
ing the *Demand* for them, in a moſt ſurprizing Manner.
For to the meaneſt Capacity it is evident, by all proper
Ways of Judging, that the Quantity at any Time hitherto
extant has been but very ſmall in Proportion to Demand.

For *Remedy* of our preſent Calamity, I propoſed to
have a *ſufficient* Quantity of *Bills*, *regulated* by an aſſigned Rate of *Intereſt*, and managed with Prudence, as the
firſt and abſolutely *neceſſary* Expedient.

The *Eſſayer* delivers his Opinion (p. 6, &c.) That *a*
Paper Credit well founded and under good Regulation, and
not larger than what the Silver Specie Currency will bear,
has been found to be a very good Expedient in Buſineſs :
But that if it exceeds this Proportion, its Effects are bad
and ruinous. And yet by ſundry Paſſages in his Eſſay he
ſeems to deliver his Opinion intirely *againſt all further*
Emiſſions

Emiffions of Bills ; declares *Barter* it felf on fome Accounts *preferable to Province Bills as a Medium* ; and ex-
prefly fays, *We have no Reafon to fear Want of a Medium,*
if the Grievance of publick Paper Credit were gradually
removed : Thus *Trade will find its own natural proper Me-*
dium, viz Silver and Gold Which is in Effect to fay, that
we fhall have noMoney at all, but the Province be left to
their laft Shift, *viz* Shop Notes, and finally be ruined ; for
we have not oneOunce of Silver to ferve as Money.

In a Word, The favourite Notion of the *Effayer*, which
runs through and animates his whole Piece, is, That the
Bills being *depreciated* in Proportion to and hand in
hand with the *multiplied* and *large* Emiffions, *this*, and
this *only*, is the *true adequate Caufe of the Rife of Silver* ;
Ballance of Trade againft us (which I call Ballance of
Debt) *not at all concerned in it.* Which is the grand general Point in Controverfy between us, and is in direct Oppofition to the whole Tenor of my Letter. The Force
of what he has offered to fupport his Opinion, I fhall
have Occafion to confider in the Sequel.

Not to take notice of fome *other* materialPoints in the
Controverfy, which he has paffed over in Silence, the
foregoing Hints may fuffice for a *general* View. I fhall
now proceed to make fome more *particular* Remarks on
his *Effay*.

His firft Paragraph, *Paper Currency at a great Difcount*
has prevailed in many of ourColonies ; and by Advocate for it
deluding the People with falfe Appearances and Reprefenta-
tions, likely to continue to greater Difadvantages than ever:
As appears by Emiffions in Maryland, New-York *and*
Rhode-Ifland.

The Word, *Currency*, is in common Ufe in the Plantations (tho' perhaps leaft of all in thisProvince) and fig-
nifies *Silver* paffing current either by Weight or Tale.
The fame Name is alfo applicable as well to Tobacco in
Virginia, Sugars in the *Weft Indies* &c Every Thing at
the *Market-Rate* may be called a *Currency* ; more efpecially that moft *general* Commodity, for which *Contracts*
are ufually made And according to thatRule, *Paper-Cur-*
rency muft fignify certain Pieces of Paper, paffing current
in the Market as *Money*. Thus he *tantalizes* the Province
under its prefent unhappy Circumftances, and would infi-
nuate that our Bills, emitted upon the beft Plan (for the
Subftance of it) that the World ever faw, and of the
greateft Service to our Well-being, are *no better than*
Wafte.

Waſte-Paper, as he elſewhere expreſſes it.   Surely according to this Way of Speaking, he might call Silver common *Earth* ; ſo the beſt Bond in the Province a *Paper-Bond,* and our provincial Charter a *Parchment Charter,* from the Matter on which they are wrote.

The Want of giving a proper *Name* to our *Bills,* has given the *Eſſayer* and others a Handle to impoſe ſuch Names as convey a very wrong and deluſive Idea of them. I ſhall therefore, by Way of Digreſſion, endeavour to ſet that Matter in a juſt Light.   And

Firſt, They are often called a *Medium of Exchange* Now tho' the Word *Medium* may be brought to ſignify a *Means* or *Inſtrument* of Commerce, yet it does not convey a juſt Notion of *Money,* as a *Meaſure of Value,* & much leſs as a *Commodity* paſſing in Trade.   For the natural and obvious Notion of a *Medium* in Trade, is a *Bill, Bond* &c. given as a Pledge, Security, or legal Evidence of the Thing promiſed in the Bill or Bond at a diſtant Time   For Example, If a Man gives an aſſigned Quantity of *Silver* for an aſſigned Quantity of *Iron,* he then immediately *exchanges* one Commodity for another : But if he gives Iron for Silver to be delivered at a *diſtant Time,* and takes a *Note* for the Payment, he then receives only a *Medium* for the preſent.   In like manner, if a Man exchanges our *Bills* for *Iron,* I ſee no *Medium* in the Caſe ; but one Commodity is immediately given for another.   Whereas if he ſells *Iron* condition'd to pay *Bills* for it at a diſtant Time, by Book-Debt, Note, &c. he then receives only a *Medium of Exchange* for the preſent

Secondly, They are called in the *Acts* for their Emiſſions, *Bills of publick Credit :* which Name upon their *original* Emiſſion was very proper, in aſmuch as they were at firſt eſtabliſhed upon the *Credit* to be given them by the Government for *Taxes* &c and that only.   But when afterwards in the Year 1712 they were with common Conſent made a *legal Tender* as *Money* (ſpecial Contracts neceſſarily except d) and ſeeing that, agreable thereto, the Government then and ever ſince made Emiſſions with a *D ſign* to ſupply the Trade with them as *Money.* I ſay, for thoſe Reaſons the naming them Bills of *Credit* ſeems not ſo proper now.   Therefore

Thirdly, Their only *true* and *adequate* Name, I reckon, ought to be *Bill Money ;* being certain Inſtruments in Writing received by common Conſent as *Money,* or a general *Commodity* for which *Contract* are made in this Province.   But to return from this Digreſſion.   He

'He says, "*Paper-Currency at a great Discount* [b]". That our Bills have undergone any *Discount*, is a wrong Supposition. For (first) By *Discount* on a Bill is generally understood an *Allowance* of —— per Cent. made to the *Debtor*, provided he pays the Sum expres'd in the Bill *before it is due*. Now as our *Province-Bills* promise no otherwise than as all other Commodities do, and differ as much from a *promissory Note*, as an Ounce of *Silver* or Pound of *Iron* does, so it is equally uncommon, and unintelligible, to say that our Bills have undergone *a great Discount*, as it would be to say, in Case an Ounce of *Silver* purchased a Bushel of *Wheat* yesterday, and will purchase but half a one to day, that therefore *Silver* has had a *Discount* to day of 100 per Cent. Indeed the Bills in *Maryland* have, strictly speaking, had a *Discount* upon them : and very justly : For they promise *Sterling* Money instead of (6 s 8 d) their old Money, yet the Payments are extended, *viz* half to fifteen Years, and half to thirty Years, by Means of which, Exchange has risen from 33 to 150 per Cent. above *Sterling* But the *Rhode-Island* and *New-York* Bills in this Sense have had no *Discount*.

But (*secondly*) if by *Discount* he means, that they will not now *purchase* so much *Silver* as formerly, I answer, It is already proved, that the *Change* of the *Rate* of *Silver* has been by Means of the *Ballance of Debt*, or its own Scarcity in Proportion to Demand ; that the *Bills* had no Tendency to *raise* it ; but otherwise, a direct one to keep it *down*, by Means of their constant Scarcity too : That *their* Rate is changed only in *common* with all other Things ; and 20 s. in *them* always have been and still are as good or better than 20 s. in *Silver*, or any other Commodity in the Market.

His next Paragraph, " *In Affairs of this Nature a true historical Account of Facts and their Consequences, is called political Experience*" &c. The Meaning of this is , he first gives a *delusive* Account of the *Bills*, and then proceeds to support it by historical *Facts*, either *foreign* to our Case, without any fair State or Application, and some of them odious in the Comparison, or else proving nothing against us, but rather *for* us (which I shall show in the Sequel) When everyBody must know that in a Case of this Kind, the Facts and Experiences to illustrate the Nature and Operation of our Bills must chiefly (if not wholly) be collected within this Province.

N:xt

Next Paragraph, " *Silver being a staple Merchandize all the World over* " &c. That Silver is an *universal Merchandize*, I allow ; and therefore that all Countries partaking of the general Trade, muſt and ought highly to eſteem it, as being one of the beſt Commodities, in which they can receive or pay their reſpective Ballances of Trade, and carry on foreign extraordinary Affairs : But it by no Means follows, that *Silver and nothing elſe* (as he affirms) *ought to be the only legal Tender*. For the Reaſons aſſign-ed by Mr. *Lock* and Mr. *Law*, why the World uſed *Silver* as *Money*, were its being lighter and cleaner than o-ther Metals, capable of taking a plain and laſting Impreſ-ſion, diviſible without Loſs &c. And the Example and Succeſs of the Banks of *Venice* and *Amſterdam* ſufficiently ſhew, that it is *better* to have it paſſing in Trade as a *Commodity*, than as *Money*. And I make no doubt but all the World would gladly reduce it at leaſt in a great Degree to a common Commodity, if they could with Conveni-ence introduce ſuch Schemes as the aforeſaid *Banks*, or even our *Province-Bills*, in lieu of it. But it is hardly practicable in many Countries. Beſides it is plain, that it's neither the beſt *Meaſure* nor the beſt *Inſtrument* in Commerce. However, a ſufficient Quantity of it in this Province, at leaſt to pay our juſt Debts to the Mother-Country, or uſe as Money (if it be found needful) is what I do now and always have contended for.

Page 2. " *Formerly in* England *the ſummary Pound was the ſame with the Pound Weight of Silver : This was in a proper Senſe the* natural *Pound* " I preſume, by this he intends to obviate my ſaying, that a 20 s Bill is the *natural* Pound of *New-England*, which he takes Notice of *Page* 17 &c. And ſo far as relates to the Money in *England*, he is right. But ſurely he ought to conſider, that *our* Caſe exceedingly *differs* from theirs We can have no *fixed* Pound under our preſent Circumſtances : And ſuch a *natural Pound*, as I mentioned, *viz.* Such as a private Man under *bad* Circumſtances can pay, always has fallen out in *England*, as well as in this Country. For a Man that then paid but one Shilling in the Pound, his natural one was Silver at 33 s. 4 d. per Ounce, inſtead of 1 s. 8 d. per Ounce.

Page 2, 3, 4 He introduces his *hiſtorical Facts*, and gives a long Detail of ſundry *Reductions* of *Silver-Coins*, that is, making them lighter by Peccinages at the Mint, by iniquitous corrupt civil Adminiſtrations in order to defraud Creditors.

Creditors, and more especially to cheat the Creditors of the Publick : And instances in *England, Holland* and *France,* and their respective *Plantations.*

That many Male-Practices of this Kind have been used in *Europe,* cannot be deny'd, nor vindicated. But what Relation has this to the *British* Colonies ? For, excepting a Coinage of *Shillings* (3dwt)&c in this Colony (*Anno* 1652) I never heard of any *Coinages* or *Recoinages* in the Plantations, or that this or any at all, ever took the *other Way* of cheating Creditors, *viz* that of *Proclamations,* making the *Pieces of Eight* when passing in Trade at 4 s. 6 d. to become a *lawful Tender,* in publick & private Payments, at the Rate of 5, or 6 s. or the like So that all the Benefit we could have from such *historical Facts* would be, to show the Curious the different Changes in the Rate of Silver in the English Mints, & by taking Mr. *Lowndes's* Extracts from the Indentures of the Mint, mentioned by Mr. *Lock.* and adding the present Proportion of Alloy, now in Use, it would then have appeared that *Anno* 28. *Edward* I. *Silver* was 20 d per Ounce, or 285 Grains to the Shilling : 5 *Edward* VI. at 22 Shillings per Ounce, or 21 (6--10) Grains to the Shilling : 43 *Eliz.* at 5 s. 2 d. per *Ounce* or 93 Grains to the Shilling; and continued so ever since.

Page 4 " That in all the *American* Colonies, at their first
" Settling and for some Years thereafter, their *Currency*
" was the *same* with their (respective) *Mother-Countries.*
" But by the *Iniquity* of some *Administrations* all of them
" have *cheated* their *Creditors* at Home ; and that in the
" *British* Plantations, in Process of Time, *they remitted* to
" their Creditors at Home a *Piece of Eight,* which is on-
" ly 4 s. 6 d. Sterling. at the Rate of 5 s afterwards at
" 6 s. and would have gone further *by Persons in Debt*
" *getting into the Administration or Power of defrauding their*
" *Creditors,* if the *Proclamation-Act* had not been obtain-
" ed by the Sollicitations of the Merchants at Home ;
" and finally, that in many of our Colonies they have
" gone greater Lengths, and *by Floods* of provincial Pa-
" per Credit or Money they have made *vile Work of it,*
&c

These are the general *Plantation historical Facts,* by which, agreable to his *political Experience,* we are to know how our Silver rose or Bills came to be depreciated. and which he has constant recourse to upon all Occasions, Now tho' I might justly object against this

Method,

Method, and tie him down (as ufual in like Cafes) to the Evidences where the Facts happened ; yet for the fake of the Ignorant in fuch Affairs, and thofe that are eafily impofed upon by Appearances that feem to gratify their prefent Intereft, I fhall once for all confider his general Account of the Plantation Moneys and our own in particular.

That our Plantations *begun* with *Sterling Money*, &c. *Silver* 5 s. 2 d per Ounce, I allow : But the *Account* he gives of the Caufes of the Changes, I utterly deny. Let us confider it diftinctly.

Firft, " *They remitted* " &c By(they)we can underftand none other than *Agents* or *Factors* for the Mother-Country, making Returns to their *Conftituents*. (For all others that remitted on their *own* Accounts, to pay a Sterling-Debt, are out of the Queftion) Now there are only two Things to be fuppofed in the Cafe : *viz.* Either (1) That they remitted Silver at the *Market Rate,* and were obliged to give 5 or 6 s for a *Piece of Eight*, inftead of 4 s. 6 d. If fo, they acted *honeftly,* and the *Rife* was owing to fome *other* Caufe. Or(2) that they bought at 4s. 6d. and *charged* their *Conftituents* 5 or 6 s.——Which to fay of them, is flatly calling hard Names   And yet all this could have no *Effect* upon the *Market,* unlefs he alfo prove them *Idiots,* as giving one Man 5 s. for a Piece of Eight, when they might have had as good from another for 4 s, 6 d.

Secondly, " *Perfons in Debt getting into the Adminiftration or Power of cheating* " &c. In this he leaves us as much in the Dark, as he did with Regard to Factors. Therefore we muft fuppofe they raifed the *computative* Value of their *Coins* by provincial *Acts* (for *Recoinages* they had none) ordering that the *Piece of Eight,* when pafing at 4 s 6 d fhould be a *legal Tender* at 5 or 6 s. or the like. Now in this Cafe he ought to have cited the particular Acts : And not only fo, but likewife proved that they were made to take in all *paft* Contracts, as well as future ones   For otherwife no Body could be hurt, as being left free to make their Bargains, agreable to the new Regulation of the Rate of Silver, in all future Contracts. But fo far as ever I have heard, and according to the prefent Circumftance of fome of our Plantations, there never were any fuch Acts made.

Thirdly, " *By Floods of provincial Paper Credit many of our Colonies have made vile Work of it.* That there have been

been *Floods* of Bills emitted in any of the Colonies, he has not proved : And I am of Opinion that in general the Quantity has been too little, tho' the Emissions something irregular But I have proved that the Quantity extant in the *New England* Colonies has been but comparatively diminutive, and the Scarcity of Bills the Cause of great Oppression : And in Reality, neither have the *Factors* remitted Silver at a higher Rate than the Market Price, nor the *Government* from time to time enacted that it should pass at a higher. So that the whole Account he gives of the Plantations seems to be full of Mistakes. And the true State of the Case is as follows.

All our Plantations at their first Settlement did, and many of them do to this Day, labour under great Difficulties by a Scarcity of Money At first doubtless they received Pieces of Eight at the Rate of 4 s. 6 d to 8 d in Proportion to the Rate of them in the Mother-Country, and *Bits* (or Reals of Plate) being 1 8th Part at the Rate of 7 d. But by Means of their Difficulties in Trade, they were soon obliged to take *light* Bits, and *light* half Bits by common Consent. And upon this (as there are in all Places People that know the Difference between light and heavy Money, and how to make Advantage of it) some People *hoarded* up the heavy Pieces, and when the Merchants wanted to purchase Returns, insisted on 1 d. or 2 d. Difference between the light and the heavy Money, which the Merchants found their Interest to give. But in Time their Pieces of Eight (as well as small Money) were *clipt*, and in like Manner the heaviest always kept up and sold with a *Premium,* and People in Trade forced against their Wills to take such Money as passed, and even to make Contracts agreable thereto. And thus by Degrees *Silver* is got from 5 s 2 d to 6 s 10 d. 2 f per Ounce in *Barbados,* to 7 s 3 d in *Jamaica,* to about 9 s. in *Antigua,* and neighbouring Islands; without any Emissions of *Bills,* or *iniquitous Administration* · And the same Cause (call it Ballance of *Trade,* or *Debt,* or *both,* at different Times, which you please) will produce the same Effects ; & that altho' Money pass by *Weight,* as in *Barbados* (the Want of which, he seems to insinuate, has contributed much to the Rise of Silver) And it wou'd be next to a Miracle if it should happen otherwise.

As to the *Colonies* that have gone into the Use of *Bills,* it is plain, that the *Reason* for their so doing was, either (1.) a common Ballance of *Trade* against them, which
unavoidably

unavoidably occafioned a great Scarcity of Money in Proportion to the Demand for the Improvement of their natural Advantages, as in *New York* : Or (2.) an actual
Ballance of *Debt* againft them, as having comparatively
no Silver-Money at all, for the Support of Government
and Trade (and even fometimes being obliged to collect
their Taxes in *Indian Corn*, and other Produce) as in the
New England Colonies, and probably *South-Carolina, Penfilvania* &c.   And the fame ftill continuing, what fhould
hinder the Rife of Silver ? And under thefe Preffures,
what could the Government do by any *Act* for the *fixing*
the Rate of Silver (or what could the *Plantation-Act* do,
however, wifely intended) even tho' the Breach of it
had been made *Felony*? Surely our Plantation-Govern-
ments could do no otherwife than they have done, as this;
and (I believe) moft others, *viz.* to oblige every Man
that makes a *fpecial Contract* for Silver-Money at a certain
Rate, to fulfil it, and where that is wanting to give Judgment for *current Money*, as Bills of Credit, or Silver at the
current received Rate in the Market. The Inftance he
gives of *Maryland*, is an Exception to the general Rule :
For their Bills promife Sterling Money, inftead of 6 s· 8 d,
Money, half in 15, and half in 30 Years, and have juftly
been depreciated by Means of their diftant Promife from
33 to 150 per Cent above the *Par* of Sterling.

  Page 5. He proceeds to fhow the *bad Effects* of Paper-
Currency being made a *legal Tender.* But if he had confidered *his own* Account of the Banks of *Venice* and *Amfterdam*, he would have found no Occafion to apply the
following Inftances to our Cafe.

  " *Baron* Gortz *about twenty Years ago had reduced*
Sweeden *to extream Mifery by impofing Government-Notes
inftead of Specie: For which, among other Crimes, he fuffer'd
Death*" This he again puts us in mind of *Page* 8. How
he came by this Piece of Hiftory, he does not tell us. I
was in *Stockholm*, the Capital, in the Year 1718, being the
laft of *Charles* XII and never then nor fince heard of any
State-Bills paffing about that Time; the Moneys then
current were *Copper Coins*, not fo large as an Englifh Farthing, called according to their Mark *Dollars S. M. (Silver Mint)* of 32 *Stivers* or Pence (their Money) and
fometimes *Mint Tickets* This Fact is univerfally known.
Monf *Devoltiere* fays, They were called *Gortz's Gods* by
the People ; which is true. And they have been frequently mentioned in Print, more efpecially in the Affair of
                                                    Woods's

Woods's Half-Pence in *Ireland*, which were compared to K *James's* Shillings, and *Gortz's* Copper-Coins.—— They were made a legal *Tender* (I think, only for *future* Contracts) upon Pain of Death ; and a Man at *Gottenberg* (I was informed) suffered capitally for the Breach of the Laws relating thereto: All the Produce and Manufactures of the Kingdom were taxed to a certain Rate by the King's Officers respectively, and the People obliged to take their Pay in this Sort of Money.

Some Time after the first Coinage (for I have seen 4 or 5 Sorts of them, and have some of them now by me) they either were really *counterfeited*, or the Ministry gave out that they were so, by a foreign Country ; upon which they made a *new* Emission, of the same Weight and Fineness, to pass at the same Rate, and *reduced* the old ones from 32 to 1 Stiver, and upon that Foot I have frequently received them. And thus they went on through several Coinages:——No Man of any Estate in the Kingdom, but detested such iniquitous Practices ; all People that could lay down their proper Businesses, did it; Strangers forsook their Ports, until in the aforesaid Year the King granted Passes (chiefly with a View to supply his own Stores with Provisions) promising to pay the Importers in *Iron* and other Produce at the King's Tax or Rate, which was strictly performed by his Officers in *Stockholm* and other Ports.

Now to run a Comparison between these *Coins* and our *Bills*, would be odious and detestable : They differ as much as Roguery from Honesty, as Folly from Wisdom, and Darkness from Light

Again, " *The arbitrary Government of* France (he says) *did* Anno 1719 *embrace Mr.* Law's *Project of a Paper-Currency ; Silver was banished by severe Penalties, and Paper made the only legal Tender. The Operation was, the Nation reduced to the utmost Confusion, Mr.* Law *disgraced* &c

What the Particulars of Mr. *Law's* Scheme were, he does not tell us, nor could I ever perfectly learn But according to my present Thought, such a Scheme as the Bank of *Venice*, &c. could not effectually be put in Practice in *France*, where the People have had so much Reason to be diffident of the publick Faith I have heard it said, that Mr *Law's* Scheme was in it self *good* and *practicable*, but *perverted* by the Ministry. Or however that was, I am positively assured by Gentlemen of Credit then at at *Paris*, and now in *Boston*, that the Bills had not only universal *Consent*, but were for some Time *better* than *Silver*, and a *Premium* of 5 to 10 per Cent above *Par* given for them. But the Fate of them was this, The *Ministry* having obtained their *Ends*, paid off the national Debts, and drawn in a great deal of Money into the Treasury, *broke up the Scheme*, upon the Appearance of great Numbers of *Counterfeits* in different Places at once, said to have been done by a neighbouring Country, refused them publick Credit, and left the Possessors to a total Loss.

Now to make our Case parallel to theirs, the Government in 1702 should have emitted a profuse Quantity of Bills, made them a legal Tender in all publick and private Payments, and to be received in both with a Premium of 5 per Cent above Silver, paid off the Province-Debts with them, given them out of the Treasury for Silver at *Par*, and lent them upon Loan; and after they had carried their Scheme as far as they could, then upon a sudden Appearance of many Counterfeit-Bills in different Places at once, said to be done by the *Mohauk* Indians, have dissolved the Scheme, refused the Bills publick Credit, and left every Possessor totally to bear his own Loss. —— This is another of his *historical Facts*, by which we are to have our Bills, according to *political Experience*, set in a true Light. But to proceed with our Author. ——

" Barbadoes *emitted* l 80000 *Bills on Land-Security at* 4 *per Cent, payable after* 5 *Years, which immediately fell* 40 *per Cent. below Silver : But by an Order from Home were all called in* " &c.

These were *promissory Notes*, and quite different from our Bills. The People were wise in taking them only at that Discount : For as lawful Interest was then 10 per Cent, so by allowing Compound-Interest l 141 1 s. of them was then only equal to l 100 Current-Money on their first Emission : And their Sentence from Home (which I have from good Hands) being that instead of 5 Years they should be paid off in 18 Months, was truly equitable, and ought to be a Warning Piece to some among us who are always hankering after *such* Bills.

Page 6 " *Our Province-Bills from the various Operations of frequent large Emissions distant Periods, & Periods postpon'd, are become* 400 *perCent worse than Sterling* " &c.

As for *large* and *sudden* Emissions, I declared against them in my *Letter*, as what ought industriously to be avoided.

avoided; and propos'd their being emitted in a *regular progreſſive* Way ſo as not hurt the Trade by a ſudden Flood. But for the *general Quantity* of Bills out at any one Time in the 4 *New-England* Colonies, it is far from being large. I could make him almoſt any Conceſſions on this Head, and I'll ſuppoſe there may be now extant and actually paſſing (tho' it's ſelf-evident that the Bulk of them are kept in a State of Stagnation) in the whole l. 650000 ; a Sum, when computed at the Rate of Silver 29 s per Ounce, only equal to l. 116000 Sterling ; which conſidering the Numbers of the People, improveable Ad- of theſe Colonies &c. is by all true Ways of Judging but comparatively a very *ſmall* Sum in Proportion to Demand. Now this being the Caſe, it muſt be obſerved, that commonly before a *new* Emiſſion at any Time could be obtained, *Trade* (by Means of ſo great Scarcity) *laboured, Debts* were *poſtpon'd* &c. and what could be the *Conſequence* upon a *ſudden* Emiſſion, but that People receiving their *Debts* in a much *greater* Proportion, and purchaſing *more Returns,* than uſual, the *Silver* and other Returns ſhould remarkably *riſe*; which is what the *Eſſayer* means by our *Province-Bills* becoming *worſe* ? (Surely this muſt have been the Event, except we had happened at ſuch Times to have *more Silver* at Market than even the *extraordinary Demand* ; then it could not have riſen.) And yet (as I have once and again obſerved) if there had always been a ſufficient Quantity of *Bills* extant, and People gone more *uniformly* to Market, *Silver* by Means of the conſtant *growing* Demand would eventually have riſen to the *ſame* Height, in an equally certain, tho' *ſlower* Manner. Beſides, we have ſundry Inſtances wherein *Silver* has *riſen* even when *Bills* as to Quantity have been at their loweſt *Ebb*. But the daily Operation of the *Market* puts the Matter beyond Diſpute : For there we find Silver every Day changing its Rate, as all other Commodities do, without any Relation to the Quantity of Bills extant. And to what other Cauſe can any Man rationally impute the *general Change,* but to the Operation of the *Ballance of Debt* againſt us ?

" *Diſtant Periods, and Periods poſtpon'd* " —— Here and throughout the whole Eſſay he goes upon the Miſtake of comparing the *Bills* to ſpecial *promiſſory Notes* ; from which they differ as much as a Commodity in Hand does from a Note promiſing that ſame Commodity at a diſtant Time.

The

The only Thing to be confidered with Regard to the *Periods* of the *Bills,* is, whether at any fuch Periods the Quantity extant was greater than the Demand. That it never exceeded, but fell vaftly fhort at all Times, is obvious to the Underftanding of every one. Therefore the *Poftponings* are mere *circumftantial* Facts ; and have never operated to lower the Value of the Bills, but otherwife, How ftrange then is the Complaint in this Cafe ? What Reafon have we for it, more than the *Venetians* have to complain, that *effective* Payments have been poftponed for many Centuries, when they can every Day in the Market have the Amount of the original *Depofitum* in Silver for their *Transfers,* with 20 perCent. more than the Sum depofited: Efpecially fince our *Bills* are of the *fame* general Nature with their *Transfers* ; both equal to Things in the Market at the current Rate ; the *Rife* of *theirs,* and the *Fall* of ours, with Regard to their firft *Par,* being wholly owing to *different* trading Circumftances, and to no other Caufes whatever ? *Poftponings* not in the leaft concerned here, as to either Cafe.

Page 9. " *So much Paper as is current in a Province, fo much really is that Province in Debt.* " —— This is a ftrange Delufion : In what Senfe can a Province be faid to run in Debt, by neceffary Emiffions of Bills ? Are they indebted thereby to *other Countries* ? Or is their *capital Stock* thereby *diminifhed* ? No certainly, their landed and trading Interefts have been thereby greatly increafed in Value : So that it would have been *good Husbandry* even if they had *borrowed* upon *Intereft* a Supply of Silver, or Bills where they were to be had, equal in Value to their Emiffions. The *Funds*-Part are abfolutely neceffary for the Support of Government, and vaftly more convenient for the Payment of Taxes (having no Silver) than *Indian Corn* and other Produce. And for the *Loans*-Part, fuppofing fome People have made a bad Ufe of their Moneys borrowed, & fuffered their mortgaged Lands to go in Payment, is not this common to all other Countries ? Bad Husbands will fell or mortgage to their own People, or any other, that will lend them Money : And in fuch Cafe it is a publick Advantage, that their Eftates fhould get into better Hands. The *Effayer's* Way of arguing is as odd, as if a Man poffeffed of 1000 Acres of *wafte Lands,* which bring in nothing, fhould refufe to mortgage 20 of them, by Means of which he might be enabled to carry on the Settlement of the whole to good Purpofe;

Purpose; saying, No, let the Lands lie waste; if I borrow Money upon them, I shall but *run in Debt.* ——

To go on

Page 14 " *We have no Reason to fear Want of a Medium, if the Grievance of publick Paper Credit were gradually removed : Trade will find its own natural proper Medium, Silver and Gold* " &c. —— If our Trade were well regulated, it might in a Course of Years get into prosperous Circumstances, and then it would produce *Silver* to pass as Money. But in order to this, it is indispensably necessary, in the mean time, to have *Bills* (having no other convenient Matter) as the Instrument for carrying on our Commerce, and improving our natural Advantages And can any Man conceive but that upon the *Want* of Bills we must run into the further Use of *Shop-Notes,* which have an infallible Tendency to increase the Ballance of Debt against us, and to drive away the most valuable Part of the Community, Artificers, Labourers, and even Husbandmen, to other Colonies and Parts, where they have Money of one Sort or other to receive for their Labour ? An Attempt of this Kind might in a dozen or a score of Years reduce the Value of the capital Stock of the Province to half its present Worth, when compared with Silver.

Having fully answered the Substance of the *Essay,* I shall now proceed to consider the *Author's* particular Remarks upon my *Observations.*

The first I shall take Notice of, is that Reflection(P.15) " *He introduces these Words,* Ballance of Trade, *on all Occasions with no true Meaning and Application*". The Ballance of *Trade* is not what I mention'd : *Our* Case being in Fact a Ballance of *Debt,* and largely explained. However, as the *Essayer* seems to mean the *same* Thing by a Ballance of *Trade,* that I do by a Ballance of *Debt,* and as the Force of his Objection turns upon that single Case, I shall give his Remarks on it a full Consideration.

" *Ballance of Trade is Cash* (Silver *and* Gold) *imported to or exported from a Country, according as the general Exports or Imports of Merchandize exceed one another.*" This I allow , and every *Ounce* of Silver imported to or exported from a Country is by *Means* of a Ballance of Trade *for* or *against* them, and this may be taken for a Day, Month or Year &c.

Again, " *The Silver and Gold which we export to* England, *are no Part of the Ballance of Trade against us, being truly as Merchandize only.* England *exports* 2 *Million*

10

to Holland *and* India, *as Merchandize, the Ballance of Trade continuing in Favour of* England *notwithstanding."* The Meaning of this is, that a Country may have a *particular* Ballance *against* them, with *one* Country and *another,* and yet a *general* one at the same time in *their Favour* with all the World. But this is *not* our Case : We have it *for* us with some Parts of the World ; and yet upon the whole we want it in *general,* with *England* &c: *Every Ounce* we export, call it *Merchandize,* or what you please, goes in the Ballance of *Trade* , and what we send Home being all together not sufficient, there still rests a Ballance of *Debt* against us.

Again, " *Ballance of Trade is also against a Country, not only when they export their Medium, but also when a Country runs in* DEBT, *by expending in fine Houses, Apparel* &c. *that which ought to have purchased Exports : This is Our present Case.*" Which Observation, if *introduced with any true Meaning and Application,* must signify that *we* run more in *Debt* to *England* than we are able to pay (a Thing allowed by every Body) and is in Effect the same Definition I gave of the *Ballance of Debt* against us ; differing only in *Words.* Now, as by this he allows us to be in a State of partial *Bankruptcy,* or the Demand for Returns in the general greater than the Quantity, must not the Rates of Silver and other Things by necessary Consequence be *raised* proportionably thereto, as in the Case of *N.* ? Notwithstanding throughout the whole of his Remarks, he cavils at the plain, natural and unavoidable Inferences.

He objects to sundry Observations in my Letter. As, Pag. 15. " *The sinking Value of our Bills is from and in Proportion to the Ballance of Trade* (or Debt) *against us.* —— Pag. 17 *A* 20 *s Bill is the natural Pound of* New-England —— Ibid. *Silver falling and rising* ad infinitum. All his Cavils at such Passages evidently and naturally arise from his not understanding his own *Ballance of Trade,* by Means of which *Silver* and *Bills* must for ever change their *Market Rate,* and 20 s in Bills or Silver be just what the Ballance for or against us makes them.

Pag 18 He pretends to quote that Passage out of my Letter ; *When Goods rise or fall in the Market, the Change must be in the Goods, and not in the Bills* He refers me to no Page, and I find no such Assertion : But the contrary. Obf P 18 " The Pound-Value (or the Value of 20s; " in the Market) is changed in all Goods, as well as in

" the

" the Bills: And 20 s. in them are as good as 20 s. in any
" other Things.

Pag 16. *Bills ought to be emitted from time to time, and
postponed till the Quantity exceed the Demand.* —— A fufficient Quantity of Bills, regulated by an assigned Interest,
I did and do contend for. But as to *postponing*, I said in
Substance, that in as much as the Government have taken upon them to 'supply the Province with Bills, they
ought to have kept always a sufficient Quantity out, upon Funds or Loans, to answer the Demands of Trade. As
the Bills promise no *effective* Payments, the *postponing* can
no otherwise be hurtful than by an *Excess* of the general
Quantity extant (which never happened) and in that
Case, whether they *call in* the Funds punctually, and at
the same time *emit* more, or else *postpone* the *Funds* already
out, it amounts just to the same Thing In this Case the
Funds or Loans are only *circumstantial* Things, and the
calling in (not the postponing) in my humble Opinion
is rather the *publick Fraud* and *iniquitous Administration* he
so frequently complains of. And as the natural *Consequences*,
of thus *reducing* the current Money of the Province, without any other good Matter substituted in its Place, must
be *long Credit, excessive Usury* and *Extortion, Idleness*, and
Intemperance, the Use of *other* Colony Bills, so as to bring
a Ballance of Trade against us, for which both our *Silver*
and *Lands* must go in Payment to them ; the ruinous
Practices of *Shop-Notes* and a *Trucking Trade* ; I say, as
these are the plain and unavoidable Consequences of a
Scarcity of Money, the *reducing* the Money of the Province may be said to be virtually *establishing those iniquitous Practices by a Law*, much more (I'm sure) than the
largest *Emission* of Bills hitherto may be said to have
been.

Pag. 23. " *The following Clauses (and elsewhere many
others) I cannot understand* ; as, *Bills made a fixed Measure of Value which Silver cannot be.* Again, *When Silver
falls, the Government may fix the Rate of it* —— Now is it
not plain to the meanest Capacity (and allowed by every
Body) that a general *Commodity* or *Money* having its own
Quantity and *Demand* always kept equal, must be a *perfect Measure* of the Value of Things ; and likewise that
supposing *Silver* to fall to 20 s per Ounce, and the Government and common Consent agree that an Ounce of
Silver shall be the N E. nummary (or Money) *Pound,*
what in the World (so long as we have no Ballance
against

against us) should hinder it to *continue* so for ever, as in
Europe ?

- But to take in the Substance of all that he says with
Regard to the *Bills* being depreciated, I must take Notice
of one Passage more, Pag. 15 " *If we find that in all
the Colonies where is no Paper-Credit, the Value of their
summary Denominations* [or the Rate of Silver] *continues
the same, and where Paper-Currencies have prevailed, their
Denominations have depreciated* [or Silver risen] *hand in
hand with their repeated Emissions, ought we to have recourse to any other Conceit (as Ballance of Trade) for the
Cause, but only to the Operation of these Bills* "? — The
Fact is, he himself owns, as I do, that Silver *rose* in the
Plantations even *before* the *Plantation-Act* ; we differ only
as to the *Cause* : And it is notorious that it has also risen
since that Act in many of them, and still continues so to
do ; that is, By Reason of their general *Scarcity* of Money,
they are obliged to take *light* Pieces, both Silver & Gold,
which is as much *raising* the computative Value of their
Coins, as if the Government did it by their Province-Acts.
And as to those that are in the Use of *Bills*, we have a
fresh Instance to the contrary of what he says, in the last
New York Emission of l. 48000 in Bills (Silver about 9 s.
per Ounce) which was not only very irregular as to the
Method, being put in Circulation all at once, and as to the
Quantity double the whole Sum they had then extant in
Bills, but also by comparing the whole Quantity & Demand
in our four Colonies with that of *New-York*, might be
thought an excessive large Emission: Yet no remarkable
Change followed. I have heard of Silver being sold as
high there before that Emission, as since : And Exchange has
only risen from 165 to 170 l the highest (for l 100 Sterling)
after two Years Trial ; the Reason, because they had Silver
enough to answer all Demands for Returns, and so no
Ballance of *Debt* against them: Which makes a vast Difference between *their* Case and *ours*   We are assured of
a Balance of *Trade* against us by the Demand we every
Day see for Silver in Returns to the Mother-Country :
And by the general Deficiency we are equally sure of a
Balance of *Debt* against us. To no other Cause can we rationally ascribe the Variation of the Rate of Silver among
us, but to the greater or smaller Operation of this Balance
of Debt, as the Demand and the Quantity of Silver in
the Market bear a Proportion to one another greater or
less : From hence we may as certainly conclude that the
                                                   Balance

Balance of *Debt* for or againſt us will for ever affeȼt the Price of Silver in this Province, as that 3 and 2 make 5.

Page 21. *He is an inexorable Enemy to Silver, becauſe it has been and may be greatly depreciated by the Exceſs of its Quantity.* —— This is intirely wrong : For *changeable* tho' it be, yet I aM along aimed at the proper Means of introducing it, and expreſly gave it its due Praiſe. For Inſtance, I ſay (*Obſ.* Page 22) *Trade is the only Means of introducing* Silver *and* Gold, *the general Treaſure of the World* &c —— I might on this Occaſion fairly retort upon him, and ſay at leaſt with equal Truth and Reaſon, *He is an inexorable Enemy to* Province-Bills. —— But I forbear. And ſhall cloſe with this ſingle Remark :

That in many Caſes it's very plain he does not underſtand the *Operation of Quantity and Demand*, and therefore one of the moſt unfit to write *Eſſays upon Money.*

POST·

POSTSCRIPT

WHILE the foregoing was in the Press, the Publick has been offered *A Discourse concerning the Currencies* &c. I presume by the Author of the *Essay*, and upon the same Plan, but I think with no great Improvements in Point of Reasoning   Now altho' I have in my *Inquiry* fully obviated and answered every Thing of Moment he has advanced in Opposition to our *Bills*; yet it may be needful for the sake of the *Unwary*, and others led by a delusive Prospect of *Gain*, who easily take up with any specious Appearances of arguing from *Fact* and *Experience*, to make some Remarks on this Piece also.

I observe, he still entertains a wrong Notion of the Nature of our *Bills*, and in the whole Tenor of his Discourse puts them upon the Footing of common *promissory Notes*, and even *such* as have no solid *Fund*, payable at distant and uncertain (postpon'd) *Periods*, and also without any Allowance of *Interest* for Forbearance: From which sort of *Notes*, it is self-evident, they *differ* in all these Regards ; as having the best Fund, *viz* common Consent, by which they are made equivalent to all Things at all Times bought and sold in the *New-England* Markets ; and thus are virtually paid off every Day , and also may be every Day let at an high Interest, either on Condition to receive Silver at a fixed Rate as in *Europe*, or to receive the same sort of Bills as he lent, which he pleases. — From the same Mistake also our Author calls them, as usual, " *Base Paper-Currency*, *fallacious Cash*, *chimerical ill-founded Medium* &c ".

He seems also still utterly unacquainted with the Operations of Quantity and Demand ; constantly complains of *frequent* and *large Emissions* of *Bills*, *enormous publick Loans* &c and yet allows (Page 26, 27.) that the Value of the whole Bills and Silver Cash extant in the 4 *New-England* Colonies, *A* 1713, was equal to 657000 Ounces of Silver ; *A.* 1718, to but 500000 Ounces ; and now *A.* 1739, the Bills extant only equivalent to 434000 Ounces
of

of Silver, or about two thirds of the Value in current Cash at this Day to what there was then. Now as I suppose, every one will allow that we may require at least three times *more* Money in Value to negotiate our Affairs *now*, than at that Time ; so according to all rational Ways of judging, we ought *now* to have three times more *Bills* in Value, than we then had : More especially since the *Quantity* did not then *exceed* the *Demand* (but probably was *less*) as may be known by the then Rate of Interest. Not that I propose the above Method as a certain Way of judging in this Case ; no, the Rate of *Interest* is the unerring Rule. And if we had a proper *Bank-Circulation*, much less Money would answer the End in that Way, than in any other.

As to *the Ballance of Debt*, the great Matter in Controversy, he introduces it in effect, *Page* 34 (and other Places) by Way of Objection, " It is not repeated large Emissions of a base Paper Currency, but the Imports exceeding the Exports, that occasions Silver to be ship'd off in Ballance ; therefore we are not to expect a Silver-Currency, supposing all Bills cancelled " &c. Under this Head he virtually owns my Ballance of *Debt*, by his Concession, that our Imports *exceed* our Exports, and proposes very justly the proper Remedy (*Page* 35) *Let us then lessen our Imports by Frugality, and add to our Exports by Industry* &c. —— But at the same time he imputes the *Cause* to the *Bills*, as giving the *Merchant Opportunity to ship off the* Silver, *which Necessity would otherways have obliged him to keep as Cash*. —— A strange Way of arguing ! Was it ever known in any Country, where they had only a common Ballance of *Trade* against them, much more where they had an actual Ballance of *Debt* against them, as we have, but that *Silver* was ship'd of in Payments ? Does not the Exigence of the Case necessarily and inevitably infer it ? And is it not so in many of our Colonies, that have had *no Bills* ? What a very trifle of *Silver* and *Gold* (and that exceeding *light* too, or else they would probably have none) have they in Proportion to their *Trade*, which may be negotiated chiefly by their *Produce*, which *curs* cannot ? What a hard Case would he reduce the Merchants to ! *Necessity* (says he) *would have obliged them*, were there no Bills, *to keep their Silver as Cash* : And yet *Necessity* too obliges them *to ship it off as Merchandize*, to pay their Debts at home. ——
Thus he does but trifle with the Objection, he proposes
to

to anſwer: and he overlooks the natural obvious Conſequence of Imports exceeding Exports, *viz* the Riſe of the
Rate of Silver and other Things: A Conſequence, that in
ſuch a State of Affairs is unavoidable. And therefore
how *ſtaple* ſoever our *exportable Commodities* are in the
trading World, whether we have *Bills* extant or not;
yet the *ſame Cauſe* juſt mentioned, if continued, will undoubtedly produce the *ſame Effect*, *viz.* the Riſe of the
Rate of Silver *ad infinitum*; as the contrary Cauſe will
the Fall of it: And as we are now circumſtanced it, is
next to impoſſible, to regulate our Trade, or carry it
on to any good Purpoſe, without a Sufficiency of *Bill-
Money*.

The grand Point, which he labours throughout the
whole Diſcourſe, is to prove by ſeveral *Facts* & *political
Experiences* relating to Paper Currencies, that (as in *Page
24.*) *the repeated and large Emiſſions of Paper Money, are
the Cauſe of the frequent Riſe of the Price of Silver* and
Exchange; further, that the *Emiſſions* and *Cancellings* of
Bills, have governed them both, and raiſed, lower'd, and
fixed them, as the Courſe of the Moon does the Tides,
plain to a kind of Demonſtration, from the following Inſtances in *New England.* —— " *After Silver had roſe (A.
1706) to 8 s. per Ounce, it continued (till 1714) at that
Rate, while Paper-Emiſſions did not exceed a due Proportion to the current Silver*". Here in the ſame Breath he
flatly contradicts his own Aſſertions: For he allows(*Pag.
26*) that *A. 1713,* the *Bills* extant in all the *N. E.* Colonies were in Value (only to be regarded) equal to 438000
Ounces of *Silver*, which is a trifle more than the Value
of thoſe now extant, and never exceeded but *A. 1718,*
and that only by 62000 Ounces; and *A. 1731,* by 32000
Ounces of *Silver*: Beſides that even in that ſhort Period
(from 1706 to 1714) there were not only *large Emiſſions*
of Bills, but (*Page 10*) a Number of *Poſtponings*, and yet
after all *noChange* in the Rate of *Silver*, the Reaſon he gives,
is, becauſe there was *a due Proportion of Concomitant Silver
paſſing with the Bills.* And what elſe is this, but to ac-
knowlege the *Ballance of Debt* (allowed by all) and in
effect to ſay, that from *A* 1706 to 1714. we had *Silver*,
either as Money or as Merchandize, ſufficient to *anſwer
all Demands* for Exportation, and therefore it did *not riſe*;
but that afterwards becoming *leſs* than the Demand, it
roſe proportionably, and continues ſo doing to this Day;
the infallible *Phaſes* of Emiſſions &c. not all ifflucnital

in

in the Cafe! —— Or in more general Terms, that from the firft Settlement of *New-England*, by Means of their own *Trade*, and in a good Meafure by the Help of *providential Supplies* (in which their Trade was not concerned) as *Silver* and other Effects imported by Means of *Wrecks, Pirates* and *Privateers, Settlers* &c. thefe Colonies were enabled fo far to keep their Credit with the Mother-Country, that the Rate of Silver was only changed from 5 s. 2 d. to 8 s. per Ounce, till the Year 1714. But that after the *War* moft of thofe Supplies *fail'd*, and our produce by Degrees *fell* exceedingly in the foreign Markets, and finally for Want of a Sufficiency of *Bills* in Proportion to Demand, we were forced into the Ufe of *Shop-Notes* to ferve in lieu of *Cafh*, and fo into an exceffive Importation of *European* Goods, which enhanced the Ballance againft us, till Silver *A.* 1739, was raifed to 29 s. per *Ounce*

N. B As to our Author's Affertion relating to the *concomitant Silver*, viz 219000 *Ounces, A.* 1713 (mentioned *Page* 26) I am apt to think it is but ill founded : For the Government in all their *Acts* refpecting *Bills*, make high Complaints of the extreme Scarcity of *Silver*, and expressly fay (*A* 1712) that *all the Silver* was fhip'd off in Payment of Debts to *Great-Britain*, and that the Trade in general had been carried on from 1705, to that Time by Means of the *Bills* : So that the Quantity then in the Market, could be at moft but comparatively fmall, and ufed only as Merchandize; not as Cafh in Circulation *concomitant* with the Bills.

In the fame Paragraph he proceeds to fay ; " *A* 1714 *we emitted* &c. " Here follow feven Emiffions in *Maffachufetts, Rhode-Ifland,* and *Connecticut,* according to which the Bills were depreciated (*Pari paffu*) till *A* 1739. One of them one Year, others 3, 4, 5, 6 Years diftant from each other. At one Period Silver rofe 1 s. 2 d per *Ounce*; at others 2, 3 & 6 s without any Relation to the Quantity of the Emiffions, or the Demand for them. Now the *Application* of thefe Facts, fuppofing his Account of them to be right, I take to be meer *Delirium.* The *Connecticut* and *Rhode-Ifland* Emiffions were never taken notice of as influential in the Cafe, till *A.* 1733 : The Reafons for doing it then, are well known. Befides in his Account of that Year's Emiffions he leaves out one hiftorical Fact, very material, I mean, the *Merchants-Notes,* value above ₤. 100000, and which may with more Juftice be charged with

with being the whole Caufe of the late extraordinary Rife of Silver, than all the other Emiffions : For it is a known and remarkable Fact, that *Silver* rofe *within about nine Months time*, that Year, from 21 s. 6 d. to 27 s which was to a very trifle the Value of thofe Notes, when reduced by nine Months Difcount. Not that I would be tho't wholly to exclude the natural Operation of *Trade* out of the Cafe : But the Obfervation I have made, may help to fupply a Defect in the Author's Hiftory and Argument, and ought to have Weight with fuch as impute the Rife of Silver to the meerOperation of the *Bills.* — As to the laft *Rhode Ifland* Emiffion in 1738, Silver did not actually rife till the latter End of *May* 1739, and the Caufe of its rifing was evidently the great Number of Payments in *Silver* and *Gold* at the annual Collection of the *Impoft* Money &c.

His Inftances in the next Paragraph (*Page 25*) in *New-England* &c. are ftrong Evidences for what I have alledg'd : For if *Returns in Shipping, Whale Oyl*, &c. be *large, and bear a good Price abroad*, has not that a direct Tendency to *lower* the Prices of *Silver* &c ? As on the contrary, the Demand for *Silver* to fupply *Agencies*, or other political Occafions, has it not the fame Tendency to *raife* Silver ? The whole of this is in fome Degree the natural Operation of the *Balance of Debt.*

He inftances in the Cafe of *Barbados*, to put his Affertion out of Difpute; which I have already confider'd, and in Fact it has no Relation at all to the Cafe

The utmoft that can be faid on this Head, is, that upon fome new Emiffions in this Province Silver rofe in *Bofton* a fmall Matter, and the plain *Caufe* (for which I appeal to Men in Trade) was the preceeding great *Scarcity of Bills*, by Means of which *Debts* due here and *Returns* to the Mother-Country were greatly *poftpon'd*, fo that on the new Emiffion People were *generally* put in Cafh, the *fudden Demand* for Returns *greater* than ufual, and the Market *proportionably* affected

The *unerring Evidence* in the Cafe, is the *Merchan's* and *Goldfmiths* Books, to which I appeal : and doubt not but they will fhew, that *Silver* has been every Day in a *changeable* State, without Regard to Emiffions of Bills.

I might here *recapitulate* fomething of what I faid on this Head in the foregoing Inquiry, *viz.* That the Bills are eftablifhed upon the Footing of a general Commodity or Money, and cannot be changed any otherways than
                                                              the y

they are ; that there has been no Change in them for the worfe by Means of a Change in their natural Proportion to other Things, or the Excefs of their Quantity above the Demand ; but they have undergone a forced Change, in common with other Things, *viz*. in the Way of rating them. That the Bills are virtually, and may actually be put upon theFoot of theTransfers of *Venice*,and *Amfterdam*,&have operated the fameWay; different trading Circumftances alone making the Odds ; all which Obfervations carry Demonftration along with them.

It is well known, that *dealing in Silver has been a Bufinefs among us*, and that frequently it has been raifed by that Means ; alfo that Silver has rifen remarkably in the *Spring* and *Fall*, on Account of the *largeft Remittances* being made at thofe Times.

To conclude this Head, I muft obferve, that fome have faid in Converfation that *they could raife Silver* from time to time, if they pleafed This is what ought, I know, to be mention'd with Caution, but is a melancholy Truth. Such a Thing, trading Men are appriz'd, might be done, and that whether the Bills be gradually funk, or there be none extant : I fay, *none at all*, becaufe when *Bills* grow a little Scarcer, they will then become a private Property, and *Silver* be fold in the *trucking* Way as otherThings are, and he that wanted to *monopolize* it, would have at leaft a good Chance to fell it for fuch Commodities as would purchafe *Silver* again : And whence comes the unhappy Affair, but from the *Ballance of Debt*, by Means of which our Imports of Silver are fmall, and the Demand frequently greater inProportion ? And by no Means from the Operation of the Bills. But to proceed ——

The long and formidable Account he has given of the *depreciating* of *Bills*, upon *Emiffions*, in thofe other Colonies, that are in the Ufe of them, as it may poffibly have a bad Effect to *biafs* fome of his Readers, I fhall therefore take fome Notice of it. But a curforyView will fuffice to evidence that nothing remarkable has happen'd as to the *Rife* of *Silver*, excepting in *South Carolina* and *New England* : And in this Cafe, I fhall not follow him through his political Remarks on their *Emiffions*, *Poftponings*, *Cancellings* &c Having already given (as I think) the moft conclufive Proofs, that the *general Caufe* of the Rife of Silver, was the Operation of the *Ballance of Debt*, in them all ; and he having offered little or nothing either to prove that the *Bills* were the Caufe of it, or to

fhew

shew *how* they could *operate* to produce the Effect he imputes to them.

In *New-York*, *New-Jerfies* and the two *Penfilvania* Governments, *Piftoles* (the greateft Article of their current Species) of 4 dwt. 6 gr. pafs for about 28 s. and in *Antigua*, *St. Chriftophers*, *Montferrat*, *Nevis* & the *VirginIflands* (which never had any Bills) *Piftoles* of but 4 dwt pafs too for 28 s. — So that the former, taking all their Species together, I reckon have the Advantage of the latter.

Maryland is intirely out of the Queftion ; their Bills being on the Foot of *promiffory* Notes ; and the Difference of the Rate of Silver there may juftly be called a *Difcount* for prompt Payment.

·*North-Carolina*, —— As to this Government I agree with our Author, that they have no great Fund (Vent) for *Bills* of Credit, thofe formerly emitted were difregarded by the People, ill-contrived, and much counterfeited : So that theirTrade has all along been in theWay of *Barter* and their *Imports* and *Exports* raifed upon *each other* in *Denomination*, without the Influence of *Bills* ; their naval Stores fold on the Footing of their common Trucking-Trade, and their beft Exports (as Tallow, Deer-Skins, Wax &c.) bartered on the Footing of *Virginia-Money*, Silver at 6 s. 8 d. per Ounce.

Thus it appears that there are but two remarkable Inftances, among all the Colonies that are in the Ufe of Bills fuch as ours, viz. *South-Carolina*, and the *New England* Colonies, whofe Bills all pafs in common : And it may not be amifs particularly to take fome Notice of the Caufes of the Rife of Silver in *South-Carolina* ; having already faid enough upon the Cafe of *New-England*.

I never could learn that frequent and large Emiffions of *Bills* were any Caufe of the Rife of Silver in *South-Carolina* ; but have often heard, about the Year 1733, that they were fo very fcarce that no lefs than 20 perCent Intereft was given for them, and the People in great Diftrefs and Confufion, till in Part relieved by a Set of compaffionate publick-fpirited Gentlemen, who circulated their own Notes in the Way of a *Bank*, tho' not without great Oppofition, and Attempts of divers Kinds to defeat their charitable Intentions. But the Caufes generally allowed are thefe—(1.) Large Importations of *Negroes* ; (2) The great *Fall* of the Value of their Produce : Either of which were fufficient to have brought about thofe bad Effects. And (3) Confiderable *Remittances* Home by
private

private Perfons, for the Purchafe of Eftates, and as a Depofitum in the Stocks. Laftly, A confiderable (both neneffary and fuperfluous) Importation of *Materials, Cloathing* &c. from the Mother-Country; together with chargeable Negotiations, Travels, foreign Education &c. all which belong to their general Account of Trade. And yet under all thefe Inconveniencies, *South-Carolina* taken in a complex View, has been one of the moft flourifhing Settlements, their capital Stock increafed in Value to a prodigious Degree; and this in a great Meafure owing to the Bills of Credit. The fame might juftly be affirmed of this Province,till fuch unaccountableNotions,as thofe of our Author, fo detrimental to the Common-Wealth, were received and induftrioufly propagated among us.

There's little elfe remarkable in his Piece, but what I have already obviated. His fuppofed *Mifchiefs* arifing from a large *Paper-Currency*, his *Arguments* (as he fays) current among the *Populace*, together with his *Propofals* for rectifying our Currency, his abufive *Reflections* &c. are all but the native Confequence of his bad Politicks, and Ignorance in the Subject he writes upon, fufficiently obvious to any judicious & impartial Reader. —— Therefore I fhall only take notice of a few Paffages, and conclude.

Page 26. " *Large repeated Emiffions of Bills are no Addition to the Medium of Trade*". Here he again contradicts his own Affertion, that in 1713 there was one half more in Value of Money, paffing then, than what there is now, and yet we may require three times more in Value now in Proportion to Demand. It is the Quantity of Money in *Value*, not in *Denomination*, that we muft regard; and every private Man, as well as every Community of People, requires a certain Proportion (in Value) of Money to carry on their Affairs. Suppofing then, that *Great Britain* required 20 Million in Silver at 5s. 2 d. per Ounce, and Silver raifed from time to time byRecoinages, Proclamations, or a Ballance of Debt, to 29 s. per Ounce, muft they not in that Cafe have 112 Million in Silver, new Money, or the fame Sum in Bills of Credit? And would there be in that Cafe one fuperfluous Shilling, whether of Silver or Bills?

Page 27 " *People who never can have any other Claim to Money, but by Fraud, the Idle, Extravagant &c call out loudeft for a Paper Medium*". This is an unjuftifiableReflection : For inFact,every Body knows,that the*Labourers* and

and *Tradefmen*, who (as he well obferves) are the *Hands which feed the Belly of the Common-Wealth*, have been oppreffed to a crying Degree, for Want of honeft and punctual *Money-Pay*. The induftrious *fair Traders* have fuffered greatly, by having their juft Debts long poft-pon'd, by being forc'd to take Goods at great Difadvan-tage in lieu of Money, and often to lofe their Debts by Infolvencies: *Widows* and *Orphans*, and even the *Clergy* many of them, have fuffered much by the diftreffing Scar-city of Money: All thefe have a good Right to defire a reafonable Currency. And the *real* Eftates in *Bofton*, and the Province in general, have of later Years been reduced incredibly in their Value, by the Operation of the fame Caufe. As for the *Shopkeepers*, they have leaft Reafon to complain, and fome of them fairly own that a Trucking-Trade is beft for them. All Men that have indifputable *Security* to give, are intitled to Money; and all Countries endeavour they fhould have it at as *low* an *Intereft* as poffible. We are perhaps the only Country, that ever dreamt of *reforming* their Trade by a *Scarcity* of *Money*, when a Sufficiency of it muft be acknowleged the beft Means of *Induftry* and (in our Cafe) of *Frugality* too.——— *Others* befides our Author have fuggefted, That *thofe who have no Right to it, are the Men who call out for it moft.* But can it be fuppofed that *fuch* will have any *lent* them? Are not the *Arts* of lending Money as well *known* here, and as much *refined* among us of late, as any where? So that there is no Danger from that Quarter, even tho' we had a Sufficiency of Bills.

Page 29. " *Long Credit is not one of the leaft of the bad Effects of Paper-Money* Ibid. *With ready Money, Bufinefs go's on brisk and eafy* ". ——— Can any Man rationally af-cribe *long Credit* to any other Caufe, but *Scarcity* of Mo-ney? Does not the Rate of *Intereft* and the length of *Credit* depend upon the *Quantity* of Money in Proportion to *Demand*, as the Shadow upon the Body? The Practice of *Holland* and *England*, and all other Countries that have *low Intereft*, fufficiently demonftrates this. Their Difcounts or Abatements for prompt Payment are but trifling, to what they are here. Indeed fome particular Commodi-ties are fo abundant in Proportion to Demand, that if Mo-ney were never fo plenty, the Seller might be glad to part with them on long Credit. Therefore the one and only Remedy in our Cafe, is a fufficient Currency, and
the

the Advantages upon that Account would be vaſtly great, and in particular to the Mother-Country.

Page 35. " *The goodly Appearance we make in fine Houſes, Equipage and Dreſs, is owing to Paper* ". This and many otherSpeeches ſaid to be made by thePopulace, are dragg'd in to gloſs his Cauſe, both in the Eſſay and Diſcourſe. I affirm he is the firſt Perſon that pretends to Reaſon and Modeſty, that ever I knew ſet the Matter in the Light he has done. His *Vulgar great and ſmall*, the noble and ignoble, even the extravagant themſelves, complain of our ſurprizing Exceſs in thoſe Particulars, own the Cauſe, and the Neceſſity of a Reformation. However, all muſt confeſs, the goodly Appearance of the Province in neceſſarySupplies and Accommodations for Life, Trade, Fiſhery, and the vaſt additional Value of our real Eſtates, &c are (next to a kind Providence) owing to our Bills.

He frequently expreſſes a compaſſionate Concern for *Poſterity*, left they ſhould be overburthened with *Taxes*, and tempted to *Mutiny*. Not conſidering, that the *Funds* ever ſince the Year 1712 have been *kept cut*, chiefly to fulfil the *Engagements* the Government then virtually took upon themſelves to *ſupply* the Province with *Bills*, to ſerve as *Money*, and that in this Regard, there never ought to be *more* called in than what is abſolutely neceſſary to defray the Charges of the *current Year*, which is no Inconvenience ; nor ſthat the Government might emit ſtill upon *Loan*, for the Bulk of the running Caſh, and upon *Funds* only for the Service of the Government, which might be punctually call'd in without the Hazard he mentions. Neither does he conſider the vaſt *Damage* the riſing Generation have already ſuſtained in the *depreciating* of their *real Eſtates* by Means of the *Scarcity of Money* : For I ſuppoſe they will not fetch ſo much Money upon Sale now (additional Improvements neceſſarily excepted) as when Silver was at 20s. per Ounce. Nor finally that they are upon the Brink of being further reduced by the ſame Cauſes, and Poſterity in Danger of being under the Neceſſity of paying theirDebts, contracted when Silver was at 20 to 29 s per Ounce, not under the Rate of Silver at 6 s. 10 d per Ounce.

Page 39. He hints at ſeveral *Schemes*. The 1ſt is *palliative, to prevent our Currency's growing worſe by bringing it to a Standard* &c. All Men are now and have been all along left to their abſolute Liberty to make *Contracts* according to the current Rate of *Silver* every Day, and the
Law

Law has always supported them in so doing; which is more equitable than a Settlement of once in 6 or 12 Months as propos'd, Some few have taken that Method in their Loans (others have gone beyond it) and that it has not been the general Practice, is by no Means the Fault of the Government, nor of the Borrower, but chiefly the *Lenders*, who instead of taking their Bonds at a fixed Rate of *Silver*, and 6 (or more) per Cent. Interest, have taken them conditioned to pay in *Bills*, from an avowed Expectation of the *Fall* of Silver, as an additional Profit —— Some such Act of Government however I am not against. Only I'm persuaded, it could never take full Effect under our present unhappy Circumstances, nor have the least Tendency to fix the Rate of Silver in the Market: For Silver, whether sold for Bills or exchanged in Barter, will always be rated according to the Course of Trade, at 20, 40 or any greater or lesser Number of Shillings per Ounce, variable till our Trade takes a new and more favourable Turn.

The Sum of what he says as to *Bills* emitted on a *Silver Bottom*, may be collected from *Pages* 43, 44, *viz.* " That however well *regulated* they might be as to *Periods* and *Discounts*, yet such Notes could never answer the Ends of a *Currency*; Nay in that Regard would be *worse than common Bills*, in Case there be any bad *concomitant* Currency, as *Rhode-Island Bills* &c or unless a *Discount* be forced on those Emissions at least for the future." ——I have already been large on this Subject, and made it appear, that *no Scheme* for emitting Bills on a *Silver-Fund*, and distant Period, whether publick or private, bearing more or less or no Interest, can effectually circulate as *Money* in our present Condition, and this whether we have other *concomitant* Bills or not: •And the Way to put this Affair to the Test may be this; Let the Government give a Sanction to those Gentlemen's Scheme of a private Bank (which I agree with him is on some Accounts better than publick Emissions) who are for a Silver-Bottom, allowing them to emit Bills in any reasonable Shape, with this *Proviso*, That they shall undertake at all Times to *lend them out on such Security* as the Bank of *England* would gladly accept of, at an assigned *moderate Interest*, and further at all Times to *supply the Trade with Silver* at 29 s. per *Ounce*, or Bills of Exchange to *London* at —— per Cent. as Returns to the Mother Country, and no other Place whatever —— Now if they will enter into and execute any such reasonable Engagements, they may attain to fix the Rate of Silver; otherwise not.   As

As to a *Discount* on *Rhode-Island* Bills &c. there's no doubt, common Confent might effect that, or might even deftroy their Credit in this Province, by refuling them any Acceptance at all ; But then it muft be confider'd, the fame might at leaft as eafily be done on their Side by Way of Reprifal : And probably we fhould be no great Gainers. —— Neither of thefe are likely to happen at prefent.

Page 42 " *Land Banks* : *The famous Mr.* Law " &c. Here he begins with a ftrange Excurfion to attack that Gentleman's moral Character, doubtlefs with a View to prejudice the Reader againft a *Land Bank*. But it's e-nough to my prefent Purpofe, that he is allowed by very good Judges, to have wrote judicioufly on Money and Trade, and concurring in his general Principles with the great Mr. *Lock*. Our Author here would palm an Ab-furdity upon Mr. *Law*, infinuating that in a Paffage quo-ted from him, he meant, that *Land* (fimply confider'd) could be negotiated as effective Money in the Market, and makes this wonderful Obfervation upon it, back'd with Reafons, viz *It's ridiculous to imagine that it can ferve as a Medium for foreign Commerce ; becaufe it cannot be fhip'd off* &c Whereas Mr. *Law* through the whole Tenor of his Difcourfe only fays, that *Land* is the beft Security or Fund for a Bank (lofing none of it's other Ufes at the fame Time) which Fund may be negotiated by *Bills* or *Transfers*. In all Countries even a common *Mortgage* may be ufed in fome Meafure as *Money*, being reducible to Silver or any otherCommodity, for domeftick or foreignOccafions. TheBank of *Scotland* (one of the beft in the World of it's Bignefs) is founded on *Land Secu ity*; and when it has happened to be fhut up on fome very ex-traordinary Occafions (as *Anno* 1715) yet their Bills have neverthelefs paffed current, chiefly from the Reputation of its Security.

I have already obferved, that we in *New England* have not one Material that can be negotiated, as *Silver* is, in the Way of a *Bank* ; and all that I underftand by *Land Secu-rity* is only a Security to the Poffeffor, that the Bills e-mitted by the Bank fhall have ready *Acceptance* at all Times by the *Bankers* themfelves ; to which if *common Confent* be added (for without that no Bills nor Commo-dity would anfwer the End of *Money*) fuch Bills would be upon as good a Bottom as any at all.

Page

Page 44. "*If the Scheme for emitting Company-Notes be paid after fifteen Years*" &c. —— It is to a Degree surprizing to find our Author patronizing a Scheme for Bills promising Silver at 20 s. per Ounce, at so long a Period, and without Interest, after he had been (in the Paragraph immediately before) inveighing against the *Merchants-Notes*, as a *Snare to many*, tho' upon a much better Foot than the Bills upon this Scheme ; and after I had been condemning the *Maryland* Bills, and above a after he had through his whole Discourse declared in the strongest Terms against all such Bills ; more particularly mentioning the Case of *Barbadoes* twice, and yet the Emission was no Ways to be compared to this now projected, being only liable to a Discount of l. 41 upon l.14 whereas these now proposed ought not to be received and otherwise than l. 238 in Bills for l. 100 in Silver at 20 s. per Ounce prompt Payment, or in other Words, these Bills promising on the Face of them 100 Ounces of Silver, only equal to 42 Ounces on the Day of their first Emission There were no *concomitant bad Bills* (as he calls them in *Barbadoes*, nor *Maryland* ; the Discounts were owing wholly to their distant Periods and short Allowances on Interest or Premium. And whatever he may propose and inculcate upon these Gentlemen as to their forcing a Discount on *Rhode-Island* Bills, or periodically raising the Value of their own Bills, *i e.* bringing them by certain Degrees in an arbitrary Manner up to their Promise of Silver 20 s per Ounce, I am persuaded it will have no Influence at all to lower the natural Rate of Silver in the Market, will be hurtful to Trade, and unavoidably will open a Door for great Oppression to Debtors of all Sorts, who shall unhappily by their Contracts be made liable to pay in these Bills, and so will become a *Snare* indeed to the People, as he often insinuates *Banks* in general will certainly prove. —— I spare all Reflections here upon the Gentlemen so zealous for a *Silver-Fund*, as to the *Views* they may have, tho' our Author is very satyrical upon those who desire a *Land-Bank*, in his Reflection *Page* 42. which perhaps might be retorted ; but I take no Pleasure in such kind of Censures ; and shall return to his *Discourse* touching a Projection upon another Foot.

Page 42 " *A Credit or Bank of Produce and Manufacture*" &c. To pass over his indecent and unjust Censure upon the Country in general, and keeping to the Point, I shall observe, that although this Bank, I apprehend, is

not

not yet fo well regulated, as it might be, yet I am perfuaded the chief Managers are willing and defirous to remove all Objections, and to make all reafonable Alterations. I am not without Hopes therefore, it may turn
out a feafonable Relief for our prefent diftreffing Circumftances.

Their *Defign* is highly laudable, and I have no Reafon
to doubt they they have an *honeft* View to the publick
Good : Their *Foundation*, Land-Security, vaftly preferable
to any other : The *Subfcribers* numerous, and principally
Men of clear real Eftate.

The general Promife of their *Bill*, viz. " *to receive this
Twenty Shilling Bill as fo much Money in all Payments,* "
is unexceptionable. Only I am of Opinion, that the Limitation to *lawful* Money might better be left out; it
appearing to me utterly impracticable under the prefent
unhappy Circumftances of our Trade, to negotiate the
Bill in an exact Conformity to fuch *fpecial* Promife (and fo
far it's liable to the fame Objection as Bills upon a Silver-
Bottom) for after all it will pafs only equal to the current Rate of Silver, and other Things in the Market.

The allowing their Undertakers to pay Principal and
Intereft in *Produce* at certain regulated Prices, may have
a Tendency to promote Induftry, and fo far be of the
Nature of a Bounty. ——

As to the Majority of the *Directors*, and the Majority
of the *Partners*, being obliged to act in *Concurrence* in
fome Particulars of the Management, which our Author
exclaims fo much againft, where is the prodigious *Incon-
fiftency* of it ? any more than in the feveral Branches of
our Legiflature having a Negative upon each other in the
Management of the publick Funds and Loans &c. The
Directors are to be firft chofen, and future Vacancies fupply'd by the Majority of the whole Society ; alfo to be
under Oath, and give Security : And I cannot conceive
then how it can hurt the Poffeffor of the Bill, but rather
think it may be a Benefit to him : However, that might
eafily be altered, if it fhould be thought requifite. —— The
whole Company are obliged to receive the Bill in all
their Dealings : But the grand Point, as to general Currency, will be *common Confent*, without which no Bills
can circulate.

Upon the whole, as this Scheme is built upon the beft
and only good Foundation we have, and has already met
with fome confiderable Encouragement from Men of
Judgment,

Judgment, of Integrity, and fufficient Eftates, I think it would be more generous in our Author, and others, who profefs themfelves Friends to the Province, to make experiment of what may be effected on the Foot of this Projection, than to raife Cavils at it without advancing a better.

He has offered every Thing to *perplex* the Affair, and *diftrefs* the Province, and nothing for it's *Relief* but what is either *impracticable*, or has a *ruinous* Tendency, by leaving us to the miferable Shifts of a *Trucking-Trade*, or *Shop-Notes*, which no Country of fo large a trading Intereft as this can long fubfift under.

The Gentleman often fhakes his Rod over us by threatning us with a *Parliamentary Inquiry* ; but I have fuch an Opinion of the Wifdom and Juftice of the Parliament of *Great Britain*, that I am in no Apprehenfion of any Severities from Home It appears they are not infenfible of the abfolute Neceffity this Province is in of having *Bills*, to pafs as Money under our prefent Circumftances ; fince *Silver* will always be fhip'd off, and none of it be kept here, till we have a Balance of Trade in our Favour.

To conclude,

Our *Author* makes a Random-Charge, that many will think unhappily recoils on himfelf (Page 45) " *Some audacioufly queftion the Power* —— *Others impudently impeach the Integrity of the Majority of our Legiflature* " &c. This would naturally lead me to take fome Notice of his own numerous and grofs Reflections upon the *civil Admini. ftration*, more particularly level'd at the *democratick Part of our Conftitution* (as he calls it) or our Houfe of *Reprefentatives* : But they muft be fufficiently obvious to his Readers, nor need any Comments to aggravate them ; and having no Pertinence to the Bufinefs in Hand, I fhall wave all Confideration of them.

F I N I S.

For Product Safety Concerns and Information please contact our EU representative GPSR@taylorandfrancis.com Taylor & Francis Verlag GmbH, Kaufingerstraße 24, 80331 München, Germany

Batch number: 08158389

Printed by Printforce, the Netherlands